Flights into the Night

Flights into the Night

REMINISCENCES OF A WORLD WAR TWO, RAF WELLINGTON PILOT

L. Anthony Leicester CD

ISIS
LARGE PRINT
Oxford

First published in Great Britain 2000
by
Crécy Publishing Limited.

Published in Large Print 2006 by ISIS Publishing Ltd.,
7 Centremead, Osney Mead, Oxford OX2 0ES
by arrangement with
Crécy Publishing Limited.

British Library Cataloguing in Publication Data
Leicester, L. Anthony (Lionel Anthony), 1923–
    Flights into the night. – Large print ed.
    (Isis reminiscence series)
    1. World War, 1939–1945 – Aerial operations,
    British
    2. World War, 1939–1945 – Personal narratives,
    British
    3. Large type books
    I. Title
    940.5'44'941'092

ISBN 978–0–7531–9408–9 (hb)
ISBN 978–0–7531–9409–6 (pb)

Printed and bound in Great Britain by
T. J. International Ltd., Padstow, Cornwall

Contents

Dedication

I wrote these stories in memory of my RAF aircrew comrades and my brother John, an RAF Hurricane pilot who did not survive the 2nd World War.

Many names of people are real but I have fictionalized events, where necessary, to make them plausible. My wife, Elizabeth, edited the manuscript to make it more readable.

Foreword

By Lieutenant General David R. Adamson
CD LOM Royal Canadian Air Force

An old 1920s flying instructor once told me about a pilot who became lost and on landing at a small, grass airfield taxied to the flight shack and asked directions to his intended destination. The manager of the airfield pointed to the east and said, "Right over there — forty-five miles," at which point the would-be pilot stepped down from his still-running aircraft, picked up the tail skid and swung the airplane around to point in the direction indicated. He then climbed back aboard and took off.

Seventy years later a space shuttle crew boards a rocket-propelled spaceship and blasts off at 18,000mph to rendezvous, with pinpoint accuracy and timing, with a space platform in orbit 100 miles above the earth. Such has been the meteoric technical achievements of twentieth century aviation and space programmes. Along the way aeroplanes have replaced ships and trains as mass people movers to the extent that the aviation and space industries, and their associated communications requirements, stand at the centre of all world commerce.

That this has become possible is the consequence of World War II and the service of thousands of 1930s high school graduates who became the aircrews required for the expanding Air Forces of the free world. Hastily trained, and operating marginal equipment under conditions of great adversity, this generation of young aviators made, against great odds, a vital contribution to winning the war and still later in becoming the essential aircrews required to man the quickly expanding commercial air transport and aerospace industries.

Tony Leicester was one of those high school graduates who trained as a pilot and at the tender age of nineteen found himself in charge of a crew setting out to make their contribution to winning the war. His blow-by-blow description of his training, and his war, provides us with a vivid account of the evolution of the aircrew training programmes and early operational deployments. That training was minimal and accidents frequent becomes painfully evident as he takes us through his experiences in Canada, Europe and across the Middle East to fight a war in the heat-infested jungles of Bengal and eastern India. Inexperience, unreliable aircraft and treacherous weather, to say nothing of a determined enemy, all conspired to severely test the skills, ingenuity and luck of these young aviators who, if they stayed alive, quickly became men.

That casualties were particularly high in the RAF and RCAF is evident from the statistics. From a force of 225,000 the RCAF lost 18,000 personnel from all causes at a rate of more than 8 per cent. A total of 10,000 of these young aircrew were lost in Bomber

Command alone. In comparison the USAAF with a total force of 2,250,000 lost approximately 90,000 personnel for a rate slightly less than half that of the RCAF. The disparity between these rates is probably due to the fact that the RAF and RCAF were in combat two years before the United States entered the war and that the aircraft available in 1939 and 1940 were vastly inferior to those that became available in 1942 and 1943. Similarly, training improved as experience was gained and technical reliability improved as the aviation manufacturing industry honed its research and skills.

This is a very personal story that serves to remind the reader of the tremendous sacrifices that were made by a young generation of aviators who joined up in their thousands, who faced tremendous odds, but who ultimately made one of the most vital contributions to the Allied victory in World War II.

CHAPTER
ONE

Turn back! Turn back!

This story was published in Fate *magazine, May 1979 and in* Echoes in the Air *by Jack Currie, Crécy Publishing Limited, 1998*

As darkness settled over the steaming Bengal jungle, I followed my crew up the ladder and climbed into the nose of our Wellington bomber. We cursed our bulky flying jackets, parachute harnesses and Mae Wests. Sweat soaked our khaki shirts, further irritating the prickly heat that plagued us all. The greatest hazards we faced were monsoon thunderstorms, heat, humidity, mechanical problems and dysentery — not night fighters, searchlights and ack-ack that flooded the skies over Europe.

Before starting the engines I called to the crew, "Give me an intercom check."

Mac sitting behind his four Browning machine guns answered first. "Rear gunner okay, Skipper."

Fane, the radio operator, and Frank, the navigator in the cabin behind the cockpit, spoke almost simultaneously. "Ready, Skipper."

My bomb aimer, Nick Rushworth, settled into the auxiliary seat beside me and gave me a thumbs up sign.

The five of us had been flying together for nearly a year, a long time by World War II standards. Although the youngest of the crew, aged twenty, I was their Skipper.

It was the night of 26 January 1944. We were setting out on an operational sortie to bomb the railway marshalling yards at Mandalay, east of the Arakan hills. We'd been told in the briefing to look for the hooded-lights of Japanese trucks on jungle roads and, if we saw any, to bomb them. The 'plane carried a mixed assortment of bombs totalling 4,000lb.

I taxied slowly toward the end of the runway, an aircraft directly ahead and another behind. The air brakes hissed as I released the pressure on the control column brake lever then, as I squeezed the handle, the brake linings squealed protesting the Wellington's lumbering weight.

I turned and lined up with the runway, a single row of smouldering paraffin flare pots served as runway lights on my left. At the ops briefing I had been given a take-off time and at that precise moment I eased the throttles forward with my left hand, pushing the right lever slightly ahead to hold the ungainly aircraft straight until I had rudder control.

As the 'plane slid away from the wavering lights and rose into the velvet-black tropical darkness, I touched the brakes to stop the wheels spinning and raised the undercarriage. The jet-black aircraft inched upward and the wheels clunked into the engine nacelles.

Inside the cockpit pale-green instrument dials glowed just enough to be visible. Outside, the two

Hercules sleeve-valve engines roared like wounded animals until I throttled them back for the long slow climb to our operating altitude, heading eastward to Burma.

The sky, a black star-studded dome, blinked and flickered like a field of diamonds. Other than an occasional routine report from one of the crew to me, or to one another, the intercom was silent.

I was leaning back in my seat with the knee rest raised under my legs, listening to the engine's steady mesmerizing beat when slowly, a strange feeling stole over me. A strange unrest I couldn't push aside. For another hour we flew on performing our respective jobs. Finally the gnawing sensation of impending danger drove me to click the microphone button and break the intercom's silence.

"Frank, give me a course for the nearest emergency landing strip," I said quietly to the navigator, "We're turning back."

It seemed ages before he answered.

"What's wrong, Skipper?" It was Fane talking from the little cubicle he shared with his Marconi radio transmitter and receiver behind me. "You have a problem up there?"

I flipped the switch. "Everything looks good on the gauges, but I've an uneasy feeling that something's wrong. We shouldn't go on."

After a long pause a sarcastic voice cut the tense silence. "Losing your nerve, Skipper?"

In the seat beside me Nick leaned forward and examined the instrument panel as if saying, what the hell's wrong anyway? I turned on the red cockpit light and noted the tightness of his jaw and the quick movement of his scanning eyes. Apparently satisfied with what he saw, he leaned back and glanced uneasily at me.

"Feel all right, Skipper?"

"I'm fine, Nick, but I have a feeling," I paused, "No, a premonition we're heading for trouble."

Nick didn't answer. I tried to analyse my unease but I couldn't. No gauge had flickered a warning. The steady drone of the engines hadn't sounded different. It wasn't fear; it was just a strange sensation. A sensation that there was something looming behind me. Some invisible force. A sensation I'd had before but couldn't remember when.

I spoke to the navigator again. "Frank. Give me that heading to Chittagong. We're turning back."

When he answered I eased the control column over, levelled the wings and settled the aircraft on the compass course he'd given me.

The intercom fell silent. I sensed the crew's hostility. I knew they were perturbed by my decision. Did they think I'd lost my nerve? Or feared enemy fighters? Or were they remembering the bad crash we had had during training back home at OTU? That one at Chipping Warden had been partially my fault, but they had never before questioned my decisions.

How could I explain to them the force that made me turn back? The engines drummed steadily as I tried to think where I had experienced the odd sensation before.

4

Suddenly it came to me. I was a little boy in Weybridge. I had just put my bicycle away in the wooden shed at the end of the garden. It was autumn, late in the afternoon and nearly dark. As I turned to leave the shed, a strange feeling made me stand perfectly still. It was as if icy fingers had touched my skin. Was someone or something behind me in that dark shed?

Afraid to look back I bolted through the door, flew over the gravel path as fast as my little legs would move me to the safety of the lighted house.

The same sensation of impending danger had prompted my order to turn back.

Ahead on the ground a few dim lights appeared. Small outdoor fires in the village of Chittagong, a native village on the edge of the Bay of Bengal near the mouth of the Ganges.

As I descended, looking for the landing strip cut into the jungle, I called across to Nick. "We'll drop the bombs, safe, on the beach over there."

Turning the 'plane towards the beach I could see the white surf breaking on the sand. Nick slid from his seat to the bomb aimer's position below me.

I moved the lever to open the bomb doors and called over the intercom. "Bomb doors open. Drop 'em when you're ready."

A moment later the aircraft lurched as 4,000 pounds of bombs fell through the open bomb-bay doors. The sudden unexpected huge orange flash of exploding bombs gave me a fleeting glimpse of land, sea and clouds — then blackness.

"What the hell happened, Nick?"

"Don't know." Leaving his bombsight he climbed back into his seat beside me. "I left the switch on 'safe' but they all went off anyway." He shook his head. "Lucky they missed the beach. Looked as if they hit the ocean some distance out."

I turned my attention to the landing. We were on final approach and there were no runway lights. I would have to get the aircraft down without any help from the ground.

As I skimmed over the trees at the end of the narrow landing strip, I closed the throttle and yellow flames spurted from the short exhaust stacks. Tyres squealed on the tarmac; it was a good landing but the crew's usual ribald comments were missing.

I glanced at Nick beside me. He was looking straight ahead, his face a sullen mask.

Ahead, near a small thatched bamboo building, a torch's wavering light appeared. I taxied slowly towards it until a side-to-side movement signalled me to stop. The hatch was opened from outside and a hand reached in to pull down the wooden ladder. No one spoke.

Quickly undoing my seatbelt and shoulder harness, I was first to step on the tarmac. I saw the double stripes on a Corporal's shirtsleeve.

"God! You're lucky you made it, Sarge," he said, flashing his torch on the left side of the aircraft.

Instead of dull black paint, the Wellington's fuselage glistened with globules of oil running down and dripping on to the ground. One by one my crew came down the ladder, stood beside me and stared silently at the shiny, black slime.

The cooling engines creaked and crackled. Then, from on top of the engine's nacelle, a voice called. "I checked the oil, Skipper. You had about ten minutes flying left before the bloody engine seized solid. There's a ton of metal in the filter. Looks like the bearings have had it."

Suddenly the crew were talking among themselves. The corporal moved close beside me, "Did you see the fighters parked alongside the runway?" he asked.

"What fighters?"

"Over there." He pointed his torch. I walked along the light's path. Sure enough, eight Spitfires were lined up wingtip to wingtip. With their wheels on the edge of the landing strip the fighter's long Merlin engines stretched several feet out over the runway.

Those icy fingers touched me again. I couldn't believe I had landed without my wingtip ripping into the marshalled aircraft.

From behind I heard flight-boots shuffling towards me. "Thanks, Skipper," a voice said softly.

A hand squeezed my arm, "Keep that crystal ball polished, Tony, we'll take it along on all our flights."

Following a wavering torch my crew wandered back in the inky darkness towards our 'plane. Before following them I stood for a moment and thought, here I was thousands of miles from home on a hot tropical night after landing on an unlit jungle runway. What a lot of things had happened to me since my brother and I heard the first air raid siren

7

sound four years ago on 3 September 1939. The wailing signal that told a nation that diplomacy had failed and we were now at war.

CHAPTER
TWO

The Ivy League

*"We are at war with Germany," the sombre voice
on the radio announced on that fateful day in September.*

At sixteen I didn't fully understand how this would
affect me, or maybe I did and that's the reason I
nonchalantly said to my brother, "Let's go for a swim."

The deserted Oatlands Park Hotel swimming pool
was all ours. We dived, swam and relished the water
until, feeling cold, we pulled ourselves out. We were
sitting on the side of the pool talking when the air-raid
siren wailed, shattering the warm afternoon silence. An
undulating sound that still brings fear.

We looked at each other. My brother, John, two and
a half years older, stood up, grabbed his towel and
quietly said, "We'd better go home."

Reality had struck us.

Later that month I went back to school and John
continued his apprenticeship at Vickers, building
Wellington bombers for the Royal Air Force. Although
this was a restricted job, he talked his way into joining
the RAF. He wanted to fly Sunderlands, the Short
Brothers four-engine flying boats that monitored the

sea lanes, protecting the lifeline convoys bringing needed supplies to Britain. But the powers that be thought differently. After he finished training at Moose Jaw, Canada, at No 32 Service Flying Training School, he got his wings. Back in England he learned to fly a Hawker Hurricane at No 55 Operational Training Unit at Usworth, and joined No 79 Squadron, a fighter squadron. A far cry from the Sunderlands he'd hoped to pilot.

As far back as I can remember I wanted to fly a 'plane. Over the years I built dozens of model aeroplanes, Sky Birds kits and balsa-wood flying models. At my prep school, Seafield Park, a fellow classmate's father was an RAF pilot. One weekend I was invited to join his family for a day's outing in Brighton. On the way from Hill Head we asked his father what it was like being a pilot. He described how he flew the big Handley Page Heyford bomber. "We have to be careful not to wave our arms over the sides of the cockpit because the propeller tips came within inches of the fuselage," he said.

Later, he showed us a picture of the Heyford, a strange biplane with its upper wing resting on the top of the fuselage while the lower wing, supported with struts, hung several feet below the fuselage. Large, ugly spats covered the landing wheels.

From Seafield Park I went on to Bradfield College; both my father and brother had preceded me there. In the summer of 1940 I left Bradfield College and on 31 January 1941 I rode my motorbike to the RAF recruiting office in Reading.

After the medical officer's examination I sat, waiting my turn to be interviewed. The recruiting office door finally opened and a Corporal appeared. He called my name and beckoned me to enter the small room.

The slightly graying, unsmiling Pilot Officer in a god-awful fitting uniform slouched behind an old, heavy wooden desk. He pointed with his pencil to a chair facing him. "Sit down Leicester," he said briskly.

Then eyeing me suspiciously he asked, "How old are you?"

"Seventeen, Sir, but I'll be eighteen in February."

"You don't look seventeen." He picked up a paper from his desk. "Well, yes I see you are." He laid the paper down and his eyes rested on my face. "So you want to be a pilot." He picked up the paper and studied it. "You've just left school and you've passed your School Cert. That's good. You did well at math. That's good. The doc says you're fit. That's good." He paused and looked up at me. "What do you want to fly?"

At school I had watched the Battle of Britain, and had even seen it on our television set. The contrails from high-flying 'planes crisscrossing the sky fascinated me. "Fighters, Sir. I'd like to fly a Spitfire."

"That's what they all say, my lad." A grin flickered across his face. "We'll see. Ever been up in a 'plane?"

I thought about the aeroplane ride I'd had when I was about six years old, in a three-engined Armstrong Whitworth Argosy. I was the only child among the twelve or so passengers. I remembered every minute, every second, every sight and smell of that short flight. Sitting in a creaky wicker chair I had gazed out through the square window as the 'plane climbed towards the bank of grey clouds. I still remembered the engine's thundering noise, the vibration that rattled everything, including the fabric on the sides of the fuselage.

When the cabin attendant had asked me if I'd like to go up to the cockpit, I chirped a quick, "Yes, please, Sir."

On wobbly legs, excited, I had followed him along the narrow aisle to the front of the box-like cabin. The 'plane lurched and a passenger, a rotund red-faced man wearing a grey mackintosh, grabbed my arm and steadied me towards the forward bulkhead where I climbed the steps up to a small door — the entrance to the open cockpit.

When the door opened a hurricane-force wind hit me full in the face and took my breath away. One of the pilots in a leather coat and a heavy-looking, round, brown crash helmet reached down with his huge gloved hand, grabbed my arm and heaved me up into the cockpit between the two pilots.

I stood in awe as the wind, screaming over the open cockpit, flicked at my tousled hair. When the cockpit door closed behind me the gale was deflected, leaving the roar from the slipstream and the deafening exhaust crackle from the radial engine in front of the cockpit.

I glanced up at the grey clouds swirling above us just as raindrops spattered and slid across the wide windscreen. Then looking down at the control panel, with its array of instruments, I was spellbound. I even dared to look over the cockpit's side at the houses with their little square gardens, the ant-like people and the black dots of cars and lorries crawling along the shiny, wet roads.

"Yes, Sir," I answered the Recruiting Officer at last. "I went for a ride in an Argosy at Croydon. I think I was six."

The recruiting officer smiled and said, "That's nice. More than a lot of the other chaps that come here can say." He hesitated, then continued. "I'm going to sign you up, but you'll be on Deferred Service. You can't start flying training until you're eighteen years four months." He pushed a buff-coloured form across the desk towards me and handed me his fountain pen. "Sign down there, at the bottom."

I scrawled my signature.

"Right. You're now an airman, an AC2 in the Royal Air Force and for joining up I give you the customary King's Shilling."

I stood up and took the proffered "bob."

"Go home," he said, "We'll call you when we need you." As I stood up he called, "Next, Corporal."

On the way home, I stopped at a pub and bought a pint of beer with my shilling. I drank slowly as I tried to imagine the consequences of what I had just done. When would I fly? As my trusty BSA Blue Star 500 motorbike took me home to Weybridge I wondered, what will it be like? Will I be able to pass all the tests to become a pilot? I had heard that a lot of chaps didn't make it and got shoved around. Some of them had to go into the army.

Five months later, in June, I got a telegram telling me to report for duty. I took the train to Devon and my training started, like many other student pilot's, at No 1 Receiving Wing, Babbacombe.

We marched, hundreds of us, across parade squares, back and forth, up and down hilly Babbacombe. We marched to breakfast; after breakfast we marched again. We did physical training and then marched to lunch. We marched when it was so foggy you could barely see the fellow ahead; occasionally some of the chaps in our flight slipped away into the fog.

We learned how to wear our scratchy uniforms correctly, to stand at ease, at attention, to salute, to clean buttons. I never had a moment to myself and, being tall, I always got selected as the right marker, which meant I always had to be on time at parades.

Our Sergeant Instructor badgered us, shouted at us, "Come on, you lads, for God's sake let's get it right!" He didn't have a watch so he was always asking, "What's the time?" and then marching us somewhere else.

In a way we hated him, but we also admired him. In just one week he'd made airmen out us, a scraggly bunch of pimpled youths now proud of our blue choker-necked uniforms. Some of our lads even got together, pooled a few bob and bought him a watch to show their gratitude.

Many times before the war ended I was to hear our Sergeant's last words, "You're posted."

Together with my fellow airmen, I boarded a train for Cambridge. The RAF had taken over part of St John's College, the quadrangle nearest the river, for aircrew students at No 2 Initial Training Wing (ITW).

Carrying our kit bags we trailed in single file through the college's magnificent front entrance and staggered through what seemed to be quadrangle after quadrangle. A few university students, clutching their books, watched our arrival.

I was impressed by the grandeur of the sixteenth century buildings and imagined the thousands of students who had studied there, many of whom, I'm sure, became famous.

In the next seven weeks we learned how the Royal Air Force functioned, how to recognize officers and NCO rank badges and how to dig latrines. We studied King's Regulations (Air) which, strangely enough, still explained how an airman should take care of his horse!

In his brand new Pilot Officer's uniform a remustered school teacher with flaming red hair, who had probably never seen an aeroplane, taught us basic navigation. The maths thinned our ranks. A few of the students fell by the wayside when exam time came around.

Supervised by an eagle-eyed Corporal, weather-beaten enough to have seen the first machine gun fired, we stripped and reassembled Lewis and Vickers machine guns. A quiet, knowledgeable Flight Sergeant told us all we needed to know about bombs, while trying not to scare us about the dangers of mishandling them.

By the time we completed the ITW course in August 1941, our group was down to about fifty. An officer told us we would have to wait a few days before we started flying. For this five-day waiting period, I joined two other student pilots, Robert and Nelson, and moved into a comfortable, old, private house on the outskirts of Cambridge. A rotund, scruffy-looking Corporal drove us there in a small van.

As the camouflaged van lurched to a stop the red-faced Corporal took off his cap, poked his head out the window and shouted to the three of us sitting on the bench-seat in the back.

" 'Op to it, look lively now. Out yer go, lads. This is it, go in there and tell the billeting lady 'oo you are. She's expecting you lot." Then with gnashing gears the camouflaged vehicle growled and pulled away from the curb. Again the driver yelled out of the window. "Be outside ready 'cos I'll be back at six to pick yer up for supper."

Robert, tall with ruddy cheeks and ruffled ginger hair, looked as if he'd shrunk in his oversized uniform. We both towered above stocky Nelson, whose neatly pressed uniform fit his figure perfectly.

We watched the van until its "Max Speed 30" sign disappeared, then we grabbed our bulging blue kit-bags and turned towards the house with ivy-covered walls. In single file we struggled up the flagstone pathway to the solid, medieval-looking, iron-studded front door. As I rang the bell I thought, this is another step to becoming a pilot, but when am I going to see an aeroplane?

Our "lady of the billets" was charming, grey-haired and middle-aged with friendly, blue eyes. She showed us to our rooms and I was gratified to see how comfortable everything looked compared to our monastic RAF commandeered "digs" at St John's College.

Before I joined the RAF, two army officers had been billeted at our home in Weybridge. They were nice fellows and each had a batman who helped around the house. Actually I think they were after the young housemaid.

Our landlady, wearing a tartan skirt, exuded an aura of gentility, but she spoke in an authoritative voice. Fixing her pale, steely, blue eyes on me, she said, "The maid will make up your beds daily. There will be no meals, and please, young men, I insist, no smoking in bed and no drinking in my house."

We nodded. Someone had to act as spokesman so I said, "Yes, ma'am. I mean, no, ma'am."

My ex-medical student partner, Nelson, with his sharp mind and tongue to match it, jabbed an elbow into my side and whispered, "Shut up, you ass."

Leading the way upstairs I quickly checked the local geography. On the good old democratic principle "first come, first served," I grabbed what I thought was the best room; it had at least one advantage in being nearest to the bathroom.

I poked the bed, examined my room and looked out the window and admired a flowerbed full of carnations and hollyhocks.

We cleaned up and adjusted our uniforms before going down the wide, curved staircase to the front door. "Rememberm, boys," the commanding voice called to us from the back of the drawing room, "The

17

front door is locked at ten every night. If you are late I won't come down to open it. Remember now."

Waiting at the bottom of the flagstone path, the Corporal seemed too preoccupied in his own thoughts to take much notice of us. On the way to the aircrew mess we asked him to stop and let us out at a pub.

After we'd sipped a couple of rounds of beer the pub closed. It was too late to get something to eat. If you didn't know exactly where to look for a place to get food in a blacked-out town, you didn't stand a chance.

Robert, like me, had been at school before joining the RAFVR and was still imbued with scholastic discipline. He suggested that we go back to our old ITW "digs" in St Johns College and try to find a place to sleep. Nelson, usually game for a prank, surprisingly didn't agree.

He reminded the two of us in an uncharacteristic voice, "We'd better get back to our billet. If we aren't there when the Corporal comes to pick us up in the morning there'll be hell to pay."

He made his point by asking, "How'd you like to be in the army carrying a bloody rifle?"

We left the pub and hitched a ride with a very drunk, unshaven farmer in a battered, mud-splattered old car. Following its one weak, blackout-hooded headlight beam, the antique whatever-make-it-was stuttered along the road.

Nelson suddenly cried out from the back seat. "You stupid bastards! We're going in the wrong direction."

We asked the driver to stop, thanked him profusely for the ride and jumped out.

18

Trying to hitchhike in England during the war could be a traumatic experience. Anyone who owned a car had, apparently, been alerted about "fifth column activities" and told not to pick up suspicious-looking persons. I don't know if we fell into that the category, but no one offered us a ride. We had to walk 3 or 4 miles home.

In the starless night, made darker by the blackout regulations, with our wedge caps stuck under our battle dress epaulettes, we swung along the empty road with parade-like efficiency. Not a light was visible from scattered farm buildings out in the ink-black fields on each side of the road.

We were good at marching. As we had to do a lot of it, I reasoned that strong leg muscles were essential for flying 'planes.

Striding down the road we talked about how as three fighter pilots we would change the war situation once we buckled up our "Sutton harnesses" and streaked our Spitfires into the air. We talked incessantly about aeroplanes. Elation, brought on by the anticipation of flying, suddenly faded when we arrived at our billet. No lights — and a locked front door.

We quickly deployed around the building to find the back door was also bolted; so were all the ground-floor leaded windows.

The "fifth column" had won again. The windows were not only locked, they were nailed shut!

Standing in front of the studded oak door, Nelson nudged Robert and me and whispered. "Look, fellows, you six-footers are way too tall for this job. I'm the

19

lightest. I'll climb up the creeper, crawl in through my bedroom window and come down and let you in."

Before either of us could say anything, he was gone. We listened to the rustling foliage and explosive cracks of breaking creeper branches above us. Leaves, twigs, and small bits of wood fell at our feet. In the dark neither of us could see what was happening above.

We heard Nelson's RAF issue shoes scuffing against the brick wall. Occasionally, from the shaking creeper above, there was a muffled, "Oh, God!"

A few more twigs fell and then silence.

I held my breath, waiting. Waiting for Nelson to fall, as surely he must. Then the front door slowly swung open.

"Psst! Hey, you clots," Nelson whispered.

As I slid through the door into the dark hallway a hand materialized. It was holding a bottle by its neck. "Come on in. Have a drink!"

"Idiot! What the hell are you doing?" My whisper echoed in the silence. At least I thought I whispered.

"Do you want to get us thrown out?" A voice hissed, "If you keep shouting like that, we will be. For God's sake, shut up!"

I shut up and slowly followed the murky figure up the stairs, wishing with each step that they wouldn't creak so much.

In almost total darkness we crept in single file along the carpeted landing keeping a finger on the shoulder ahead like three old-time yeggs, expecting at any second an explosion of light and discovery.

A hoarse, strangled call came from ahead. "In here."

I followed the voice into the bedroom and carefully closed the door just as a switch clicked and the room filled with light.

"Anyone care for that drink," Nelson glanced quickly at the label, "of port?" settling on the bed and leaning back on soft pillows and overstuffed bolsters. With a glass in his hand and his tunic unbuttoned, our serious-faced, ivy climber continued, "Hanging out there with one hand I had a hell of time getting the window open and worming my way in."

"Lucky it was your room," I said, reclining in a chair and taking a sip of port. "What would you've done if it'd been Mrs what's-her-name's?"

Nelson shrugged and continued. "I closed the window and tiptoed into the hallway." He stood up and pantomimed his actions high-stepping on his toes like a stage comic. "I crept down the stairs trying to keep them from squeaking and at the bottom I got lost. I couldn't remember where the damned front door was. Feeling my way I swung my arms slowly back and forth like this." He demonstrated. "Suddenly, I touched something. Whatever it was started to fall. I grabbed it." He held out the bottle. "It was this." He looked at the label, "Hmm . . . Sandemans."

Next morning we were up early. One always got up early in the services. I suppose the idea was if you're going to waste time, waste all day, not just part of it.

The three of us were standing outside the front of the house waiting for transport to arrive when our landlady, wearing a light brown suit, suddenly appeared in the doorway.

"My, my!" she said, stepping outside and glancing crinkly-eyed at the side of the house. "We must have had a bad storm last night." Then raising her hand to shade her eyes from the low early morning sun she looked up towards the second floor windows. I followed her gaze to the wall, bare in spots and streaked with early morning shadows.

"A lot of creeper has pulled away." She fixed her blue-gray eyes on the three of us. "But I didn't hear any wind, did you?"

As our official speaker I replied. "No, ma'am. We didn't hear any wind, it was a beautiful night, we were . . ."

"Shut up," a voice rasped in my ear.

I shut up! But I've always wondered if, somehow, she knew what had happened that night.

CHAPTER
THREE

Going solo

Our group of about fifty airmen left No 2 ITW on 13 August 1941. Promoted to Leading Aircraftsman we now sported student pilot's white flashes tucked in the front of our field service caps. After a march of about 5 miles from St John's College along country roads to Marshall's Flying School, we arrived at No 22 EFTS (Elementary Flying Training School), just outside Cambridge.

Swaying along in step someone started a marching song and our resonant voices filled the warm, afternoon summer air. A few small boys trailed alongside us, swinging their gangling arms, trying to keep in step.

When the song changed to, "Cat's on the rooftops, cat's with the piles," the Sergeant marching in front, turned his head and shouted out of the side of his mouth, "Knock it off, lads, if you can't do better than that."

Arriving at the barracks I knew, at last, this is where I would learn to fly.

We were split into small groups and assigned to a Flight. At the edge of the grass aerodrome each Flight had its own dispersal hut, tucked in among trees near the boundary hedge. In front of the green-painted wooden huts stood a row of yellow Tiger Moths waiting for us.

Flt Lt Liversidge, my first flying instructor was tall, slim and slightly debonair. He was also the Flight Commander. In those days, when a Corporal directed every moment of our lives, a Flight Lieutenant seemed like God. It was almost beyond a student pilot's comprehension to be in the same aeroplane with such a high-ranking officer, especially one who wore frayed pilot's wings on his well-worn battle dress.

After the first few short flights, however, I became disillusioned. Liversidge wasn't the perfect instructor I had believed him to be.

On each training flight, before we climbed into the Tiger Moth, Flt Lt Liversidge explained, in detail, the exercise we were going to fly. "This morning we're going to do powered approach landings, precautionary landings and some instrument flying." Using his hands he illustrated how the 'plane would turn, dive or climb.

Later, in the air, flying from the front seat, he demonstrated the manoeuvres while giving me the instructor's "standard patter" of what he was doing and why. Then, with his voice coaching me through the Gosport tube — a thin pipe connected to the headphones in the pilot's helmet — he made me follow the manoeuvres with my hands and feet on the controls. Finally he had me fly the aircraft and go through the exercise again. But while I was flying he constantly berated me, using foul language and telling me that everything I did was wrong. "You clot. Watch your airspeed." . . . "Silly bugger, I didn't tell you to do that."

One morning, while going through the seemingly endless "circuits and bumps" and battered with constant criticisms, I did a bouncy landing and he yelled at me, "I've got it!"

He shoved the throttle forward and with a roar from the four-cylinder Gypsy engine we lurched back into the air and went around again. With my hands on the controls, on the circuit's downwind leg, I felt a movement in the control-stick move and I knew that his hand was on the dual-controls.

I banked and turned across wind and I again felt his hand on the controls. I turned into the wind, closed the throttle and started my glide approach. The wind whistled by the open cockpit. I watched my throttle lever inch forward, then back. "Keep the wings level," he shouted me. I eased the stick over.

"Level, you silly bugger!" Liversidge shrieked through the Gosport tube. I let go of the stick. The wings levelled and the aircraft continued its approach. Then, the 'plane rounded out over the grass landing area, but too late. The wheels hit the ground hard and we bounced back into the air.

"You bloody little fool! I have control," Liversidge screamed, adding a string of foul oaths as he shoved the throttle forward.

At that point I almost lost what little confidence I had in my flying ability. On the next circuit he constantly nagged me over the intercom. I was supposed to fly the aeroplane and make my own mistakes, but he was flying it for me!

I didn't get angry very often but now I was furious, no livid, at the attitude of the foul-mouthed man in the front cockpit.

The next time he shouted at me over the intercom, I lost control of my anger. I took hold of my Gosport and bent it around the side of the windscreen so it faced forward into the slipstream. A strong gale shot into Liversidge's ears, ballooning his leather helmet like a football. In the little rearview mirror I could see part of his enraged face. That's done it, I thought. I've had it now. I'll probably be court martialled.

As we landed and taxied towards the small wooden dispersal hut near the line of parked aircraft, I reasoned that I'd probably be sent to the Glasshouse in Aldershot, or worse, into the army. With false bravado I snapped the cockpit side panel open, flipped up my goggles and climbed out. Nonchalantly I heaved my parachute over my shoulder and followed Liversidge as we left the 'plane in strained silence.

I went straight to the Flight Sergeant in charge of the dispersal hut's office and told him, curtly, that I wanted to change my instructor. He listened attentively and patiently to my story, nodding his greying head once or twice. "I'll speak to the Flight Commander," he said and left the office. After a few moments he returned and told me that he'd made the appointment.

Then, in a kindly, fatherly way, he added, "Put on your cap." I followed him into the inner office. There behind a small wooden desk Flt Lt Liversidge sat stiffly, his thin face expressionless. His well-worn, stained hat rested on the desk beside his right hand near the full "IN" basket. On the other side of the desk was an empty "OUT" basket.

I stood rigidly at attention in front of his desk and saluted. There was a moment's pause while the Flight Sergeant left the office and closed the door. I braced myself for the unpleasant confrontation I was sure was about to take place.

When Flt Lt Liversidge, unblinking, finally spoke, I was stunned. Instead of the foul-mouthed instructor who had sworn, cursed and received an earful of slipstream less than an hour ago, he now spoke with a calm and well-modulated voice as he changed roles from flying instructor to flight commander.

"Flight Sergeant McCann tells me that you wish to change instructors." He leaned forward slightly. "Why?"

Still taken aback by the situation I heard myself speak as though I had never seen this officer before. "I'm not progressing with my flying, Sir." I hesitated, and then hurried on, afraid my voice would falter, "There's a personality clash between me and my instructor."

He glanced at me, picked up a buff-coloured file from the blotter on the desk, leaned back in his chair and studied it. His face showed no emotion as he slowly turned each page of my progress report.

Nervously, I shifted my weight a little to my left foot and waited, certain that the full wrath of military discipline was about to descend on me. My flying career would end in this very room.

Finally he looked up and I thought I spotted a trace of a smile. "Leicester, your progress, so far, is fine. Your instructor has made very favourable comments on your flying. You will become a good pilot."

He snapped the file shut, dropped it back on the desk and looked me squarely in the face. The mask-like expression returned. "I'll arrange for Sergeant White to be your instructor."

Before I could decide whether I should say "thanks", or keep quiet, he snapped, "You may go."

With an inner sigh of relief, I saluted, turned to the right and quickly left the room. Little did I know that I would be in that office again — soon.

Sgt White was short and rather stocky with quick-moving blue eyes, and several years younger than Flt Lt Liversidge; but to me, at eighteen, he looked rather old, at least twenty-three, maybe twenty-four!

During our first session of circuits and bumps he noticed I was having difficulty in "rounding out" — the first step in landing from a gliding approach when the aircraft is flown level to the ground. I couldn't seem to tell how far from ground the wheels were and I rounded out too high. He pushed the stick forward a little and shouted through the Gosport tube, "Hold it there. Watch until you can see the blades of grass."

It worked. The aircraft sidled onto the ground in a perfect three-point landing, wheels and tail-skid hitting the grass at the same moment. My confidence was restored.

White's flying ability inspired me. One of the student pilots said, "I heard White's done a tour of Ops flying

Spitfires. He's also credited with shooting down an Me 109."

"Yeah," another student chipped in. "He's got another confirmed as damaged. Smoke was pouring out of the engine. Jerry probably didn't make it home."

We student pilots regarded instructors with a great deal of awe, especially if they had been on Ops. Every move they made was watched, whether flying or on the ground, and we tried to emulate them. We even wore our issue silk flying gloves without putting on the heavy leather gauntlets, as the fighter pilots did.

Two days after my confrontation with Liversidge, Sgt White had me do several take-offs and landings in Tiger Moth N6714. After we'd landed I taxied back to the dispersal, the tail-skid grating on the ground. I swung the tail slightly left and right so I could see ahead, because the engine blocked the pilot's view from the rear cockpit. I pulled into line beside the row of parked 'planes and stopped with the engine still running, waiting for White to tell me to cut it. Instead of shutting down, he climbed out of the front cockpit, reached back and buckled the loose ends of his Sutton harness and leaned towards me.

"Off you go, Leicester," he shouted over the exhaust crackle, "You're on your own. Fly over the field a couple of times . . . get used to it . . . if another kite's near you on final . . . or taxies onto the landing path . . . go around again." He slapped my shoulder, "Good luck."

Taxiing out, bumping across the grass to the take-off point, I felt exhilarated, or was it nervous? Perhaps it was both. I should've taken a leak, but that would have to wait now. This was the moment I'd been waiting for — going solo.

There was no head sticking out the cockpit in front of me. I was totally in charge of my destiny. I had to fly the aeroplane alone, if I made a mistake there would be no friendly voice to remind me what to do.

I knew I could do it!

Without looking back I sensed that Sgt White was watching.

At the end of the take-off strip I stopped, facing crosswind. Then, holding the stick fully back, I opened the throttle to 1,600rpm and quickly snapped each magneto switch "off" and back "on", as I had done a dozen times before. No mag-drop. The small biplane had no brakes so I closed the throttle quickly before it lurched forward.

I ran through the pre-takeoff check, HTMPFFG — "Here're . . . Two . . . More . . . Prostitutes . . . Free . . . From . . . Gonorrhoea". As I called out each word — Hydraulics, Trim, Mixture, Pitch, Flaps, Fuel, Gills — I touched the appropriate control, or substituted an action if I didn't have that particular one. The mixture control lever, for instance, was wired in "full rich" so student pilots couldn't move it into "lean". For higher altitude flying, forbidden to us, the engine's mixture should be leaned. Incorrect use of the mixture control could cause engine failure; not recommended for a student pilot!

As I waited my turn to take off wisps of smelly, oily exhaust blown back by the idling propeller stung my nose. I looked to my right and watched several landing Tiger Moths line up on final approach like birds returning to roost. One after another they plopped onto the grass ahead of me, turned and cleared the landing strip.

I glanced quickly at the white windsock, pushed the throttle lever slowly forward with my left hand, kicked the rudder and turned the 'plane into the wind.

Solo!

For this moment I had stood as right marker on parade squares, polished boots — the tops, and the soles, because I was told to — written test paper after test paper and saluted at pay parades.

This was it!

I eased the throttle fully forward. The Gypsy Major engine growled as the revs climbed to 2,100. The frail fuselage vibrated. Then the tail slowly lifted as the small biplane readied itself for flight and the tail-skid stopped scraping the ground. I glanced at the airspeed indicator. Before I could ease the stick back for take-off I realized I was already airborne. Of course! No instructor's weight, the 'plane was lighter.

I was flying solo!

I climbed straight ahead at 66mph to 1,000ft and banked gently to the left, and throttled back to 1,950, the cruising rpm. I started to relax and enjoy being all alone in the sky.

I looked down at the aerodrome. Toy-like yellow Tiger Moths crawled across the green grass lining up for take off. I glanced up at the fuel gauge in the middle if the wing above me. A small, black ball bouncing in a thin glass tube indicated half a tank.

Ahead the propeller swirled. What if it suddenly stops? Why should it, I reasoned, it hasn't stopped before? Besides, hadn't I done several simulated forced landings, just in case?

I quickly eyed the vibrating white-lettered cockpit gauges, making sure the oil pressure's needle was between 40 and 45lb. Confident that all was well, I relaxed and gazed outside at the smooth, white fluffy cumulus clouds above me.

I was flying solo!

I couldn't believe it was true. But wait — it doesn't count until you've landed!

I circled the field three times, revelling in every second of the flight. I was sure that White would be down there watching, trying to figure out which was my 'plane.

On the circuit's downwind leg I did my pre-landing check, GBUMPF — Gas . . . Brakes . . . Undercarriage . . . Mixture . . . Pitch . . . Flaps. Of course I didn't have brakes, undercarriage to lower, propeller pitch control or flaps to lower, but the next 'planes I would be flying would have them.

Then I turned cross wind and throttled back. Suddenly, about 200 yards away to my right, a Tiger Moth appeared from out of nowhere. I opened the throttle slowly and smoothly and climbed away. Didn't White instruct me to go around again if anyone was with me on final approach?

On the next final approach, I was all set. My 'plane was gliding towards the aerodrome boundary, down to about 200ft when a yellow 'plane swung into wind for take-off right in front of me.

"Damn it!" I muttered aloud as I opened the throttle, eased back the stick and climbed back to circuit height and went around again.

On the next approach, watching the blades of grass, I eased the stick back. I felt the aircraft rise. A quick glance at the vertical speed indicator told me I was going up when I should be going down! Of course, there was no instructor's weight in the front cockpit. I grasped the stick tightly and eased it forward and rounded out a second time. My palms were clammy. I was so hot I wanted to unzip my flying suit.

"Make sure the throttle is closed," I said aloud giving myself instruction. "Ease the stick back. Watch ahead, the nose is still sinking. Ease the stick back."

"Back! Ease it back! Hold it right back."

The 'plane was sinking, but the downward motion stopped almost as soon as it began when, with a gentle thump, the tail skid and wheels touched at the same time. A three-point landing! The 'plane ceased to be a smooth-flying machine as it bumped, grumbled and vibrated rolling across the rough grass field.

"How'd it go?" Sgt White asked as I climbed out of the cockpit. "Thought you'd never come back down," he added, grinning.

"Piece of cake, Sarge." My wet palms and overheated flying suit already forgotten.

I'd made my "first solo."

Although Tiger Moths sometimes finished up on their nose after a bad landing, our group at Marshall's Flying School got through the course without a fatal accident. During the initial screening process instructors weeded out students who obviously weren't cut out to be pilots. One aircraft stalled after a very high landing bounce, nose-dived and finished up with its upper and lower wings draped around the cockpit with a dazed student pilot inside.

Another student, I think his name was McWhurter, a tall, curly-headed non-stop talker, got lost and decided to make a forced landing in a farmer's field. On final approach he misjudged his height and flew through the tops of several trees, stripping most of the fabric off the lower wings, but he landed safely. The 'plane was so badly damaged it had to be hauled away on a low-boy. McWhurter continued flying and went on Service Flying Training School. I'm sure he learned his lesson and never made that mistake again!

With my solo flight under my belt and recorded in my logbook, the next phase of dual instruction started. With Sgt White in the front cockpit, we left the circuit for the local low-flying area. He showed me how to make low-level steep turns, to watch for the wind effect and not to be misguided and either under, or over, control by pulling the stick back and getting a high-speed stall.

He demonstrated the risk of a high-speed stall in a tight turn at about 20ft. The 'plane shuddered momentarily. I noticed he eased the control forward and kept the aircraft safe during that fraction of a second between flight, a low-level stall and a crash.

"Don't ever let the aircraft get ahead of you. Always be in charge," he shouted over the intercom, "And don't ever try this when you're solo." I vowed to myself that I wouldn't.

Flying over the flat Cambridge landscape we circled a group of Womens' Volunteer Service (WVS) Land Girls working in a field. Land Girls, dressed in riding britches and white shirts, had taken over many of the farming jobs left by men who had gone into the services. Every bit of arable land in England was cultivated to grow food.

Sgt White turned and we flew by them again with our wheels skimming the grass. They looked up and two of them waved. White suddenly pulled the stick hard back. We shot up and flipped into a stall turn, straightened out and whizzed by them again skimming the ground. They waved. I could see they were shouting at us.

Sweeping low over the ground was both exhilarating and frightening, but I knew White was in control.

We flashed by the girls once more, waggled the wings and we both waved. Then Sgt White opened the throttle and eased the stick back. The 'plane shuddered slightly as we started to climb. He levelled off at 1,000ft and we headed home.

Sideslipping over the trees he crabbed towards the ground. The wind whistled across my face. Near the ground he kicked the rudder and quickly levelled the wings; the 'plane dropped on the grass in a perfect three-point landing.

As the wheels touched the ground the 'plane suddenly slewed sideways, flinging me against the side of the cockpit as it slid across the damp grass and skidded to a stop. White turned the engine off, threw his Sutton harness and parachutes straps over the back of the cockpit, then jumped out and peered under the trailing edge of the bottom wing. "Christ! Look at that," he called out. "We must have hit a barbed wire fence. Left tyre's burst. Got a big gash in it."

On our way to the dispersal hut, carrying our 'chutes, White looked at me and winked, "Burst on landing, didn't it?"

One of our training exercises in the Tiger Moth was a "solo cross-country". With two fellow student pilots we planned to fly the 40 miles from Cambridge to Hatfield in formation.

Unauthorized formation flying by students was forbidden. So we waited until we were out of sight of the airfield and then edged our 'planes in close V-formation. I positioned myself on the right as planned.

In slight turbulence we bounced our way at 70mph over the flat Cambridgeshire landscape. Approaching Hatfield we broke formation, joined the circuit, followed our leader and landed. After a cup of tea at the NAAFI waggon I said to one of my fellow students, "I'm going over and take a look at that Mosquito." As I walked towards a de Havilland fighter-bomber parked near the edge of the tarmac, a voice boomed out, "Hey, you! Stop! Get away from here."

An airman guard, with a set, businesslike look on his face and an even more menacing rifle in his hands, trotted over and blocked my path. I shrugged, turned and rejoined my tea drinkers.

Later, back in the air we again jockeyed our 'planes into formation and headed back to Cambridge.

In the late afternoon haze, with barely a mile visibility, the formation leader suddenly dropped a wing and made a tight spiral turn to the left. I watched him for a few seconds and then lost sight as the yellow-painted 'plane disappeared in the gloom.

I hadn't been paying attention to my map reading. I didn't have a clue where I was, so I relied on the other pilot on my left and followed him. After a few miles he looked towards me. Light glinted off his goggles as he waved his hand, waggled the wings, turned and disappeared into the haze.

Now I was really lost!

I glanced down at the clipboard strapped to my knee and read the log I'd made for this cross-country flight. I was flying the correct compass course, but I hadn't jotted down my take-off time and I had to guess how long I'd been in the air.

Looking over the side of the cockpit I tried to match the ground to my map. Green fields slid by underneath and once in a while a blacktop road suddenly appeared through the haze, then disappeared just as quickly. Finally, I picked out a prominent village on the map, about where I thought I should be, and looked around for it on the ground. That didn't work either. I couldn't recognize anything. The fields all looked alike.

A feeling of uneasiness crept over me. I didn't want to admit it; I was lost and in trouble if I didn't quickly find out where I was. This apprehension made me think, what if I'm attacked by a roving German fighter? Several training 'planes had been shot down near here.

I remembered my instructor's words, "If you're lost, look for a good place to make a forced landing. Land before you run out of petrol, find a telephone and call me."

I glanced up at the petrol tank's fuel-gauge. From the position of the little black ball, bobbing up and down in the glass tube, I figured I had about twenty-five minutes flying time left.

Through the smoky haze I spotted a railway line to my left. I dropped down to about 300ft, low enough to see the wooden sleepers between the rails. But I didn't know which line it was on the map. Railway lines, like fields and roads, were everywhere and they all looked alike!

After flying parallel to the tracks for a few minutes, I spotted a village green and circled the large grassy area with its thatched-roof white pub on one side and a road on the other. I couldn't identify the village on my map but I reasoned it was a perfect place to land. There was plenty of room and not many trees in the way. I'd make a practice approach.

I set up a circuit pattern, and as I shot by the front of the pub, in a low pass at about 50ft, several people rushed out and waved. I waved back.

I had about twenty minutes of fuel left so instead of landing, I decided to continue down the railway line for ten minutes. Then, if I couldn't find out where I was, I'd turn back and land by the pub.

Visibility got worse. I watched through the thick haze as unidentified villages and hamlets came and went below. I was feeling desperate when I spotted ahead what I thought was an aerodrome with a grass field. As I approached I noticed several parked Tiger Moths!

What a relief! I wouldn't have to call my instructor from a pub in the middle of nowhere!

A yellow Tiger Moth loomed ahead. I turned and followed it into the traffic pattern. As I neared the field ready to land, I had a feeling of *déja vu*. Through the haze I spotted wooden dispersal huts, a familiar landmark. "Stupid clot!" I yelled into the slipstream. "You're home. It's Cambridge!"

In the late afternoon murky light I taxied to the dispersal hut, threw off my harness and climbed out of the cockpit.

Sgt White, with his hands in his battle dress pockets, stalked over and stood by the wing. "Where the bloody hell have you been?" he glared at me. "You're not just late. You're overdue."

"Well," I stuttered, "It's pretty hazy up there. I got a bit lost and it took me a while to find my way home."

The way Sgt White tilted his head slightly I knew he knew more than I'd told him.

As he turned and joined the Chief Instructor standing close by, I heard the CI say, "Well, at least he's back, but we've still got one missing."

It turned out that our formation leader knew where he was when he peeled off and headed straight home.

The second student pilot had got lost, as I had, but he had landed at a Bomber Command aerodrome; home of a Stirling bomber squadron.

Later, he told us how he had taxied to a dispersal, stopped beside a towering four-engined Stirling, shut off the engine, climbed out and asked an airman working on one of the bombers, "What's the name of this 'drome?". The airman answered and gave him a quick salute. He'd probably spotted the "OC'B' FLIGHT" stencilled across the back of his flying suit and thought he was an officer. Taking advantage of the situation he told the airman to get him a can of petrol.

The airman quickly found a can of petrol and filled the tank on the top of the wing. The student pilot got into the cockpit and called out to him. "Okay. Give the prop a swing." Then, knowing where I'd landed, he swung the 'plane back on the runway, took off and flew home.

The incident had taken a quite a few minutes so when he arrived at Cambridge, he was long overdue and it was dark. There wasn't a flarepath because there was never any night flying at Cambridge.

He landed without any trouble, taxied to the dispersal and climbed out to be greeted by an angry Chief Flying Instructor and his livid-faced instructor.

When he told them what he'd done, they gave him hell for not having reported where he was so that his instructor could have gone and fetched him.

Later, he told us, "After they'd raked me up and down a few times and tore a large strip off me, the

Chief Instructor said, 'Bloody good show. Nice landing'."

I heard that after he got his wings he became a night fighter pilot!

On another solo flight it was a perfect September afternoon. Light winds blew a few small cumulus cloud across the blue sky. I was reluctant to end my solo flight. As I joined the circuit I noticed the almost limp windsock. On final approach I mimicked my instructor and pushed the stick all the way over to the left, holding the nose up with lots of right rudder, sideslipping towards the trees and the black tarpapered roof of the dispersal hut. Slipstream blew into the cockpit as the 'plane crabbed sideways towards the grass aerodrome. Wind whistled in the wing wires. I peered through my goggles at the ground and judged my angle. I aimed to land just beyond the parked Tiger Moths, lined up in front of our dispersal hut, their long, late afternoon shadows stretching over the grass.

My judgment was perfect. I kicked the rudder straight while pulling the stick back and levelling the wings in a perfectly synchronized manoeuvre. The 'plane settled gently on to the ground in a perfect three-point landing, rolled a few feet and stopped; just the way Sgt White had done it, or maybe even better. I gave a short burst of engine, swung the 'plane around and taxied across the grass into the last position on the line of parked aeroplanes. The end of a perfect flight.

As the propeller shuddered to a stop I heard someone yell.

"Leicester!"

I looked around for the booming voice and spotted Flt Sgt McCann standing in the doorway of the wooden dispersal hut. "Get over 'ere, on the double." He bellowed again. "The Flight Commander wants a word with you."

As I dropped my 'chute at the steps of the hut it crossed my mind that maybe the Flight Commander was going to tell me about my new posting; a Service Flying Training School where I'd get my wings.

The Flight Sergeant stepped back to let me pass. "You're in for it this time, me lad," he said, eyeing me. "Put your bloody 'at on and follow me."

In the Flight Commander's office I saluted with an inward sigh of relief. It wasn't Liversidge behind the desk. It was one of the other officers acting as Flight Commander. He smiled, "Superb approach, Leicester. Fantastic landing."

That's pretty nice of him to notice my good flying, I thought, wondering which SFTS it would be.

He stood up suddenly, leaned forward with the palms of his hands resting on the desk, and bellowed, "You stupid clot."

He glowered at me, "With that kind of flying you could've hit this bloody roof, you nearly did, and killed yourself!" I stood rigidly at attention in front of him, arms stiff to my sides, he lowered his voice slightly "More important, killed me too. You could have written off all those kites on the flight line. Don't you know there's a bloody war on and we need 'em!"

I remained rigid. I didn't know if I was expected to say something, answer his question, or whether it was rhetorical. He solved my dilemma.

"If I ever see you do anything like that again, I'll have your balls for bookends. Get out!"

I got out.

I always thought that one should learn something new every day and was I learning fast — instructors could get away with things that student pilots couldn't!

The course ended with a one-hour final check flight by Sgt Steed. Then, with a Summary of Flying Assessment in my logbook showing I'd completed my course at 22 SFTS and the annotation, "has shown aptitude as a pilot," signed by no less than Flt Lt Liversidge, I was off to No 2 PDC Wilmslow, and on my way to Service Flying Training and my wings in Canada.

CHAPTER
FOUR

Anson is as Anson does

A photo of the accident described in this chapter appeared in the November 1942 issue of TEE EMM, the WW II Service Training Memorandum issued by the Air Member for Training.

His Majesty's troopship *Pasteur*, the French luxury liner of the 1930s, rolled day after day across the grey-green Atlantic swells heading towards Canada. On deck, along with a group of fellow student pilots, I huddled against the wind with my greatcoat collar pulled up against my ears. Leaning on the rail we watched as lease-lend destroyers, spewing white smoke from large single funnels, ploughed in and out of the convoy's lines of ships churning a white wake behind them.

Once in a while a destroyer would leave the convoy to chivvy a straggling tanker. Occasionally they roared down between the tight line of ships, going in the opposite direction and shooting off depth-charges. The black rubbish bin-like canisters — one, two, three — arced into the air, moments later a white spume of water burst upwards as they exploded in the depths.

This was a little disconcerting for us ship-watchers; were subs that close? Below decks the clanging depth charges sounded like a giant wielding a sledgehammer on the side of our ship.

One morning I wandered on deck and looked out into a thin Atlantic fog. I couldn't see the convoy, all the ships had disappeared along with the escorting destroyers. The *Pasteur* was alone in the grey, fog-streaked, rolling ocean. A rumour shot round the ship that we were close to the American coast and, because she could outrun German subs, the *Pasteur* had left the convoy and was heading directly for Halifax harbour. I felt more comfortable when a Coastal Command Canso dropped out of the solid overcast and stayed circling us.

I arrived in Canada on 24 October 1941, after eleven days of zigzagging the Atlantic, and immediately boarded a troop train at Halifax docks.

Chugging out of the city, the little houses and apartments slid by. Then the scenery changed to green, open spaces and fields. The heated compartment was too hot for me and the lack of humidity dried out my nose. The air, full of thick, blue cigarette smoke, didn't help.

When I opened a window for a breath of fresh air, hot cinders from the enormous engine ahead blew in and my carriage mates yelled, "Shut that bloody window."

In my diary I recorded a description of the changing scenery as we thundered across rocky Quebec, through lake-strewn, wooded Ontario, on into Manitoba's miles and miles of open prairie. Thundered, perhaps, wasn't the right word. The train rocketed along at full-speed for a while, then we'd be shoved on to a siding and would wait for hours while east and westbound trains roared by making our train rock in their slipstream. During those stops we were allowed to leave the train and walk about, but there was quite a nip in the air so we didn't linger outside.

As the train clacked along we read, told stories, smoked and wondered how much longer would it take to get to Carberry in Manitoba. No one seemed to know how long it would be, or where we'd stop next. We lost touch with the outside world. What was happening in England? Was the Luftwaffe dropping more and more bombs?

It was nearly dark when the train pulled slowly into the Winnipeg station and rattled to a stop as the carriages bumped one another. We clambered out on to the platform to be met by a group of smiling, friendly people — the city's hospitality group.

A middle-aged couple, hands outstretched ready for an introduction, approached me and my two newly-found friends, Don Kirkland and Geoff Ingleton. "We're the Brockies and we'd like to show you Winnipeg." We were whisked downtown in their car to a city of bright lights, flashing signs, honking cars and crowded sidewalks. How different from blacked-out England!

We stopped in front of Moore's restaurant's brightly polished copper doors. Inside we were treated to a sumptuous meal and questions, "Where are you from?

— What do think of Canada? — Do you find it cold here?"

The meal tasted so good after the food we'd had on the train. After many handshakes and sincere "thank yous", we were driven back to the station and reboarded our waiting train.

Bill and Mary Brockie, our host and hostess, gave us their Winnipeg address and insisted we stay with them when we had time off. We did.

A lingering memory of this brief stop in Winnipeg was the crisp, dry air and the smell of the cars' exhaust; it smelt quite different to English exhaust!

Once we arrived at 33 Service Flying Training School (SFTS) at Carberry, 100 miles west of Winnipeg, the Chief Instructor, Wg Cdr Cox, told us, "You fellows have arrived here two weeks too early to start flying, but we'll find something useful for you do to do until the course ahead of you finishes."

The "something useful" for us budding pilots was day after day washing down muddy twin-engined Ansons. As I crawled around under engine nacelles knocking lumps of mud and slush off the undercarriages, I wondered when I would get to fly again; hopefully, before I had forgotten all I had learned on Tiger Moths at Cambridge.

We were quartered in an H-block. The building had a wing, with rows of double bunks, on each side of the central toilet facilities. We gorged ourselves in the Mess; the unrationed food was excellent and plentiful. We were told we could have as much as we wanted, but not to take more than we could eat. Eggs for breakfast, every day if you wanted them. Canned tomatoes were my favourite addition to eggs and bacon.

On 10 November 1942, I had my first flight in an Avro Anson with my instructor, Sgt Sarre. Compared to a Tiger Moth the twin-engined Anson seemed huge. From the cockpit, looking back into the cabin, it seemed like the inside of a bus with windows all the way down each side, but there were only two or three floor-mounted seats. The cockpit gave the pilot a wide panoramic view of the sky. Sgt Sarre nursed me through my familiarization flight and then instructed me doing circuits and bumps.

At first it was a strange feeling landing on a runway instead of grass. Near the ground I discovered the Anson tended to float, not wanting to settle on the runway. I soon discovered, with just a little coaxing, it was best to let the 'plane land by itself.

After six hours and five minutes dual instruction I flew with another instructor, Flt Lt Barton. He came over to me in the crew room, "Sergeant Sarre says you're ready, so I'm going to give you your solo test. If it turns out okay you'll go off on your own. Solo."

We flew around for thirty minutes reviewing all the items Sgt Sarre had asked me to do. When we stopped in front of the hangar Flt Lt Barton undid his seatbelt and said, "Okay, off you go. Do a few solo landings."

I wasn't as nervous doing this flight as I had been when I soloed the Tiger Moth. But when I taxied in after the flight I felt greatly relieved. I'd passed another hurdle in getting my wings, but there were more to come.

Flt Lt Harnett, the Flight Commander, became my next instructor.

I got on well with Harnett though as a Leading Aircraftsman (LAC) I was still somewhat overwhelmed flying with a Flight Lieutenant, but not as much as I had been at Cambridge with Flt Lt Liversidge. It is extraordinary how a little service indoctrination will completely realign your thinking.

Carberry, stuck out on the open, treeless prairies, was freezing most of the time. I was never so cold in my life. The Anson, being British built, had no cabin heating so I really appreciated the protection of my leather flying suit and warm flying boots. The 'planes had been fitted with special carburettor heaters to combat the sub-zero temperatures. The pilot had to pull a couple of small levers to turn on the hot air on final approach, otherwise the engine might get so cold it would fail, especially if it had to open up to climbing power for an overshoot.

The perspex cabin windows often cracked when the 'planes were pushed out of a warm hangar into the subfreezing air. Maintenance, apparently unconcerned about cosmetics, didn't bother to repair them. They just doped a strip of fabric over the cracks.

The cold cabins had another unsettling effect. When flying with another student pilot, one of us sometimes had to take a leak using the relief-tube at the back of the cabin. This discharge tube had a venturi device under the fuselage which tended to freeze up. But when you've got to go, you've got to go! Frozen urine on the floor sometimes made moving around the back of the cabin a little dangerous. I wondered what happened when they put the aircraft back into a warm hangar. Did a group of student pilots, early arrivals like us, get to clean the cabins?

One night, while doing circuits and bumps under a clear, crisp, star-studded sky, I had difficulty landing. I just couldn't get the aircraft down on the ground; I rounded out at the right height but floated longer than usual along the runway before landing. Later, in the crew room, I asked some of the other pilots who came to sign the log, if they had experienced any difficulty landing.

"Yeah, I did," one of the students said.

"There was hardly any wind, but perhaps we were landing downwind," someone offered as a solution.

The officer in charge of night flying walked into the crew room. "How'd you like the new kites?" he asked with a big grin on his round face. "You're the first to fly 'em."

I mentioned the problem most of us had had with our landings.

The officer's grin widened. "You were landing too fast. Didn't you notice the airspeed indicators? They're in knots. K-N-O-T-S. Not miles per hour. You were landing too fast."

It would have been nice, I thought, if someone had mentioned this before we took off.

It was a few days before Christmas when Flt Lt Harnett sent me off for an hour's solo flight to make single engine, flapless and short field landings. The sun was shining so I decided I'd be warm enough wearing just my leather jacket over my battle dress. In case I needed them I dropped my leather gloves on the co-pilot's seat.

My hour was nearly up as I positioned myself in the circuit pattern for my last landing. I was starting to feel chilly and looked forward to thawing out the warm crew room.

The endless, white expanse of the Canadian prairie's winter cloak, 1,000ft below, slid slowly by as I followed the brown and yellow camouflaged Anson ahead of me as it banked, turning left on to the crosswind leg of the traffic pattern.

As I followed it onto final approach I thought of summer days in England at Elementary Flying School. They had been busy, exciting days for a student pilot. Chasing around the sky in a Tiger Moth over the flat fens around Cambridge, pondering what training came next. Service Flying Training? Graduation, dreaming of the ultimate Wings Parade and going on "Ops". Realizing, too, that there was a war on and lots of people, pilots like me, were being killed every day.

But today wasn't the day to worry about the war; I had other things to do. As the twin Cheetah radial engines clattered steadily, I lowered flaps and settled down on my final approach, looking ahead over the Anson's long nose at the grey, concrete runway bordered with dirty brown snow.

A quick glance at the airspeed indicator, 80mph, then back to the runway. My perspective had changed. The runway now looked wider and flatter.

As I crossed the runway threshold I estimated my height to be about 30ft. Bit too high, I thought, I'll float quite a long way before touchdown. Hope Harnett's not watching. He'll tear a strip off me. He's told me over and over again to touch down on the first third of the runway.

My silk-gloved right hand eased the throttles back. Student pilots, like me, were supposed to wear issue leather flying gauntlets; but most RAF fighter pilots, whom we all hoped to emulate, wore only the white silk linings.

Keeping my right hand on the throttles, I eased the control column's small wheel slowly back with my left hand and held it steady while looking ahead through the windscreen to see if I'd over- or under-corrected. Would I float upwards from the speed-streaked runway, 20ft below, or sink down to it for a landing?

Suddenly a small bright speck, smaller than a pea, fell on my knee. Against the blue of my RAF battle dress trousers it looked like a tiny drop of water.

In a fraction of a second my mind tried to resolve how water could get inside an Avro Anson's cockpit; it was below freezing outside. The cabin wasn't heated and in spite of my leather flying jacket I was cold.

In that split-second it dawned on me it wasn't a drop of water. It was a chip of perspex from the overhead canopy.

A quick flash of light caught my eye and I glanced up.

The tip of a whirling propeller was just 4in above my head.

52

While the blades chipped the sunshine into patches of flickering light the slow-motion reaction to impending disaster took over.

A quick glance out of the left and right side windows assured me that a propeller spun in front of the engines' cowling on each side. My mind tried to rationalize the presence of an extra propeller above my head.

What was happening?

Suddenly, with a wave of fear, I realized there was a 'plane directly on top of me.

The survival instinct took over. I heaved back on the throttle to drop down, to get out of the intruding propeller's way. But the whirling scythe slowly moved downwards banging like a machine gun, slicing deeper into the plexiglas canopy and its fragile aluminium frame. Little chunks of metal and plastic showered down on me.

I let go of the control column, swung my left hand towards the middle of the windscreen, grabbed the shiny brass ignition switches and knocked them to "off", killing both engines. Simultaneously my right hand let go of the throttles and pulled my Sutton harness release-pin.

Free from the seatbelt I twisted to the right, rolled over and fell between the two pilots' seats and finished up face down in the cabin.

A thunderous banging erupted, a combination of grinding and splitting sounds — rubber tyres squealing. Then a violent, shuddering jolt, like being dropped 50ft to the ground inside a steel drum.

Moments later, except for the soft hissing of air escaping from the brakes system and gentle clicks from settling, torn metal, it was silent.

I noticed the smell. A mixture of old oil, hot exhaust fumes and leather.

The slow-motion scene stopped. I was lying, dazed, on the cockpit floor between the two pilots' seats, facing the tail of the aircraft, half sprawled over the main spar which separated cockpit from cabin. A thin jet of acrid liquid squirted inches from my face. Was I alive? Nothing hurt. Could I move? I could, and did.

I grabbed the hissing fire extinguisher, rolling around on the floor in front of me, and scrambled to the back of the cabin.

I shoved the cabin door open and jumped out into the bright sunlight. As I dropped about 3ft to the ground the crisp, cold air stung the inside of my nose.

Bewildered, still not fully understanding what had happened, I turned and looked at my aircraft.

It squatted, almost in its normal attitude on one wheel, the front end was hidden and its left wing pressed against the ground, flattened by another 'plane. An Anson lay on the back of my aircraft like a huge praying mantis with its tail cocked in the air, nose resting on the ground.

Both aircraft had slued 180 degrees and now faced the approach end of the runway.

Squinting in the bright sunlight, I looked around the snow-covered aerodrome and located the control tower. Then aware of the hissing red fire extinguisher in my hand, I pulled the knob on top and it stopped spewing carbon tetrachloride.

Fire! The smell of leaking petrol and the thought of fire propelled me to action. I ran as fast as I could and swerved around the end of the wing to the front of the coupled aircraft. I looked in through the windscreen of the other 'plane.

The student pilot sat completely still in his cockpit. His blue eyes stared straight ahead.

My God! I thought, he's dead!

I leaned forward and peered through the unbroken windscreen. There was no blood. I tapped on the glass with my silken knuckle. He didn't move.

Then, suddenly noticing me, his dazed eyes widened and he mumbled, "Where'd you come from?"

"You clot!" I shouted, pointing. "From my 'plane, under there!" Then I realized that from his tilted-forward position he couldn't see anything below or behind him.

"Get out!" I shouted, waving the fire extinguisher. "Open the hatch! Get out!"

He moved slightly in his seat.

A hand touched my shoulder. "You okay, mate? You're bloody lucky to get out of that mess."

The crash crew had arrived.

Instead of removing the escape hatch over his head, the dazed student pilot climbed up through the cabin to the 'plane's back door and opened it. Twenty feet above ground he gazed down stupidly, waiting for the crash crew as they struggled to position the ladder.

The stocky airman who had just spoken to me, pushed back the hood of his parka and climbed onto my damaged aircraft's fuselage to steady the wooden ladder. After helping the pilot climb down the airman jumped onto the wing 4ft below. With a splintering sound and a yell of surprise he shot, feet-first, through the wing and finished up standing on the runway. Up to his chest in broken plywood and torn yellow fabric, he stood scraped, bleeding and cursing while the crash crew cut away parts of the wing to get him out. Tension and suppressed fear rolled away as I, along with everyone else, roared with laughter.

I moved around the piled-up aeroplanes and climbed back inside my 'plane's cabin door to get my gloves from the cockpit.

I was numbed by the sight. The windscreen, pushed down by the weight of the 'plane on top, had sheared off the front of all the gauges on the instrument panel.

The brass ignition switches I'd turned off moments ago now rested on the throttle quadrant. Pointed, jagged shards of glass from the windscreen were everywhere. The crushed and shattered perspex roof was little more than a foot above the green leather seat where I'd sat only minutes before. I tried not to think of what would've happened to me if I hadn't rolled out of that seat.

The crash crew took several minutes to pull the still cursing airman clear of the punctured wing. With cuts and bruises he was the only casualty of the whole incident.

With squealing brakes the ambulance arrived. The other pilot, the scraped and bleeding airman and myself were bundled into back of the grey-painted "blood-waggon" and whisked off to sick quarters. After a thorough medical exam the MO found me undamaged. But the accident had really shaken me up.

An officer on the Board of Inquiry instructed me to write a detailed report of the "prang", explaining in my own words what had happened. Then, to add to my nervousness, he told me this information could be used by the Board as evidence against me.

A few days later, when I was feeling a lot better about the accident, I learned from the grapevine that at a preliminary meeting, the Board had more or less decided that I was responsible for the collision. I gathered I was to be accused of taking off in front of the landing aircraft which hit me.

Although my instructor, Flt Lt Harnett, couldn't act as counsel on my behalf, he advised me what to watch out for.

"You've told me what happened and I believe you. You're a Leading Aircraftsman," he continued, "So don't let the officers of the Board coerce you. Just tell 'em what happened. You'll be okay."

From the moment I marched into the room, saluted and stood before four stern-faced officers seated at a long table, I had the same feeling I'd had when I stood in front of the Flight Commander's desk at Marshall's Flying School; I knew I'd had it. There was no doubt in my mind that, as far as they were concerned, I was guilty of causing the crash and my flying days were over.

"Sit down," one of the Flight Lieutenants said gruffly. Another officer spread dozens of photos over a table. After the accusations had been read to me one of the officers leaned forward and said, "Now you tell us what happened."

"I was doing a normal landing, Sir. After crossing the end of the runway, and before touch down, I realized there was a 'plane right on top of mine."

I described how the small chip of plastic fell on my knee.

One of the officers leaned forward. "So you weren't taking off?"

"No, Sir. I was landing."

The officers chatted for a few minutes. "Go on, Leicester, tell us what happened next," one of them said.

From a photo of the interlocked aircraft I pointed to the fully extended landing flaps on my aircraft.

"See. With full flap there's no way my 'plane could have taken off and been airborne at that point on the runway."

As I spoke I illustrated with my hands the positions of the two 'planes on their final approach. "The collision occurred while both aircraft were in flight just about over the middle of the runway."

"Weren't you landing rather long?" an officer asked.

I admitted that I might have been "landing long", "But," I added, "If the other aircraft hadn't hit me it probably would've landed at the far end of the runway and ended up in the snow-covered over-run area."

"Look." From a photo I pointed at my 'plane's short radio antenna. "See, it's just aft of the pilot's perspex escape hatch and it's stuck straight up through the wing of the 'plane on top."

The four men moved closer and looked at the photo. "If the wing hadn't come straight down on top of me wouldn't the antenna have been sheared off?" I added.

The officers stood up and huddled away from the desk. I fidgeted anxiously in my seat as they talked amongst themselves for what seemed an eternity.

What were they thinking? I asked myself. Hadn't I made myself clear? Then the officer I'd spoken to turned to me and nodded. "That does it, Leicester. You can go." When he spoke I thought I saw a trace of a smile. The first I'd seen from this severe-looking group.

The next day, in his office, the Commanding Officer, Gp Capt Brill told me that I had been clear and concise in explaining the accident to the Board.

"They absolved you of any blame for the accident. You will continue your flying training."

He paused and grinned. "The Board's officers were impressed with your, er ... presence of mind ... stepping out of that crashed 'plane with a fire extinguisher in your hand!"

I tried to keep a straight face as I saluted and left his office.

The next day my wrecked Anson lay like a dismembered bird on a lowboy truck behind the ground school building, a constant reminder to me, and other student pilots, what a close shave looked like!

On 30 January 1942, at the age of eighteen, I received my RAF wings, and an assessment in my logbook as an "above average" student pilot. As a result of this midair collision, all RAF training aircraft in Canada under the Commonwealth Air Training Scheme were painted bright yellow instead of drab brown camouflage.

CHAPTER
FIVE

Aircrew screwed by airscrew — a Nickel raid on Nantes

(The "prang" of Wimpy BJ 665)

After leaving Carberry, Manitoba, we newly-graduated Sergeant Pilots and Pilot Officers were given ten days off and told to report to Halifax to board a ship for our return to England. I had an invitation to go to New York from an acquaintance of my mother, and I took along two friends. On the way we stopped over in Montreal. In New York the three of us were put up in a nice, and I'm sure expensive, hotel and royally wined and dined. We visited the Stock Exchange, the Waldorf Astoria and dined in the Rainbow Room.

Arriving at Halifax one of the group was discovered to have chickenpox; God knows where he had picked that up. We immediately became pariahs; quarantined and banished to sealed wooden huts near a runway at No 3Y Depot at Debert, Nova Scotia about 60 miles from Halifax.

The maritime OTU at Debert flew Hudsons. We gazed longingly out of the window through swirling snow watching 'planes land and take off, wishing we could go out and get back to England. The MO visited us and cheerfully said, "You'll have to be confined here for two weeks, unless someone else develops chickenpox, then it'll be a further two weeks."

I must say we were well looked after. They brought us books, the food was good, but who wants to be confined in a barrack block for two weeks with thirty, thoroughly bored, newly-graduated pilots eager to fly! Days of our sentence were religiously pencilled off on a large calendar on the wall as though we were long-term prisoners in a cell.

Finally, they let us out. Since we'd missed our troopship we boarded a Canadian ship, the SS *Beaverhill*. Instead of swinging in a hammock at night on mess deck, I shared a comfortable cabin, ate in the dining room and had a pleasant sea voyage home; *and* there were several pretty nursing sisters on board. The only real excitement of the voyage was the discovery of a condom on the deck. There was a lot of speculation from then on as to who did what to whom and when!

Then, more waiting. Nearly a month at No 3 PRC in Bournemouth. Our group got split up, I suppose because we were going to different OTUs (Operational Training Units). The powers that be were reluctant to tell us exactly what was going on; maybe they didn't know themselves. On 21 April 1942 I was sent north to No 7 PRC in Harrogate, Yorkshire, for another three weeks. By now I hadn't seen the inside of an aeroplane for nearly four months. Wasn't there a war on? Didn't they need pilots?

Suddenly the picture changed. I was told to report immediately No 3 AFU (Auxiliary Flying Unit) at South Cerney in Gloucestershire. There I received intensive refresher flying in an Airspeed Oxford. I liked the Oxford, smaller and much lighter than an Anson, it was nimble and nice to fly. One of our course pilots crashed and was killed in what appeared to be a power dive that finished up beside the control tower. There wasn't very much left of anything and we were badly shaken by the accident.

Two days after finishing the refresher course I was flying an Oxford at No 15 BAT (Beam Approach Training) at Swanton Morley in Norfolk. I knew I'd been recommended at Carberry to fly "heavies", but I still hadn't been told which OTU I was slated for. Then, one morning the Flight Commander called me into his office. With a telegram in his hand he said, "You're posted to Chipping Warden, you'll be flying Wellingtons."

At No 12 Operational Training Unit, Chipping Warden, my first contact with a Wellington was the "Wimpy Crew Trainer." An old fuselage, raised majestically on a wooden stand, sat in one of the hangars like a partially decimated whale. Stripped of its fabric, parts of its geodetic frame were removed to better display hydraulic lines, fuel and electrical systems.

Each student crew member at the OTU — pilots, navigators, wireless operators, bomb aimers and rear gunners — spent time individually examining their specialties, later they revisited the recumbent whale for crew training.

The "whale's" instructor, a grizzled Flight Sergeant pilot sporting a huge, ginger, walrus moustache, meticulously conducted drills and training procedures. Although he had a gammy leg he moved easily around the airframe with the aid of a thick, Irish-looking walking stick. To us students he oozed technical knowledge.

"You know Flight got shot down on Ops and got badly bashed in a Wellington crash landing," One of the student pilots told me.

After a few visits to the stripped airframe I became quite familiar with the Wellington's guts. I felt at home in the pilot's seat. I knew where all instruments and switches were located and I could touch them with my eyes shut. Back in the cabin I could arrange and rearrange the cumbersome fuel system's fuel cocks to satisfy two or one engine flight, and I knew how to pump oil from the auxiliary tank to the engines; this job, I was glad to find out, was detailed by the Captain to a crew member.

After seven hours of dual instruction I soloed in a Wellington Ic. Another solo flight under my belt.

In the middle of my OTU course I was told that my brother, a Hurricane pilot, had been killed at El Alamein in the Sahara Desert on 27 July. I got only two days leave to be with my mother. The loss of my brother was a tragic event in my life. It brought home to me what war meant as I joined so many others in their loss of a family member.

After I "crewed up" we did crew drills for bailing out and ditching; we did a simulated dinghy drill in a nearby swimming pool. After this training each crew member was supposed to know exactly what to do in an emergency. Little did I know I was going to put them to the test more than once!

During Initial Flying School (ITW) and Service Flying Training School (SFTS) my Morse sending and receiving was quite good. Very good compared to some of the other pilots because at college, not being a devout follower of the religious dictums, when in chapel I would practice turning everything my roving eye could read into Morse.

Wireless operators had to work regularly to keep their ear in tune and their Morse up to scratch. The Harwell Box, a training-aid about the size of a telephone booth, was designed for sending and receiving Morse signals. Sparsely furnished with a small desk, a Marconi wireless like the one in the Wellington, headphones, Morse key and a chair, it simulated working in an aircraft. The operator sent messages, in code, over a few hundred yards to another wireless operator.

"Let's go to the Harwell Box and try your hand at sending Morse" said Fane Solomon, my newly-acquired wireless operator.

I was very nervous when he put me in front of the Morse key, but after a few minutes I was both pleased and surprised when I actually sent a message over the air that an another operator could understand. I also received several five letter groups and decoded the message. This experience gave me a better appreciation of the wireless operator's job as he sat stuffed in a cramped space behind his wireless set in the Wellington's cabin, trying to pick out a faltering Morse signal from radio static above the roar of the aircraft's engines.

Like the emergency pumping of oil to the engines, I was glad I didn't have to do a wireless operator's job.

The Wellington, first flown in 1937, was nicknamed "Wimpy" after the Popeye cartoon character J. Wellington Wimpy. Halfway through bomber conversion course No 36 at No 12 OTU, Chipping Warden, our old Wimpy Ics, with their Pegasus engines, were replaced with the Bristol Hercules XI-powered Mark III Wellingtons fitted with the new Rotol electric propellers.

My first flight in one of the newly arrived Wellington IIIs took place on the night of 17 August 1942. Out at the dispersal site, in the English blackout darkness, I climbed into aircraft BJ 665 with my newly-formed crew for a long, night cross-country training flight.

Frank Prescott, the navigator, was an ardent bridge player with a dry sense of humour, and was a wizard with numbers. He came from London and had the blackest hair and the palest face you could imagine.

Frank Rushworth, the bomb aimer, was short and wiry and the oldest of the crew. He had a broad stubborn chin, a shock of unruly hair and he always looked as if he needed a shave. He trained as a pilot but "washed out" for low flying. He then got his navigator's wing, but they'd trained too many navigators so he became a bomb aimer, a newly-formed aircrew trade. Because of his cross-training he was a good man to have on the crew; I felt comfortable when I put him in the pilot's seat. We called him "Nick" because we couldn't have two Franks answering on the intercom.

Fane Solomon, my wireless operator, the smallest person in the crew, came all the way from Nassau in the Bahamas to England to join up. The RAF wouldn't train him as a pilot, so they asked if he'd like to be a navigator. Much to the training staff's surprise he said he'd rather be a wireless operator.

The fifth member of the crew, Graham MacNab, the rear gunner, was a brash red-faced young lad from Scotland. With short blond hair, Mac looked sort of chubby, but he was solid muscle. Muscle he'd obviously put to good use taking care of himself on Grangemouth's docks.

At nineteen, I was the youngest member of the crew. We settled into our respective places in the 'plane ready for take-off.

At the end of the runway I did a run-up and detected in the port engine some unusual rpm fluctuations in excess of the maximum permissible drop of 50 rpm. I tried the recommended procedures for clearing fouled spark plugs, but with no success.

Since my 'plane blocked aircraft waiting to take off, Plt Off Cowshill, OC Night Flying, climbed on board and asked me to move the aircraft out of the way. Sitting in the pilot's seat, he tried the same procedure I'd used to clear fouled plugs. He also operated the manual and electric pitch controls several times to see if they were working correctly. Nick, standing in the cabin and leaning into the cockpit, listened as Cowshill explained how an electric motor in the Rotol propeller hub changed the propeller's pitch as well as feathering it.

"You can choose to change pitch by using the conventional pitch levers beside the throttles, or by a three-way position electric control-switch," he said.

Pointing to the switch, he continued. "In the electrical control 'Fixed' position, the propeller's pitch stays where it was set, as do the engine's rpm. Engine revs can be changed by moving the spring-loaded electric toggle-switch to 'Increase', or 'Decrease'." He clicked the switch. "In the 'Auto' position the propeller's electric motor maintains set engine rpm and the engines stay synchronized."

Plt Off Cowshill changed the propeller's pitch several times; the rpm fluctuations decreased until they were barely noticeable. "I don't think you had a mag drop. I think your problem was something to do with the pitch controls. Looks okay now, doesn't it?" he said.

I had watched what he had done and to me everything seemed in order. "What do you think caused the fluctuations?" I asked.

"I don't know. These kites with electric props have just arrived. We don't know much about 'em."

After Cowshill left Nick closed the forward hatch and I swung the aeroplane out on to the runway and took off.

I decided our engine trouble was a bad attack of Gremlins. Gremlins were the RAF's aerial hobgoblins who'd make you do a heavy landing by pushing the runway suddenly upwards, or they'd pour oil on your spark plugs to make the engine sputter. They'd obviously fiddled with my engine and then jumped out of the 'plane when the instructor climbed in!

Our six-hour cross-country flight returned us to Chipping Warden at about five in the morning. It was pitch-dark but the sky was clear, visibility good and the wind calm. In blacked-out England not a light could be seen. I descended to circuit height and joined the lighted DREM circuit (A ring of hooded lights around the aerodrome that could be seen only by a pilot looking ahead). On the downwind leg I performed the pre-landing check and called to the crew.

"Ready for landing."

We had been instructed to cruise with the electric propeller control in the "fixed pitch" position although this caused the engines to constantly go out of synchronization. Adjustments then had to be made on the three-way toggle-switch to increase, or decrease, rpm to get the engines synchronized again.

As part of the pre-landing check I moved each engine's switch to the "Auto" position. Then, with the manual pitch levers, I could increase engine rpm by putting the propellers to the full-fine position. The starboard engine responded but the port engine remained at 1650rpm, cruising rpm for the Hercules engine.

No amount of persuasion would budge the port engine's rpm so I put the electric switches for both engines back to the "Fixed" position.

Mistake number one!

On the downwind end of the circuit I reduced my speed to 120mph, lowered the undercarriage. I followed the hooded DREM lights, flying along the lighted ring around the aerodrome, until I picked up the final approach lights and the runway appeared dead ahead with a row of lights down each side.

With both propellers now in the "Fixed" position, I couldn't increase power too much without over-boosting the engine for that rpm. I was slightly low on my final approach, nudging the glide-slope indicator between green and red, so I elected not to lower flaps.

Nick, sitting in the second pilot's seat beside me, had watched my efforts to restore the port engine's revs. I called across to him, "I can't get the revs up so I'll do a flapless landing."

Mistake number two!

Using what power I could safely use, I maintained my air speed and crossed the aerodrome boundary still slightly low. Over the end of the short runway I rounded out for a flapless landing. As I levelled out the landing light showed a layer of white mist about 3ft thick covering the aerodrome. I was too high above the ground.

Mistake number three!

I had an uneasy feeling I was in trouble. I closed the throttles and eased the 'plane down. But by the time we sank into the mist and the wheels touched, I was almost halfway down the runway. There was no wind and I was still going like hell!

With both engines in "Fixed pitch" there wasn't time to move the electric switches to "Auto" and increase rpm using the manual pitch levers. It was impossible to abort the landing, open the throttles to climbing power and go around again. I knew if I tried to do this I risked over-boosting the engines and I'd probably have a double engine failure. I had no choice. I had to try and get the 'plane down on the ground and stop it before I ran out of runway.

Rolling down the runway at breakneck speed, wisps of mist swept by the windscreen. I held the control column fully back and squeezed the hand-operated brakes as hard as I dared. ON, and when the tyres squealed, OFF. Then ON, OFF, ON, OFF.

The situation was grim; I knew I was going too fast to get the 'plane stopped before I overshot the end of the runway. I kept a firm grip on myself, telling myself — don't panic — hang on — it's up to me to get us out this mess.

The words of Flt Lt Harnett, my instructor in Canada, flashed through my mind: "If you're going to prang, stay in control of your 'plane for as long as you can."

Should I ground-loop?

No. I'd probably tear the undercarriage off and risk catching fire, or hit a parked 'plane.

Should I try and stop in the over-run at the end of the runway?

Yes. Good idea. As the runway lights on either side flew by I knew we were still going too fast and I was about to "prang".

We shot over the red lights across the end of the runway. The wheels rumbled on the grass over-run and I shouted over the intercom, "Hang on. I'm going to belly her in. Here we go!" Confused, excited — I grabbed for the undercarriage lever to pull up the wheels, instead, I caught hold of the wrong lever (mistake number four!) and put down full flaps.

The aircraft, still moving just fast enough to fly, lifted slightly. I was airborne! I glanced at the airspeed indicator; the needle was falling back, back, back. "Oh no! We're going to stall!"

"Stay in control," Harnett had said. I slammed the control forward and looked ahead; there was nothing but inky blackness.

I don't remember hitting the ground. I was thrown forward against my safety harness. Suddenly I smelt earth and heard the tortured squeal of tearing metal. All the instrument panel lights went out . . . then silence.

For a moment I was too stunned to move. My God! We could catch fire! The thought of fire brought me quickly to my senses. We had to get out, and quickly. I undid my Sutton harness and threw open the escape hatch above my head. "You okay back there?" I shouted.

I looked to my right. "Christ! Where's Nick?"

I heard the sound of seatbelts snapping open and Fane's voice called out. "We're all right."

Then I saw Nick. He was curled in a ball below me under the instrument panel. "You okay, Nick?"

He grunted. "Yeah, I think so."

I climbed up on my seat and called, "Who's coming out?"

There was a mad scramble in the darkness and four of us, one by one, stepped on the pilot's seat and wiggled through the overhead hatch, slid over the top of the fuselage and stood on the tilted wing. In the inky darkness I could just make out its leading edge resting on the ground.

I jumped to the ground, "Anyone hurt?"

Although it was dark, almost black, I noticed a spinning wheel protruding straight up through an engine nacelle, sticking into the air like some monster's head.

"Where's Mac?" I called. "Quick! Get back there. Look for him."

Before anyone could move a strong Scottish brogue came out of the blackness. "I'm here! I'm okay." I heard Mac stumbling towards us. "Forcrissake," he spurted out. "What the hell happened? I fell out of my turret on my arse."

"Yeah," I said. "And looks like we're in a potato field."

I walked with him to the tail of the aircraft and he pointed to his gun turret silhouetted against the night sky about 20ft up in the air. "I thought it was just a bit of a rough landing and when we stopped I opened the turret doors and stepped out."

When we joined the others Nick discovered a large gash in his leg, blood ran down over his shoe. I waved my torchlight along the side of the fuselage looking for the first aid kit symbol. I found it, tore open the emergency kit, ripped apart his trouser leg and applied a compress bandage.

While the cooling exhaust pipes clicked and crackled, I spotted Fane holding his head as blood oozed around his fingers. He had a small, deep gash on his forehead and was bleeding profusely. He muttered, "I hit my head on the damned radio. Marconi is probably stamped on my forehead."

I patched him up. Meanwhile, Frank was sitting on the ground, complaining that he'd twisted his back. The navigator's desk faces the side of the 'plane and he had been thrown sideways when we crashed.

Inspecting the aircraft I noticed the nose section forward of the windscreen, including the front gun turret, was flattened into the ground. This is where Nick had finished up.

Suddenly a shrill voice called out of the darkness. "You nearly hit my house!"

An apparition came into view; even in almost total darkness its brightly coloured silk dressing gown was visible. It identified itself as Squadron Leader somebody-or-other.

He peered at the twisted wreck, "Would you like a glass of water?" he asked in a more conciliatory voice.

That's a stupid remark, I thought, but before I could reply an approaching vehicle's headlights cut through the hedge grove. The engine stopped and several wavering torches stabbed the darkness. The lights approached and someone shouted, "Where are you? Anyone hurt?"

"Here! Over here," Mac called out.

The crash crew finally found us although we were near a country road only a few hundred yards from the end of the runway. Shadowy figures scrambled over the hedge into the potato field and we were spirited away in an ambulance to sick quarters.

I'd never had an experience like this. I'd had one or two minor "prangs" on my motorbike, but they had involved only me. What had happened tonight could have killed all of us. Had I done the right thing, or was it finger trouble on my part? Whatever had happened we were bloody lucky to walk away.

Was I afraid? There wasn't time for fear, it all happened so quickly and I was too busy.

The following day a Board of Inquiry convened to consider the write-off of the crashed Wellington. I gave the required written statement, giving my version in detail. I asked that Plt Off Cowshill explain to the Board what he had noticed in the pre-takeoff run up, and the mag drop. I was told that he "wasn't available".

I was never again interviewed by the Board and never knew of their findings until, one day, I went to the training office to write some Link trainer time in the back of my logbook. I was flabbergasted to see on the last page an endorsement that read:

"Pilot misused his controls. Was in "S" blower for 5 hours at low altitudes — also misused airscrew control. On landing overshot — Did not use flaps."

75

Beside that in large red letters it read:

GROSS CARELESSNESS. Authority: AOC 9Gp.
   *Signed by Wg Cdr D.M. Morris. CO Training
Wing.*

I immediately went to the Chief Flying Instructor
and asked, "What's going on, Sir? Why wasn't I brought
before the Board and told of their findings instead of
discovering my logbook had been endorsed."

The CFO became evasive. He wouldn't answer my
questions and he suggested that I "let sleeping dogs
lie."

"I want to put in for a redress of grievance, Sir," I
said.

"You'll only make it worse for yourself, Sergeant, if
you ask for that," he replied curtly.

I left his office, furious. As a Sergeant, what could I
do without support from someone?

I spoke to Flt Sgt Fairchild, my flying instructor. He
was more frank. "You've been had, chum! Forget it. You
all got out alive. They haven't grounded you. So forget
it!"

I tried to forget it.

The station hospital kept Frank and Fane for a few
days. Fane told me later that when he arrived at the
hospital he went into a room where a nursing Sister
dropped a pair of pyjamas on the bed and told him to
put them on. Fane said, "I'm already wearing pyjamas,
Sister."

The Sister, cajoling him because of his head wound, again suggested he get undressed and into the pyjamas. Fane repeated he had them on already. After the third request he undid his tunic, pulled it open, much to the surprise of the Sister, and displayed blue pyjamas. "See! Pyjamas! I wear them all the time!"

He did too! He said he didn't like the feel of the uniform's rough material, so he wore pyjamas. Top and bottoms. On an earlier occasion on parade an officer doing inspection asked him, "Airman. What's that sticking out from the bottom of your trousers?"

"Pyjamas. Sir!"

The officer paused for a moment, as if about to say something, but thinking better of it, shook his head and moved on down the line.

Added to my concern for Fane and Frank in hospital was the discovery that one of our parachute packs couldn't be found at the wreckage site. But, lucky for me, after the usual sheaf of paperwork it was finally written off.

Several weeks later I was in the control tower and spotted a muddy parachute pack lying in the corner. The missing 'chute! Apparently someone had brought it in and just left it there without saying anything. I returned it to the pretty blond WAAF corporal in charge of the parachute section. Since it had already been written off already she said it would help balance her inventory deficiencies; more likely, I thought, she'd make it into a dressing gown. Anyway she was very, very grateful to me, in a loving sort of way, for bringing it in. I would liked to have seen *her* in that dressing gown.

Like falling off a horse and getting back on before you lost your nerve, three days after the crash I flew with an instructor for an hour and a half doing circuits and landings. On 30 September we were back flying as a crew on a six-hour night cross country, carrying a simulated "War Load."

Although I had been told to forget the findings of the accident, I couldn't. I was upset because no one seemed to believe my story about the problem I'd had with that damned electric propeller.

A few weeks later a "boffin" from the Rotol factory gave the OTU instructors and student pilots a lecture on their electric prop now used in the Mk IIIs. He brought along a beautifully made, full-size cut-away clear plastic model that showed the propeller's guts, gears, electric motors and miles of coloured wire.

After the lecture I told him about the events that led up to the prang of BJ 665. I explained how the propeller hadn't worked for me, but after the investigating team dug it out of the potato field and tested it, they claimed the pitch-control motor worked.

The Rotol man listened to my story and asked lots of questions about operating the propeller controls.

"See that wire," he said, using his pencil as a pointer. "That wire used to short occasionally, here, and caused the symptoms you experienced." He then explained, "Thicker insulation was added to prevent it happening again."

I told him about the red endorsement in my logbook and how important it was to me to be exonerated and get it removed. "Would you tell the Chief Flying Instructor what you've just told me?" I asked. He was sympathetic, but said he wouldn't because of the chain reaction it would set up and because it would be a bureaucratic nightmare for him. He suggested I forget the whole matter.

"As long as you and your crew know that you hadn't misused the controls as the endorsement stated, that's all you need."

The incident gave me valuable experience. I never again overshot on landing! It also taught me that if trouble occurs, look out for the big cover-up!

Besides, I must have done something right — not everyone who gets a red endorsement for writing off an almost brand new Wellington gets to continue flying!

As a recently-graduated Operational Training Unit crew, we now waited for our posting to an operational squadron. On 16 October 1942 all the new crews were summoned to the OTU's briefing room. As we sat down I turned to Fane and said, "This is it. I wonder which squadron we'll go to?"

When the Chief Flying Instructor walked in, the room fell silent. He paused, cleared his throat and said, "I know all of you are waiting for your postings. They haven't come in yet. But," he continued quickly, "you'll get to go on Ops sooner than you thought."

There was a rustling sound as the crews fidgeted in their seats.

The CFI continued. "Tonight you will participate in a massive air raid over Europe, similar to the 27 May thousand bomber raid on Cologne."

I felt a wave of excitement. I hadn't expected to hear anything like this. The CFI continued. "This is what you've been trained for, but tonight you'll not be carrying bombs. You will doing something that's vital to the war effort; you'll be flying a "Nickel" raid, a code name for a leaflet drop. Tonight propaganda leaflets will be dropped on the French town Nantes. You'll get all the details at the Ops briefing at fourteen hundred hours."

He paused, "Check the aircraft roster on the board, then go and do an air test and," he cautioned, "Do not repeat to anyone what you've just heard."

Although leaflets would be the first "missile" we'd drop on enemy-occupied territory, we took it seriously. To us they were as important as 500lb bombs, and the risk no less dangerous.

For this night operational flight I had been assigned BJ 703, a Wellington III with Bristol Hercules XI 1,375hp engine. We readied our equipment to make our first "operational flight air test."

On the flight line we all tried to appear "operational" in front of the nearby OTU "sprog" students getting ready for a "mere training flight." Out of the corner of my eye I saw their admiring glances, and I wondered, how did they know?

The 50-minute test flight was successful. We were ready for our first "Ops" briefing. At this briefing the CFI and his staff showed us the routes certain aircraft would fly to prevent too much airspace congestion. Navigators were given their special charts and the bomb aimers their detailed target maps. Wireless operators were briefed on frequencies to use and when to make transmissions.

Evening came quickly and it was soon time to climb aboard the aircrew bus, loaded with parachute bags, Mae Wests, leather flying suits, gauntlet gloves and sheepskin-lined suede flying boots. We fell silent as the driver trundled us down the flight-line and dropped us off at our aircraft; one of several lined up nose to tail on a taxiway in the inky darkness of England's blackout.

While the crew checked their equipment, I walked slowly around the 'plane, with torch in hand, making my external check. I'd done this walkaround before every flight, but this one was special. I wanted to make sure I didn't miss anything. I shone my torch up into each undercarriage bay, carefully checked the wheels and tyres and then headed towards the tail of the aircraft.

Suddenly a staccato burst of machine gun fire from the rear turret stopped me in my tracks. I watched, horrified, as tracers arced in the air towards the Chipping Warden church.

I dashed to the turret and found Mac struggling to climb in. At the same moment the officer in charge of night flying appeared.

"What the hell's going on?" he bellowed.

Mac lowered himself to the ground and said sheepishly, "I grabbed the gun's hand grips to pull myself into the turret and accidentally pulled the trigger."

"Let's hope you didn't hit the village," the officer said jotting something down on his clipboard. I guess he didn't hit anything important because we heard nothing more about the incident.

With our parachutes stowed, oxygen masks connected and seatbelts secured we waited anxiously in the aircraft for the briefed "engines on" time.

Finally it came. I started the engines, released the brakes and slowly followed the aircraft ahead of me. After take-off I flew in a steady climb, heading towards the English Channel. Frank leaned into the cockpit and handed me a slip of paper and said, "The course to Nantes." This was a rewarding moment for all of us. Wasn't this the reason we joined the RAFVR — to fight the enemy? Well, at least, dropping leaflets over enemy-occupied territory was a beginning.

Somewhere over the Channel we lost hydraulic pressure and the bomb doors fell open. I couldn't get them closed and their drag slowed us down. I'd heard tales of crews' bravado on their first Ops; some of them never came back! I didn't want that to happen to us. Even though I had little experience as a Captain I now had to make a vital decision. I called the crew on the intercom. "We shouldn't try to get to Nantes, two hundred miles away, and then fly another three hundred miles back home with the bomb bay doors open. I've decided we'll drop the leaflets over the first part of France we reach and then go home." I paused.

"Frank," I called, "What's the nearest large French town ahead?"

Moments later he called out, "Cherbourg," and gave me an alteration of course.

Later, Frank alerted us that we were approaching Cherbourg and Nick moved down into the bomb aimer's position. Nearing our target I could see the coastline and had a strange, ominous feeling because that was enemy territory. I descended to our assigned altitude to avoid scattering the leaflets over the whole of France.

"Mac," I called to the rear gunner. "Keep your eyes peeled for night fighters."

From where he lay below, Nick's voice cut in, "We're almost over the city. I can see the harbour clearly. Bit to the right, Skipper." He paused as I swung the aircraft. "Bit more, Skipper, about five degrees." Then he pressed the switch and called over the intercom, "Leaflets gone." The leaflets dropped from the bomb bay containers. I hoped someone would read them; even though the information may have been specifically addressed to the citizens of Nantes.

I turned back out to sea, fully expecting anti-aircraft gunfire to open up. It didn't. As I climbed back to 12,000ft, Frank gave me a homeward-bound course to steer, along with our ETA to the English coast, near Brighton. The night was clear with small patches of cloud below us. The moon reflected off the English Channel; ideal for enemy fighters, I thought. But we would soon be close to the English shoreline where we should be safe from German night-fighters.

Although fully alert, we were all nervous and jumpy because of our inexperience. We hadn't learned to work as a team yet. Some time after leaving Cherbourg I called on the intercom, "Where are we Frank?"

I waited several minutes before he called back in a constrained, woolly voice, "Hold your present heading, Tony." Later, a long time later, he called again in the same guarded tone, "Steer two seven zero, Skipper."

This heading surprised me. "Why two seven zero?" I called back to Frank. "Where the hell are we?"

He mumbled something over the intercom. I should have asked him to repeat it, but somehow it didn't seem important.

In the darkness I concentrated on the instrument panel. Nick, sitting beside me, kept a lookout through the windscreen. Suddenly he nudged me and pointed ahead, "I thought I saw something move over there."

I peered over the aircraft's nose. At first I couldn't see anything. Then I thought I saw an aircraft closing in on us rapidly. I pressed the intercom button. "Unknown aircraft approaching fast from ahead. Action stations." Adrenalin flowed.

In seconds Nick scrambled forward and climbed into the front gun turret. I watched the turret swing left, then right, as he tested it. Fane left his radio and scrambled back to his station between the two beam machine guns near the astrodome. From the rear turret with its four Browning's machine guns, Mac called, "Guns ready."

Frank, watching for course changes, leaned into the cockpit from the cabin. He had to notice any course changes I made.

The aircraft came closer. "What is it Nick?" I asked.

"Dunno," Nick replied. "It's a twin. Can't see any markings."

Slowly it turned away from us. Good, I thought, greatly relieved. Then, suddenly the 'plane's navigation lights came on and it swung back quickly, closing in rapidly.

"It's a Mosquito," Fane called from the astrodome. "I saw the roundel but couldn't identify the letters."

It moved in alongside of us, about 100 yards away, and shot three Very signals, the coloured balls trailed off into the air. Relieved, I called over the intercom, "It's one of ours."

From my tunic top pocket I pulled out tonight's code signals printed on rice paper, which I was supposed to eat if we fell into enemy hands, and gave Frank the reply code over the intercom. He reached up and fired off a series of coloured cartridges from the roof-mounted Very pistol.

As the last fiery ball trailed into the sky behind us the Mosquito turned off its lights, rocked its wings, banked and peeled away into the night. We immediately lost sight of it.

"I expect some clot's lost," Mac's voice came over the intercom. It sounded strange, I thought. Was it slightly slurred?

We continued flying west. I was totally relaxed. The air was smooth, the cockpit was warm, the engines droned evenly. We were heading home. What more could I ask for? As we scudded along the cloud tops a rasping squeal came over the intercom. Within seconds Fane called out, "Hey! Skipper, that's 'squeakers'. We're near a balloon barrage."

I jerked back to reality and shoved the throttles forward and started climbing. I glanced out the window and through a gap in the clouds below I saw a silver trace of a river. Reflected in the moonlight, a few thousand feet below us, were several large, grey, sausage-like balloons. At least we're over land, I thought, and levelled out.

Later, dead ahead in the clearing sky, a blue-white searchlight flicked on. The bright vertical path of light slowly arced down towards the ground. Then another vertical beam stabbed at us and dropped, pointing in the same direction as the first one. When a third beam lit the sky it was a long way off to our left.

"Another clot lost!" Mac's curiously indistinct voice came over the intercom.

We droned on. Nick, peering through the windscreen spotted, just before I saw it, a slowly flashing, dim red light on the ground. "Frank," he called out, "I see a 'pundit'. Take a look."

Frank leaned between Nick and me and gazed ahead at the light. Shielding his torch he checked his code book, identified the pundit and gave me a course alteration to the southwest.

"Head home!" he called out, "Man is not lost," jubilantly quoting the navigator's motto.

We landed at Chipping Warden, taxied to the inky-dark dispersal and I climbed stiffly out of my seat and down the ladder onto the nice, solid tarmac.

The ground crew helped pull out our parachute packs and pile them in front of the 'plane, ready for the crew bus. "You chaps are overdue," a Corporal called to me, "What happened?"

Before I could reply the crew bus arrived and a voice called out of the darkness. "Leicester. The CO would like to see you and your crew. Right now."

An uneasy feeling that all was not well crept over me. In the bus on our way to the briefing room I told the crew. "I'm not sure what's up, but whatever it is, I'll do the talking."

Those who wanted their "post op" rum entitlement took it, Mac had his — and mine — before going into the debriefing room to see the CO.

The Group Captains' broad chest draped with rows of multi-coloured medals below his pilot's wings, sat behind a long wooden table. A map of the British Isles and Europe covered the wall behind him.

He leaned forward and looked straight at me. "You're quite a few hours overdue. You've caused a lot of people a great deal of trouble and I want to know what happened." He paused. "What went wrong?" he asked.

I was confused. "We lost our hydraulics, but I didn't know anything had gone wrong, Sir."

"Why did you fly along the south coast?" He continued before I could reply, "And then pass between Dover and Calais up towards Norway before turning back?" As he spoke the Briefing Officer behind him traced our course on the map. My God, I thought. We did that?

"You then flew over the North Sea and crossed the coast near the Wash. Why?" The briefing officer pointed to Norfolk's coastline.

"Because of the hydraulics I elected to drop the leaflets on Cherbourg, then we came home. North Sea? Wash?" I glanced at Frank's bewildered look.

"At this point," he continued as the briefing officer pointed to the map, "You were intercepted by a Mosquito night-fighter we'd sent up after you. Did you see it?"

"Yes," I replied. "We thought it was a lost aircraft."

Why hadn't I tried to contact the Mosquito by radio, he asked? I didn't even remember whether the radio was turned on, and I know the thought never crossed my mind. Gradually it dawned on me that we were the ones lost — badly lost. Why hadn't Frank said so? Hadn't he known? I wondered what else we had, or hadn't done!

The story got worse. Apparently the SANDRA searchlights were also for us; SANDRA was an emergency system set up to direct lost aircraft to the nearest aerodrome. A lost pilot merely had to call on the radio for "Darkie" and a finely-tuned team went into action. Many Allied aircraft in trouble were saved this way. Apparently, we had bypassed the system by not following instructions, and this had upset quite a lot of people.

When the CO finished he leaned back in his chair. "Now you tell me what happened."

I tried to keep things low key, but Mac, fortified by two rum rations, swayed slightly as he tried to embellish everything I said. The rest of the crew finally eased him to the back of the group before my credibility was destroyed.

As I told my story I thought I noticed the CO raise his eyebrows slightly at one point as if in disbelief. Was my story that incredulous? It sounded pretty good to me.

After I'd finished the CO tilted his chair back as if in deep thought, then, apparently digging for information, he asked, "Did you use oxygen?"

"Yes, Sir. I turned the oxygen system on and checked the regulator gauge as we taxied out for take-off."

When the Group Captain asked if I was sure that the system was working, I could only state that the regulator gauge indicated oxygen was flowing. Lack of oxygen had never crossed my mind until that moment. The CO, obviously suspicious, said he would have the aeroplane checked. Before sending us off to bed he asked Frank to hand over his navigation log.

The next day I learned that the engineering officer's report stated the oxygen system was not working; that's why we had done so many strange things that night. We had flown at 12,000ft without oxygen long enough to get anoxia; hence the mistakes and our apparent lack of concern. The effect was as if we had knocked back several gin and tonics!

I discovered that another crew had previously reported a leak in the oxygen system. When oxygen tubes, attached to the aircraft, were not in use each one was snapped into a clip which pushed in a plunger, cutting off the flow of oxygen. If the pipe is pulled out of the clip and pushed into the oxygen mask's hose bayonet fitting, oxygen flow is restored.

But to prevent oxygen leaking someone had inserted a small wooden cotton-reel into each oxygen pipe clamp, closing the shut-off plunger. In the dark we had hooked our masks to the loose connector pipe not realizing the valves were locked closed.

An investigation showed that the regulator, in front of me in the cockpit, indicated that oxygen was flowing when it wasn't! We were lucky to have made it back to Chipping Warden. We might easily have finished up somewhere in Norway and run out of petrol.

I could just hear the BBC radio announcer . . . "and one of our aircraft is missing."

The incident taught us all a valuable lesson. I learned the seriousness of my responsibility as the aircraft's Captain and my crew learned the need to work together as a team. From then on I always checked with each crew member to make sure all the aeroplane's systems were in working order.

As an operational bomber crew with an operational flight recorded in our logbooks, albeit a not very successful Nickel raid, we left the OTU at Chipping Warden and reported to No 1446 Flight at Moreton-in-the-Marsh in Gloucestershire. Our next contribution to the war effort was to take a Wellington from England to Egypt.

I was assigned aircraft W5453, a Mark II Wellington, powered by two Rolls-Royce Merlin X engines. The Mark II, with its inline-engines, had sleek, streamlined engine cowlings, a change from the Hercules radial-engines in the Wellington IIIs we had been flying.

Flight Lieutenant Leysmon, an instructor at 1446 Flight, came over to me in the crew room. "Leicester, you've never flown a Wimpy Mark Two, so get your crew together and I'll give you a quick check-out."

We climbed up the ladder and he settled himself in the left-hand seat. He did some spectacular low-flying which didn't impress me. Low-flying for fun was exhilarating, but it has killed a lot of pilots, and this foolhardy demonstration certainly wasn't a productive familiarization flight.

After we landed he said, "Okay. Leicester. Take your crew and do some 'circuits and bumps'."

As I slowly taxied out to the end of the runway I noticed that the 1,145hp, twelve-cylinder Merlin engines sounded quite different from the radial Hercules I'd flown at OTU. The Merlins purred and a sharp crackle came from the stubby exhaust stacks on each side of the engine — a different, but not unpleasant sound.

At the end of the runway, with pre-takeoff check completed I called over the intercom, "Okay, chaps, here we go."

I opened up the throttles and the 'plane swung smartly to the left off the runway and onto the grass infield. Feeling slightly embarrassed, I stopped, taxied the aircraft back on the runway, lined it up and tried again.

At the third attempt we took off! The crew cheered.

In Mark III Wellingtons the pilot, compensating for the swing to the right, had to open the throttles with his left hand and use his thumb to push the starboard throttle ahead of the port throttle. On the Mark II the propellers rotated the other way and the aircraft tended to swing to port on take-off; of course no one had bothered to mention that! By leading the starboard throttle I had induced an even larger swing to port; one which I couldn't hold with the rudder.

Once I got the hang of it I found the aircraft handled well. It was responsive to the controls and nice to fly. The Merlin engines had a throaty roar on take-off, but they were pleasantly quiet at cruising rpm even though, with their long engine nacelles, the props were closer to the cockpit.

Using a boost override control was a new experience. On take-off, just before opening the throttles, I pulled a lever, increasing the maximum boost pressure. After take-off I reduced power, pulled back both the throttles and pitch controls, and then disengaged the boost override.

I discovered that if I engaged the boost override during the take-off roll, the boost-pressure gauge needle nearly jumped off the gauge as the aeroplane leapt into the air. I'm sure this method of engine handling was frowned upon by engineering officers.

A long-range overload fuel tank had been fitted in our aircraft's bomb bay to increase its range; extra fuel cocks were added to the Wellington's already confusing fuel system. Before leaving England for the Middle East we had to calculate our fuel consumption. To make this test flight a small quantity of petrol had been pumped into the overload tank. I took off using fuel from the main wing tanks, climbed to 5,000ft and switched to the overload tank. Frank was responsible for checking fuel gauges and Nick for switching tanks. We cruised along waiting for the fuel in the tank to run out. When that happened Nick, waiting in the cabin, would switch us back on the wing tanks while Frank calculated our hourly fuel consumption.

To my surprise an American B17, Flying Fortress bomber, suddenly appeared nearby on our left side. I nudged Frank, sitting beside me, "Look. We've got company."

The Fortress eased over to our wing tip in formation. As the pilot tucked his huge wing in close to ours the crew waved. The Fortress pilot must have been amazed when both of our engines ran out of fuel and stopped. Propellers still windmilling we dropped like a stone falling below and behind the huge American 'plane.

Nick, waiting in the back for the tank to run dry, quickly switched over to full tanks, worked the wobble pump and called over the intercom, "Back on the mains."

The engines caught immediately and we zoomed back up beside the American bomber.

We came back so close and so quickly, I could see the startled expressions on the crew's faces. Maybe they figured it was a new RAF evasion tactic.

In the thirteen days we spent at Moreton-in-the-Marsh we made several cross-country flights to get the feel of our aircraft in preparation for our overseas flight. Now ready to go, we flew our aircraft to Portreath, Cornwall and reported to No 1 OADU (Overseas Aircraft Delivery Unit).

CHAPTER
SIX

England to Gibraltar

A week later on the night of 27 November I sat with my crew in our Wellington Mark II at the end of Portreath's bleak runway waiting for take-off clearance. Our mission: to deliver the aircraft to Cairo, stopping en route at Gibraltar.

High winds in the Mediterranean had already delayed our departure for two days. On the third day the winds abated slightly and the decision to go, or not to go, was left to the pilots of the waiting aircraft. Along with two others, I decided to go. A heavy responsibility for a nineteen year old.

I completed the run up, set the throttles of the twin-Merlin engines to a fast idle, and we waited in the darkness. Finally, from the aerodrome controller's yellow caravan beside the runway, came a steady green light. Our turn to take-off.

I clicked the microphone switch on my oxygen mask and called out, "Here we go chaps. Take a last look at Old Blighty."

Slowly I opened the throttles and we lumbered down the runway between the flarepath lights. The aircraft's tail rose and the rudder became more responsive making it easier to hold the 'plane down the centre line. As the rumbling wheels left the ground and the runway lights slid behind us, I touched the brakes and raised the undercarriage. We climbed out over the Bristol Channel into the inky darkness. Our Wimpy felt sluggish and heavy; with full wing and nacelle tanks we carried 750 gallons of petrol and some freight. Each of my crew reluctantly admitted to having more than the regulation 65lb aboard. I owned up to being overweight as well.

At 5,000ft I levelled out, eased the throttles back to cruising power and the snarling Rolls-Royce Merlin X engines gave way to a comforting purr.

My navigator, Frank, leaned forward between me and our bomb aimer and checked the compass. The dim cockpit light emphasized his pale complexion.

In the crew's cabin right behind me the radio operator was "listening out". At the aft-end of the Wellington's long fuselage, "Mac" sat hunched in his turret behind four Browning machine guns.

"You still with us, Mac?" I called on the intercom.

"Aye," he replied. Mac was a sturdy Scotsman of few words.

As the coast of Cornwall slid from underneath us I wondered how many months, or years, it would be before the five of us returned to England. Perhaps none of us would make it back. We might not even make it to Gibraltar. "Jerry" had shot down quite a few aircraft on this run down the Portuguese coast. We'd been briefed that we might also encounter enemy fighters flying near the desert battles between Gibraltar and Cairo.

Since the RAF required only one pilot for the Wellington, there was a single control column. When the bomb aimer wasn't lying on the forward hatch, peering through the bomb sight, he sat in a jump seat beside the pilot.

It was dark and cloudy and we were somewhere over the Bay of Biscay when Frank, standing in the astrodome, called me on the intercom. "Skipper. There's a Wimpy above us, to our port."

I peered out of my side window and then twisted my body and looked up through the cockpit's plexiglas roof, but I couldn't see it.

Flashing the top identification lights I signalled "TR9" in Morse code, asking the Wimpy crew to switch on their TR9 radio. No reply. Either they couldn't read Morse, or my code sending was worse than I thought. Later I found out that this aircraft landed at Gibraltar ahead of us and reported seeing a Wellington flashing SOS!

Between gaps in the clouds, an occasional star showed itself long enough for Frank to take a star shot with his sextant. He was a whiz at quickly figuring out our position and he was usually bang on.

When night finally broke into a watery, grey dawn Frank leaned into the cockpit. "Over there," he pointed at a dark misty shape to our left, "That's Cape Finistére."

As morning light filled the cockpit "George", the automatic pilot, was flying the 'plane. "He" did a good job holding course and keeping the 'plane straight and level. But if the pre-set trim adjustment was off the aircraft yawed slightly and raised, or lowered, the nose when I engaged it, slowing the airspeed and wasting fuel. "George" could, and did, go berserk sometimes and had to be quickly disengaged.

Sitting at the controls I was relieved that we had passed over the Bay of Biscay without seeing any Luftwaffe 'planes, but now I worried about the weather conditions at "Gib". Quelling my anxiety I twisted my head to loosen a stiff neck. I had been sitting in this seat for several hours and I needed to loosen up, move around. "Keep an eye on things, Nick," I said, lifting the arm rest so I could slide out of the seat. "I'm going to stretch my legs and take a leak."

"Okay, Tony. Good idea. I'll go when you come back." Nick slid from his seat and lowered his wiry frame down into the bomb bay in order to swing his folding seat out of my way.

The seat jammed. "Oh, for God's sake." He yanked at the seat. It wouldn't budge. "The stupid boffin that designed this contraption should be made to get in and out of the bloody thing." Nick thumped the seat viciously with his hand and tried again to fold it against his side of the cockpit. "S★★★! Now it's really stuck." He grabbed the aluminium tubing and shook it. With a crash it suddenly unfolded.

I pushed by him and then he swung up and sat in the pilot's seat mumbling, "Those people at Vickers."

In the cabin I found Fane with a screwdriver in his hand and the "innards" of his Marconi radio spread over his desk. Deep in concentration he didn't look up.

"What's wrong?" I asked.

"I don't really know." He glanced up at me with a puzzled look on his face, still tanned from the Bahamian sun, and pointed the screwdriver at the radio. "It wasn't working so I'm having a look inside to see if I can find out why."

That seemed logical so I moved out of the back end of the cabin and let him to get on with it. Whatever he did must have been right. Later he called over the intercom, "Got the radio working loud and clear."

Making my way down the Wellington's tunnel-like interior, it looked like the inside of a large animal's carcass with its criss-cross, geodesic, aluminium frame. I climbed over the main spar and down the narrow wooden catwalk to the Elsan. Using the round, tub-like chemical toilet mounted on a wooden platform on the port side, one felt a bit exposed. If the rear gunner looked through the window at the back of his turret he could see you perched majestically on the throne.

Back at the controls, I called Frank. "What's our ETA to Gib? Clouds are thickening and I think we should descend and try and stay under them."

Frank eased himself between Nick and me and held out a folded map.

"We're here." He stuck his finger on the drawn track line. "We altered course here, we've got less than a hundred miles to go." He paused and looked out at the lowering clouds ahead. "Yes. Stay under the clouds if you can so I can pinpoint the coast."

I eased the throttles back and started a slow descent to get below the layer of grey strato cumulus looming ahead of us.

Before we departed England the Briefing Officer had told us that the weather conditions at Gibraltar would be "rather poor" for our arrival. His guess was right. I had to go down to 800ft to get below the clouds and we flew in light rain above the choppy sea's whitecaps.

Nick suddenly called out. "Look! Straight ahead. It's the Rock!"

Sure enough, right on Frank's ETA, Gibraltar's majestic grey "Rock" loomed dead ahead of us, about 5 miles away.

Before entering Gibraltar's control zone we exchanged the appropriate identification signals with a lookout point on the Rock's south side. Nearing the aerodrome, with its single east-west runway, I took a quick look across the harbour at nearby La Linea in Spain.

"The German Consul sits in La Linea with a wonderful view of the Rock, harbour and aerodrome," the Portreath Briefing Officer had told us. "Day and night he watches our aircraft come and go and there's nothing we can do about it."

Will he log us, Wellington W5453? I wondered.

I called the crew on the intercom. "There's a hell of a wind down there coming in off the Med. I'm going to make a practice circuit to check out drift."

Flying in and out of light showers, with windshield wipers clanking, I headed towards the end of the runway. The runway's west end jutted out into the harbour and as I approached it I skimmed over ships' masts.

"My God!" Nick called out. "Look. Over there." He pointed towards the towering rock. "Some poor bastard didn't make it."

Lying off to the side of the black runway a badly mangled Wellington rested on its belly with a wing torn off. My hands involuntarily tightened on the wheel.

Not exactly an encouraging sight, I thought, as I faced a dicey landing situation. I don't like this squally wind and that's one hell of big piece of rock off to the right of the runway.

Above the drone of the Merlin engines the windscreen wiper's rhythmic clatter back-and-forth was the only sound in the cockpit as I flew along the runway. Over the Mediterranean I circled right to go around the Rock.

"Keep an eye out for other kites," I called to Nick. "Vis is pretty poor."

At the end of the downwind leg I lowered the undercarriage for final approach, greatly relieved to see the three tell-tale green warning lights showing the undercarriage was down and locked.

Just off the end of the runway, in the lee of the Rock and lower this time, heavy turbulence suddenly caught us. The aeroplane rolled and then pitched violently. I wrestled the wheel and pumped the rudders, struggling to hold us straight, shoving the throttles to full power to control a sudden rapid sinking in a wind gust. When the aircraft soared up like a seagull, I hauled the throttles back. Little by little I sidled down closer, closer to the runway.

Just as the wheels touched the ground the east wind, whipping down the runway, caught the aircraft and gently lifted it 20ft into the air. Gripping the control column I realized I'd got to hold this bucking monster and make it go where I wanted it to go. I heaved on the wheel and managed to level out, but we hit the runway hard; not once, but several times.

Thus in a gut-wrenching downdraft we arrived at Gibraltar with a sigh of relief. I say "arrived" because my efforts hardly resembled a landing. When the wheels finally stayed on the ground we rolled about 40ft and stopped.

The intercom clicked on. "Pretty fancy landing. Trying to make us seasick?"

Mac's Scottish brogue came through.

Eight hours and forty-five minutes after leaving England we had reached Gibraltar.

We took care of arrival formalities, climbed into the aircrew bus and headed for the transient quarters. There we found beds and without showering we dropped into them and slept until evening.

The roar of a 'plane taking off woke me. For a moment I didn't know where I was. Then memories of the long flight reminded me I was at Gibraltar. Feeling refreshed I suggested to the crew, "Let's go downtown and see the sights."

Compared to blacked-out, cold England the town seemed like a dream. The air was warm, shops ablaze with lights, their windows full of clothing, shoes and other wonderful things we hadn't seen for a long time. We found a restaurant on Main Street and ordered the biggest steak possible and washed it down with lots of beer. Nick, a good eater, remarked, "What a hunk of beef, lot better than the rationed stuff at home."

With our appetites satisfied by good food, we left the restaurant and ambled down the street looking for a cosy bar.

Sailors outnumbered the army and air force in most of the bars. A thin red line of "red caps", military policemen, representing the three services, waited outside near the main street's watering holes.

We were halfway through our first beer when there was a scuffling at the far side of the bar. Glasses and bottles crashed to the floor as some soldiers started a free-for-all with a bunch of sailors. The fat, harassed bar keeper tossed his drying cloth on the bar and rushed into the street. A few moments later he returned with several army and navy MPs. Cudgelling the wrestlers with their night sticks the MPs separated the yelling, warring group and hustled them outside. Order restored, drinking resumed.

During the three days we were at Gibraltar noise echoed and the ground rumbled from heavy calibre and anti-aircraft guns firing intermittently from emplacements on the face of the Rock. At what I don't know.

A constant flow of arriving and departing aircraft kept the single runway busy. Many of the 'planes were destined to join squadrons for the North African desert campaign's "push to the west". Others headed for India where the Japanese in Burma edged nearer to India's eastern borders.

At night searchlights poked out from the Rock's north side, sending beams sweeping back and forth, stabbing the darkness above the runway. Caught in the glare, hundreds of parked aeroplanes looked like grotesque toys. The steady, dazzling light must have annoyed the German Consul across the border in Spain.

Our aeroplane was inspected soon after we arrived; however, while doing a routine run up, I noticed a large mag drop on the port engine. A mechanic worked on the engine and the mag drop cleared up, but the engineering officer suggested, "Since we can't pinpoint the cause, do an air test to make sure the engine will operate properly in all speed ranges under engine-load."

Not wanting to make a test flight with freight aboard I asked to have all stowed items removed, including a heavy, white, wooden box, about 2ft square with "medals" stamped in large black Government lettering on the lid and sides. It had taken four men at Portreath to lift it onto the cabin floor where it sat in everyone's way.

The test flight was never made and no one bothered to put the box back on the 'plane, and I never reminded anyone. I was happy to see the last of it. (After the war I learned that about the time I left England gold had been flown to Cairo. Perhaps that box contained some of it!)

The reason for the mag drop was never found. After several run-ups it was now within limits and I was satisfied it wasn't a problem. The aircraft had been pronounced serviceable and I had accepted this decision by signing the maintenance form F700.

Three days after our arrival at Gibraltar we were ready to leave the Rock and head to Egypt.

With several other crews, in a mixed bag of 'planes — fighters, Lockheed Hudsons, a Liberator and other Wellingtons — we received a detailed briefing for our non-stop flight to Cairo. Because of the large number of departing 'planes that night we faced a long wait for our turn to take off.

The night was warm and balmy. Wearing battle dress we sat on the ground near our 'plane. Between us and the end of the runway several Spitfires were parked, their long Rolls-Royce Merlin engines protruding out over the edge of the runway. Aircraft taxiing to the end of the runway for take-off had to stop when they reached the Spitfires, wait for a green Aldis light clearance before swinging out to the middle of the active runway to go around them. When they reached the end of the runway they turned, headed east towards the Mediterranean and waited for a green signal; clearance to take off.

I saw the Aldis lamp flash a green dah-dit-dah, "K"; take-off clearance to the aircraft sitting at the end of the runway.

As the pilot started to roll down the runway the crisp, blue-white exhaust flash lit up a patch of ground around the 'plane as it accelerated along the runway towards us. At that moment I caught a movement from the corner of my eye. Another Wellington had pulled out on to the runway and was taxiing in front of the parked Spitfires, heading straight for the oncoming 'plane.

"Look out," I shouted, leaping to my feet. "They're going to hit." The five of us turned and dashed into the maze of parked 'planes behind us.

I glanced back over my shoulder just as the two Wellingtons collided head on. The bang sounded like a building collapsing. All four engines suddenly stopped leaving total silence.

Nick, beside me, shouted, "Let's go!"

We turned and ran towards the crash.

The two black Wellingtons stood interlocked head on. Neither undercarriage had collapsed but one damaged wing drooped helplessly on the ground.

Tortured metal creaked and cooling exhaust pipes crackled. Then from inside the fuselages came voices. Some stridently shouting orders, others yelling for help.

Through a windscreen I spotted the white blur of the pilot's face. A propeller blade had sliced through the side window and the fuselage and pinned him to his seat. Poor bastard, I thought, looks like he's had it.

Light caught each yellow Mae West as, one by one, the crew crawled out of the small emergency exit at the aft end of one of the 'planes. The last one wormed his way out on to the petrol-soaked ground and called out. "The navigator's still inside. He's hurt. Get him out."

Nick and I struggled in through the emergency escape hatch and crawled along the catwalk to the front of the plane. In the dimly lit cabin we found the injured navigator huddled in his twisted and bent seat, wedged against the broken navigation table. From his ashen face and tortured expression I could see he was in a lot of pain.

As Nick and I struggled in the cramped cabin to pull him clear; he cried out, "Christ! My leg. Take it easy mate!"

Somehow the two of us heaved him out of the small cabin back to the astrodome. I shoved the plastic dome open and with great difficult we shoved him up through it and eased him down onto the wing. I slid down the wing on to the ground. Nick pushed the groaning navigator towards me. Then Nick jumped down and with our joined hands, we carried the injured navigator in a fireman's lift to a waiting ambulance.

Laying him down on a stretcher, I said, "Careful, Corporal, he's got a compound fracture of the left leg."

The Corporal cocked his head as he turned to look at me. "How do you know? Do you think you're a bloody doctor?"

"Stupid ass! I can feel the broken bone sticking through his trousers, that's how I know, Corporal," I snapped, and spread out the palms of my bloody hands.

As they placed the navigator into the ambulance a crowd of aircrew and ground crew from nearby waiting 'planes quickly gathered. Hushed voices speculated as to what had happened. Suddenly a searchlight beam stabbed down at us, the heat from the intense light warmed my face.

Under the harsh, bright light the two 'planes, welded together, looked like a stage prop in a theatre. Petrol pouring from the gashed fuel tanks sloshed around our feet. Two airmen stood nearby, one pulled out a cigarette and stuck it in the side of his mouth.

"Hey!" I shouted, "You, over there! You want to blow us up? Get to hell out of here!"

Someone in the crowd said he'd heard that the propeller had sliced through the fuselage, hit the pilot and pinned him by his thigh, but he was alive. The back and forth rasp of a hacksaw came through the cockpit window and I could just make out the Medical Officer and another person trying to cut the pilot free. It took about half an hour to release his leg. Bystanders, concerned about the leaking petrol, watched in silence.

When the pilot was freed he had enough strength left to drag himself out of the twisted cockpit and down on to a waiting stretcher. I learned he was a Canadian, a tough one too, I thought. The propeller had stopped at just the right moment, his leg was broken but not cut.

If the aircraft had caught fire the damage would have been devastating. Both crews would have perished and hundreds of 'planes would have gone up in flames, including ours. There was no space anywhere to move the parked aircraft, the parking area was full. The fire engines wouldn't have had a chance.

This was the end of flying for that night. Badly shaken by the crash we grabbed some of our kit from the 'plane and headed back to the transit aircrew quarters.

Our turn would come tomorrow night.

CHAPTER
SEVEN

The Atlas Mountains, Sahara Desert and Cairo

Soon after dark the following day, our lumbering, jet-black Wimpy rolled down the runway for takeoff, leaving Gibraltar and the memory of last night's horrendous accident behind. Carrying two full overload fuel-tanks in the bomb bay, an extra 280 gallons of petrol, we were heavier than when we left Portreath. With 1,030 gallons we had sufficient fuel to fly, non-stop, the 2,200 miles from Gibraltar to Cairo.

To bypass the desert battle in Tunisia, Gibraltar's Briefing Officer pointed out our route on the map; southeast across a short expanse of water to Morocco, over the Atlas Mountains and then east, across the northern edge of the Sahara Desert to Cairo.

After crossing the Mediterranean I levelled out at 14,000ft, a few scattered clouds floated above us. I eased the nose down to build speed and get the aircraft on the "step". The boost pressure gauge needle, one of many fluorescent-green dials on the instrument panel, moved anti-clockwise as I gently eased the throttles back to cruising power.

109

Suddenly the aircraft lurched and swung violently to port. The left rpm gauge reading dropped to zero.

Oh God! I thought, this is a hell of a time to lose an engine!

I snapped off my oxygen mask and shouted to Nick, beside me. "Fuel cocks. Nick, hurry!"

With a series of crash, bangs and curses Nick abandoned his ridiculous jump-seat and in seconds his voice came over the intercom, "Cocks changed Skipper. Overload off, mains on, balance cock B off."

To maintain altitude, I followed the engine failure procedure, pitched levers to "full fine", and both throttles to "full open". The port engine roared back to life.

After a short period I throttled it back to cruising power, thinking that an air lock might have caused a fuel starvation.

The port engine stopped!

Again Nick did his theatricals with the seat and rushed to the back of the 'plane. I quickly determined the fuel system was not the cause of the engine failure; but Nick, now on oxygen, remained in the back ready to switch isolation fuel cock "H", in case he had to use the manual fuel pump.

I punched the feathering button and the propeller windmilled and stopped.

If it wasn't a fuel problem, what had made the engine cut out? I wondered. Could it be spark plugs? Not likely, I reasoned because there was no mag drop on run up, I got full take-off power and everything went smoothly on the long climb to our cruising altitude.

110

Dirty fuel? No, I decided, I would've seen some indication on the climb when the engines were really sucking up petrol; besides, that would effect both engines. There was no indication of overheating, in fact, the two Merlins had behaved beautifully. That is, until the bloody port engine stopped!

I realized I hadn't a clue what was wrong, but I wasn't about to let my crew in on my doubts.

The altimeter showed that we were losing height at about 300ft per minute. I closed the oil cooler shutters to reduce drag. That helped. Our rate of descent slowed, but to maintain altitude I lost airspeed. I called on the intercom, "Frank. Where are we?"

Without hesitating he replied, "We're right over the Atlas Mountains."

My mouth went dry. At this altitude, we were less than 2,000ft above ground. We were losing height and if our starboard engine acted up we'd be in hairy situation.

I pressed the intercom call light. "Fane," I said to the wireless operator. "Get our exact position from Frank and send out a distress signal." I kept my voice calm and forced myself to speak slowly not wanting to show my anxiety. "Give our position, report that we're on one engine and losing altitude."

The intercom was silent. Then, bleeding faintly into my earphones I heard Fane's transmitter — dit dit dit — dah dah dah — dit dit dit. That SOS, I thought, means if anything drastic happen to us at least someone somewhere would know.

Nick and I peered through the side windows into the black night, looking for a glimpse of land below. We saw nothing. I flashed the intercom warning light again and gave the order. "Stand by to bail out."

The crew called an acknowledgment.

We each wore a parachute harness. Nick passed me my chest-pack parachute and I clipped it on. The bulky pack just fitted between me and the control column.

Following the procedure outlined in the Wellington's Pilot's Notes, and keeping my voice as calm as I could, I called over the intercom. "Nick, you leave first — out of the forward hatch. Frank, you're next — take the Very pistol and maps. Fane, you follow Frank. Mac, be careful when you go out of your turret." Then I added what didn't really need to be said, "I'll be right behind you, Fane, so don't waste any time."

If we had to jump the idea was for all of us to get out of the 'plane as quickly as possible to avoid getting too spread out on the ground and unable to find one another.

We waited in silence as the 'plane slowly lost height.

The situation didn't look good. I had to try something, anything, so I unfeathered the port engine and worked the controls. I quickly discovered the engine would continue running if I kept the throttle at almost full climbing-power. With both engines producing power we stopped losing altitude.

The heterodyning from two engines running at different revs was noisy as hell. A pulsating vibration ran through the whole aircraft — and us. Tension slowly lessened and the crew chatted for a moment over the intercom.

I turned to Nick, now back in his seat beside me. "That vibration's a lot better than the sound of one engine, isn't it?"

He grinned. "Sounds pretty good to me."

But we still had a serious problem.

I wondered if we could see the ground so I turned on the landing light located in the port wing. It pointed straight down for a moment before swinging its beam ahead to the landing position. I shone it down a couple of times and picked out barren, jagged rocks. Nick looked out of his window and then turned to me. "Don't like the look of that. We're better off staying up here." I nodded in agreement.

I'd always presumed from discussions on leadership with school mates, that people in charge had authority and they somehow always knew what to do in an emergency. I now realized it didn't work that way! I was in charge but I didn't automatically know what to do. I was the aircraft Captain; if I didn't do it right we all died!

We flew on for about a half an hour. When I was sure we were clear of high ground and no longer had an emergency, I called Fane, "Looks like we're okay now, cancel the distress call."

The intercom clicked as Fane sent out his coded Morse message.

We unclipped our parachutes and Nick stowed mine in its rack down in the bomb aimer's compartment. I'd been very uncomfortable sitting trussed up like a turkey with a parachute on my chest.

We had solved the immediate problem of staying airborne, but with one engine at climbing power we were gobbling up fuel at an alarming rate. We'd either have to turn back to Gibraltar, or land somewhere in the desert short of Cairo. Making some quick calculations Frank announced, "With this increased fuel consumption we can't make it to Cairo, or even Mersamatru, two hundred and fifty miles this side of Cairo. We'll have to land somewhere closer."

I sent Nick to the back to switch fuel cocks to the fuselage overload-tanks. I planned to use up the fuel from the bomb bay tanks first so that, in case of an emergency, they would be empty.

The next decision. Should I turn back and land at Gibraltar, or continue to either Benghazi or Malta, the en route emergency aerodromes given to us in our briefing?

I imagined trying to return to Gibraltar against a stream of 'planes taking off. I didn't like that idea at all! I'd have to make a night single-engine landing with all those aircraft parked down the side of the runway, and that big rock sticking up into the darkness! The memory of last night's dreadful accident, the head-on collision of the two Wellingtons on the runway at Gibraltar, didn't help. I'd also have to jettison fuel, but I couldn't jettison fuel from the overload tanks because the Wellington's fuel jettisoning system only drains the main-wing fuel tanks.

If we continued we'd burn off fuel instead of jettisoning it. That I liked. Our ground speed would pick up as the 'plane became lighter; I liked that idea, too. Our landing, wherever it was, would be in daylight and I liked that very much.

We would continue.

To alert the crew I flashed the emergency call light, "I've decided we're going to press on. Anyone disagree?" No one did.

With the Atlas Mountains behind us I descended to 8,000ft and told the crew I'd turned off the main oxygen valve, and they were free to smoke.

Nick's oxygen mask, unclipped but still attached to his flying helmet, swung back and forth when he turned to me and said, "That's better. I hate sucking oxygen through that thing. It dries up my throat." He lit two cigarettes and passed one to me.

Approaching the Gulf of Gabes I had to make another decision. Which emergency airfield should I select? Benghazi? Malta?

I decided Malta was out. The little island was frequently the target of German air raids. Ground ack-ack gunners were likely to shoot at any aircraft near the island and ask questions afterwards. Besides, I'd heard stories of navigation errors that put aircraft over the German-held island of Pantelleria, 125 miles west of Malta. Jerry would give the aircraft a green light to land and as the crew climbed down the ladder they found themselves looking at the wrong end of German held rifles. Then it was off to a prisoner of war camp.

Going to Benghazi, however, could mean either flying a longer passage over the sea, or flying over the desert near the ground battle somewhere east of Tripoli.

I compromised. We would fly fairly close to the coast, giving Tripoli a wide berth.

I ran the crew through our dinghy drill and then relaxed, as much as I could, listening to the engines' undulating roar.

We flew on in the darkness below scattered high cloud. As we approached Tripoli artillery flashes in the desert off to our right looked like distant fireflies. Nick and I scanned the sky constantly for German night-fighters. From the movement I felt in my flight-controls I knew Mac was slowly turning his turret back and forth, looking for that night-fighter that might spot our exhaust flash and sneak in behind us.

Ahead in the distance, between the coast and us, sheet lightning chased weakly around the sky. Maybe we'd be lucky and the electrical disturbance would discourage Luftwaffe fighters in the area.

As we droned on the desert battlefield slid away on our right and the dim flashes of gunfire to the south faded. Lots of poor sods were being killed down there, I thought.

Dawn came as a streaked, yellow glow ahead of us. The morning light caught small puffy cumulus clouds below, turning them into little yellow islands on the dark blue-black sea. One by one, the stars faded as the sun's red ball slowly eased out of the horizon. It rose becoming a mass of golden fire gradually changing the sky from orange to blue. The fluffy, white clouds below accentuated the blue of the sea; a sea as smooth as a mirror.

An hour later the sun, now well up in the sky and dead ahead, heated the cockpit. We cursed the unbearable glare through the windscreen. I wedged a folded map to block out the sun's glare. Nick shielded his eyes and peered ahead as we neared our ETA on the coast. Within seconds of spotting landfall he found a pinpoint. "We're here," he said, stabbing a finger at his neatly folded map.

We didn't have to alter course because we were tracking straight towards Benghazi. In a shallow dive I descended to 1,000ft and looked at the instrument panel clock. We'd been flying for nearly nine hours.

With the port engine still screaming we passed over Benghazi at about 1,500ft. A dead city — no vehicles moved, no people in the streets, just a few goats wandering around between palm trees and the low, flat-topped, yellow and white buildings. I circled to the south of the city and spotted an aerodrome squeezed in between buildings on three sides. Several small, damaged aircraft lay on the ground.

Our maps didn't have a lot of detail and our Gibraltar briefing had been a bit vague concerning the emergency aerodrome's exact position. While listening to the briefing I never expected I'd be looking for a place to land in the desert.

As I circled the aerodrome I called over the intercom. "Who was the clot at briefing who said we'd be able to land at Benghazi? From the looks of it that 'drome is just for light aircraft. How's our fuel, Frank?"

Frank had been keeping an eye on the fuel gauges.

"Not too good, Skipper. We're pretty low, actually we're almost empty. We'd better find somewhere to land — and soon!"

"We can't land at that small aerodrome, so before we run out of fuel we'll have to head out into the desert where we can make a forced landing if we have to," I called back to the crew, "Everyone keep your eyes peeled for a flat place."

Nick and I hunched forward staring through the windscreen.

"Look!" Nick suddenly called out pointing ahead. "Over there! See those 'planes?"

My weary eyes, following the direction he indicated, spotted several hard to see crashed and burned German 'planes dotted across the orange desert. I recognized an Me 109. Cautiously I circled what was obviously an aerodrome, but I couldn't pick out a runway. Our briefing hadn't mentioned anything like this.

I finally picked out the landing strip. At the same time I noticed a parked "stickleback" Wellington. It moved slowly, taxied a short distance then stopped and the engines shut down. From its slipstream's blowing sand I noted the wind direction and set up a landing pattern.

On final approach to the ruddy-brown landing strip, I lowered the wheels and throttled back. The port engine stopped. I punched the feathering button and continued for a single engine landing.

The wheels touched gently on to the hard sand and the 'plane rolled to a stop.

"Pretty good, Skipper," Nick said, grinning. "With a little practice you'll make a perfect landing one of these days."

I tried to fire-up the dead engine to taxi, but it wouldn't start.

Ahead, in the distance, a jeep sped towards us trailing a plume of sand. When it was about 100 yards away it stopped.

I opened the emergency hatch above my seat, stood up and waved. The driver cupped his hands around his mouth and shouted, "DON'T . . . MOVE! . . . YOU . . . ARE . . . IN . . . A . . . MINE . . . FIELD!"

We obviously weren't going anywhere for a while so I switched off the starboard engine; it was starting to heat up anyway.

Sitting on the ground in the sun we started to feel the heat inside the 'plane. I stuck my head in the cabin. "It's getting bloody hot. Open the astrodome and the rear hatch. Nick, open up the forward hatch. Let's try and get some air circulating." The crew peeled off their leather jackets and battle dress tunics.

We sat sweltering in the morning sun and waited. There's nothing like a black painted aircraft to heat up quickly.

Finally a small group of men appeared. The mine disposal squad had arrived. They moved slowly towards us crossing back and forth and sweeping the ground with their mine detectors. As they moved along they stretched a ribbon of tape down either side of the swept area. One of the men stuck his head under the forward hatch and called out, "Okay, Skipper, start your engines and taxi ahead between the tapes."

I started up the starboard engine. It's pretty difficult to taxi a twin-engine aircraft on one engine and follow a straight line, but when I thought of the mines that might be tucked in the ground outside of those tapes, I suddenly became very good at it.

Out in the clear I taxied in great arcing loops and followed the jeep as it headed towards the black-topped road running east and west through the desert. An airman raised his arms and marshalled me towards a vehicle parked close to the road. I stopped, shut down the engine, locked the parking brakes and snapped the control lock over the wheel and rudder pedals.

Nick opened the forward hatch lowered the wooden ladder and I climbed stiffly down to the ground.

I looked back up at Frank waiting at the top, sleepy-eyed and paler than usual with a stubble of beard; he seemed exhausted. I wondered if I appeared as haggard as he did.

Gazing around at the dry, hot Saharan landscape I realised that although we hadn't made it to Cairo, we were, at least, safe. Our Wellington, parked near a field kitchen, would be "home" for the next ten days. Across the road were a dozen or so one-man tents.

A Squadron Leader wearing a khaki shirt, baggy kneeshorts and long socks, climbed out of his jeep.

"Lucky you didn't roll further down the strip or you'd have finished up further into that minefield we haven't swept yet." He looked at our 'plane. "Where are you from?"

"We've come from Gibraltar on our way to Cairo, Sir. I lost an engine over the Atlas Mountains and had to land here because we were short of petrol."

He looked at the feathered propeller. "Sorry I can't find you a tent, everything's being sent west to chase Rommel. There's nothing I can do right now about your engine. You chaps get some grub from over there," he turned and pointed to the field kitchen. "Get your heads down for a bit and we'll talk later."

Exhausted from our long, tense night flight, no one was hungry. We lay down on the sand in the shadow of the aircraft and slept. It was about 3 o'clock when I woke up. We went over to the cookhouse and were given some biscuits, jam and hot tea.

Fully refreshed I followed the Squadron Leader's instructions and found the Ops room nestled in a small, sandy cave in the side of a *wadi*.

The cave smelt musty and the furnishings certainly weren't luxurious; three badly stained folding canvas chairs, a map tacked on a sheet of plywood, a rusty, old Italian typewriter and a massive black-stained, straight-backed wooden chair with highly ornate carvings. It looked as if it had been pinched from a Moroccan palace.

The Squadron Leader sat in the "kingly chair" behind a desk made of a wooden door propped on wine crates. He was a bit portly, sort of Henry the VIIIs shape. With his ruddy complexion and bristly moustache he looked somewhat like one of Bill Hooper's RAF Officer caricatures published in *Tee Emm*. I put him in his early forties, probably a regular who might have flown Wapitis in India.

When I asked about getting my aircraft repaired, he replied, "I'm afraid it doesn't look too good, Sergeant. I've no mechanics here who can work on your Merlins, they just do radial stuff. We've got a couple of Beaufighters and one Wellington here so far." I'd told him earlier we were *en route* to Cairo; he now seemed disappointed that we were not assigned to his unit. After a long pause he blurted out, "I've got an idea."

He reached for the field telephone at the end of the desk and cranked the handle viciously. Someone apparently answered because he started shouting into the mouthpiece.

When the one-sided conversation ended he pushed his fingers into his khaki battle dress top pocket and pulled out a packet of Craven As. I took his proffered cigarette and offered him a light.

Blowing out a cloud of smoke he said, "A fitter from 33 Squadron will come over. They've got Hurricanes and can handle your Merlin."

"How ironic," I said. "My brother was with that squadron, killed at El Alamein. Shot down by an Me 109."

"Bad luck," he mumbled, dropping his eyes away from mine. Then he looked back up at me. "Must be your older brother? You look as if you're just a kid. How old are you?"

"Nineteen, Sir."

"How old was your brother when he was shot down?"

"Just turned twenty-one, Sir. His birthday was in July, he was killed on 27 July 1941."

"Sod of a war, isn't it? Especially for you young chaps. You hardly get your wings when you're sent to some Godforsaken place like this. Or you climb into an aeroplane and get blown out of the sky."

Neither of us spoke.

Suddenly he stood up and broke the tension. "Look, old chap, er, Sergeant. I'll do my best to get someone over here as soon as I can to look at your duff engine."

A couple of days later a Corporal and an LAC, 33 Squadron's fitters, arrived in a beaten up 1,500-weight lorry.

I explained to them in detail about the mag drop at Gibraltar and that no one had discovered the cause for it. "Do you know exactly what the mechanics did to the engine?" the Corporal asked, looking at the aircraft's travelling log.

"No," I replied, "but everything worked fine until I throttled back at fourteen thousand feet."

"Too bad you didn't do that air test," the airman chipped in, "they'd have found out what was wrong before you left Gib."

"Let's take a look," the young Corporal replied, moving towards the port engine.

With shirts off in the warm sun they set up a ladder and changed all the spark plugs; this was a day's work. When they finished and had the engine cowlings screwed back on, I started the engine for a run-up; ground crew were not allowed to do engine run-ups. When I flipped off the magneto switch, the engine banged and backfired and shook so badly in its engine mounts that I was afraid I'd damage the engine so I quickly flipped the switch back on.

Next day they brought in a new ignition harness and installed it. I did another run-up but the engine still backfired.

The following day an unflappable, weather-beaten Flight Sergeant arrived with the two mechanics. He listened in silence to my story and said, "I'll take a look."

Later, I went back to the 'plane and found the Flight Sergeant wrapping something in an oily rag. He looked around at me with a big grin on his deeply suntanned face. "I've found the problem. The slip-ring in the magneto's stuck. It kept the spark fully advanced."

No wonder the engine had cut out over the Atlas Mountains when I'd throttled back to cruising revs.

"It's probably going to take several days to find parts to rebuild this mag. I'll do what I can." Then, for the first time, he smiled and with a reassuring look added, "In the meantime have a holiday by the sea."

As he turned to climb into the lorry, he paused and looked back. "Oh. The Corporal says your name's Leicester. We had a Sergeant Pilot Leicester. Got shot down in the desert back east a few months ago."

"He was my brother," I said, quietly.

At the cookhouse we'd scrounged some "irons" from the cook. One knife, two forks and two spoons to share

124

between the five of us, and we each acquired a cup, and a round biscuit-tin lid for a plate.

The cook served bully beef three times a day. At each meal he cooked it a different way and when he exhausted his repertoire, the cycle started again. Who ever said RAF cooks have no imagination?

I got cold at night sleeping on the ground under the 'plane so I moved up into the cockpit, removed the control locks and tried sleeping in the pilot's seat. The padded leather seat was very comfortable and, sometimes, on long flights I had found myself dozing off for a few seconds, but it was no place to sleep all night. After a couple of nights I gave it up.

Except for Frank Prescott, who made himself a nest in the centre of the fuselage on the wooden catwalk that led aft to Mac's rear gun turret, the rest of us slept on the hard ground. I suppose Frank was comfortable inside there, but in the morning when he squeezed his way out of the small emergency hatch he looked a crumpled sight.

While waiting for our Wimpy to be repaired the five of us entertained ourselves swimming in the chilly Mediterranean. The water looked blue and inviting but, God, was it cold! We swam hard to stop ourselves freezing.

I asked if the area had been swept clear of mines and I was told that Jerry left in such a hurry he only had time to put a few down near the landing strip. Since it appeared safe we went exploring. We climbed around wrecked German and Italian aircraft, examining them in detail, and discussed design and construction differences from aircraft we had flown. An airman told us that German pilots usually carried a Luger in the cockpit so we looked for hidden pistols.

One day, with great difficulty, the five of us removed a wing-mounted machine gun from a badly damaged Me 109. Since we didn't know how to dismantle the gun it took us hours to get it out of the wing. When we'd finished our hands and arms were covered in grease. Water was severely rationed so we cleaned up using fuel found in a bomb-damaged, three-engined Ju 52. One engine had been knocked out of its mountings.

I discovered, when I turned on the fuel cock, that fuel flowed from a broken line. The synthetic German petrol smelt quite different from our own, but it cleaned our greasy hands. I turned to Fane, who was beside me, "Look at this." I reached up to the top of the front of the radial engine. "Look at this plaque. It's a Pratt and Whitney American-made engine. I wonder where Jerry bought it! How long before Pearl Harbour had engines been sold to Germany?" (I found out, later, that in 1937 the German BMW company had made Pratt and Whitney engines under licence.)

Empty wine bottles, ammunition and rifles, dropped by fleeing Italian soldiers lay around everywhere. One afternoon we each selected a rifle, grabbed a handful of bullets and went down to the beach for a little target practice.

If you hit the bottom of the overturned barge that was lying a few hundred yards offshore, there was a puff of rust and, moments later, a satisfying loud clang.

126

I thought firing these rifles might be dangerous because the Italians' bolt action locking mechanism seemed rather crude; it consisted solely of a small sear that locked the bolt when the first pressure was taken on the trigger. There was no rotation of the bolt as in the sturdy British Lee Enfield rifle to positively lock the breech before the rifle fired. I was afraid that one of us might get an eye blown out.

One morning, just at dawn, a terrific barrage of anti-aircraft gunfire woke us. We scrambled up to watch the sights.

The guns must have been hidden in a nearby depression back in the desert. Each time they fired we felt the muzzle blast and smoke from the guns drifted over us. Puffs of black ack-ack burst in the sky over Benghazi a few miles away. Suddenly there was a muffled explosion and a red burst of light filled the sky. Then, a second later, an even louder explosion and a white glow overshadowed the dawn-breaking sky, followed by a huge pall of black smoke.

We heard later that a supply ship in Benghazi harbour had been hit and the Luftwaffe was determined to sink it. The early morning raids by Jerry became a ritual for several days.

There were no interceptor fighters at Benghazi. The Wellington (a Mk VIII stickleback mine destroyer) that taxied the day we arrived hadn't moved since. I never did find the pilot. A couple of twin-engined Beaufighters were parked near the landing strip. The whole operation seemed pretty casual to me.

One day I watched a Beaufighter, returning from a sortie, come in for a landing. The pilot, it seemed to me, was going too fast when he rounded out. When the wheels touched ground the undercarriage collapsed and the aircraft slid across the desert in a cloud of sand.

After the dust settled I expected to see a pile of wreckage instead, the 'plane, undamaged, lay on its belly. Within seconds two figures climbed out, dusted off their flying suits and walked around the 'plane assessing damage. Later, I heard it had been hit by one cannon shell, a lucky shot in a vulnerable spot in the hydraulic system.

An almost continuous flow of east and westbound traffic moved along the road beside the aerodrome. One afternoon I said to Fane and Mac, "Let's hitch a ride on a convoy and see what the desert's like to the east?"

We stood by the edge of the road and thumbed a ride towards Cairo. We were soon picked up, but after about twenty minutes bouncing in the back of an empty open lorry I called out. "This is too uncomfortable and too hot. I've got dust in my eyes, ears and mouth. Had enough?"

Both Fane and Mac nodded. I banged on the roof and shouted to the driver to stop.

We waited beside the road until a large, westbound supply lorry came into view. I stuck out my thumb. The vehicle crawled to a stop and we scrambled up on top of neatly piled boxes, a load of supplies heading towards the fighting zone. I pulled back the heavy tarpaulin, "Hey look at this," I called out, "Fresh tinned fruit!" We grinned.

Within minutes we had prised off the lid with our fingers and removed a few cans of fruit. As we neared our field-kitchen we tossed the cans down onto the side of the road, banged on the driver's cab and shouted we wanted to get off. The three of us jumped down, waited as the lorry ground its gears and pulled away in a cloud of black diesel exhaust. We then walked back a few hundred yards and retrieved our ill-gotten gains.

That night, along with our bully beef "cook's special", the five of us enjoyed sweet, juicy tinned peaches from California.

One overcast morning I was walking towards the Ops room when it started to rain. It was an extraordinary sight. Big raindrops plopped on the sand and sank, leaving dark red-brown spots. After a few minutes the ground was soaking wet. Then, as suddenly as it had started, the rain stopped and the ground glistened in the sun and a fresh, clean smell came up from the ground. The smell reminded me of walking in the rain-wet woods at Oxshot with our two fox terriers.

The next day I noticed small green tufts of vegetation sprouting in the sand. It made me wonder what might grow in the desert if it could be irrigated.

The Flight Sergeant finally brought the magneto back and he and the two fitters soon installed it. They closed and locked the Merlin's cowlings. "Okay, Sarge," the Flight Sergeant called up to me in the cockpit. "Start 'er up and let's see what happens."

I did an engine run-up. Not a trace of a mag-drop. With the travelling copy of the F700 signed, we were now serviceable and could leave Benghazi. Nine days after our landing in the minefield we were ready to take off for Cairo.

Full of bully beef, we left Benghazi on 11 December and headed east to Mersamatruh, and then on to LG 224, Cairo's new aerodrome. We took along five airmen going to Cairo on leave.

The Wellington, a medium-heavy bomber, had no seating aft in the fuselage so the men had to sit wherever they could find room; not the safest way to travel but, as they said, it beat riding for several days in the back of an open, dusty lorry. I had to agree with that!

After our arrival at Cairo I signed in at the reception desk. It had taken us 37 hours and 27 minutes of flying time from England to Cairo, and seventeen days to complete the trip.

The CO, an engineering officer, came out of his office and said, "Would you give us a hand and fly your 'plane over to the RAF aerodrome at Heliopolis?"

On our way over I took a sightseeing swing around the Pyramids and Sphinx. Flying at 1,000ft we saw the awe-inspiring ancient monuments as they loomed out of the haze.

At Heliopolis I got a signature for the delivery of one Wellington, twenty-four spark plugs and two aircraft clocks. A vehicle then took us to No 22 PTC in Cairo, a large tent camp for transient aircrew. In our assigned tent, about 15ft square, we each had a camp bed with legs stuck in the sand and a small wooden table. This would be our home for the next few days, or would it be weeks?

The day after our arrival I said to my crew, "Let's go into Cairo."

We hitched a ride and I was amazed at the hustle and bustle, the wild traffic, honking horns, the crowds of yelling, pushing people. Strange smells came from charcoal braziers. Everyone seemed to be busy either selling something, carrying something, or pushing a cart.

Little kids pimped for their elder sisters and beggars were evenly spaced along the pavement; saying *imshi* didn't get rid of pleading beggars, but "F★★★ off!" barked in English did!

To get away from the noise and the crowds I suggested we go to the cinema to see a French film. The Arabic subtitles fascinated me. A long French conversation gave a correspondingly long English subtitle but only a few Arabic letters, yet a brief sigh from the lovesick heroine caused the Arabic letters to fly across the screen.

The highlight of the entertainment came after the film ended during the Egyptian national anthem. While the respectful audience stood, a slightly drunk British Army Corporal in the stalls, sang, off key, at the top of his lungs, "Up your pipe, King Farouke, hang your bollix on a hook . . ." Even the Arabs were amused!

Since we had successfully completed our "ferry flight" I hoped we would be sent back to England to pick up another 'plane and deliver it to the Middle

East. Instead, after a two-day rest, we found ourselves back at LG 224 with orders from the CO of No 1 Ferry Unit to take a Wellington to Karachi, India!

Stories about Kipling's India had always fascinated me. At Prep School one of the masters, who had been stationed there with the army, told tales of snakes, tigers, rain and heat, palaces, old forts and adventure. Tales to set a boy's imagination spinning! Now I was going there!

But first I was told to choose one of several Wellingtons parked in the sand-blown dispersals around aerodrome LG 224. I didn't like the look of the first one. The floor, instruments seats, everything was covered with sand. Sand had been forced through the smallest cracks by the wind. The 'plane looked as if it had been sitting there for months. It had a totally "clapped out" look.

After carefully examining each of the remaining aircraft I realized they were even more dilapidated and decided the first one wasn't so bad after all. I'd take it!

These Wimpies had probably done several Ops tours over Europe. Now that four-engined Lancasters and Stirlings were bombing Germany, the Wellingtons were slated for action in India.

My crew and I spent three days helping the ground crew clear sand from the engine nacelles and tidying up the mess inside. Mac dismantled all the machine guns, cleaned out the sand and reassembled them. I hoped they would work if needed. Fane cleared sand from the radio and checked it to make sure it was in working condition.

The ground crew finally pronounced NF 814, a rather bedraggled Mark Ic Wellington, clear of sand and serviceable.

We were ready to head for India.

CHAPTER
EIGHT

Christmas in Bahrain — Arrival in Karachi

After an external check of Wellington Ic HF 814, the aeroplane which was to take us to India, I climbed the ladder and slid into the pilot's seat. This old Wimpy looked a bit bedraggled; sitting for God knows how long, the Egyptian sun had badly faded her paintwork. She looked well worn, but she was serviceable. The crew had gone over each piece of their equipment thoroughly, and I had spent time with the ground crew as they worked over the Pegasus engines.

Frank leaned into the cockpit and pointed at a folded map in his hand. "We'll leave Cairo, head across here to Port Said, then follow the coast." He flipped the map over. "We'll look for the pipeline, here." He pointed to the thin line on the map. "It runs from the Mediterranean to Kirkuk. Before reaching Kirkuk we head south to Habbaniyah. I estimate about six and a half hours. Here, Nick. You take this map, I've got another one."

After take-off we climbed to 2,000ft, leaving Egypt's green delta behind, flying over sand and scrub towards

134

the Mediterranean. About an hour later, as we followed the Mediterranean coast, Nick peered inland towards the desert looking for the oil pipeline. The Briefing Officer jokingly said, "You'll have no trouble finding the pipeline to Kirkuk, it's the only black line stretching across the desert."

Nick tapped my arm and pointed. "There it is. Over there."

The Briefing Officer was right. It wasn't just "the only black line"; it was the only "thing" distinguishable against the drab, brown desert.

The pre-war RAF Station at Habbaniyah, about 60 miles west of Baghdad, was our first Middle East stopover point. After landing I taxied to the parking apron in front of the hangars. The Liberator pilot who landed after us swung his aircraft's bulky fuselage around and parked on the ramp beside our 'plane.

I was standing at the bottom of the ladder helping Nick unload our gear when, suddenly, a series of sharp cracking sounds came from the parked Liberator. I swung round just in time to see the heavy aircraft lurch as the right wheel broke through the concrete apron and dropped into a large jagged hole.

The aircraft sank to the ground resting on the two starboard engine nacelles and a couple of badly bent propellers.

One by one the crew of the damaged 'plane jumped out and stood huddled in a group, staring at their pride and joy lying on the ground like a large, wounded bird. The concrete apron, stressed for aeroplanes like the

Fairey IIIF's biplanes of the early 1930s, was no match for the heavy, four-engined Liberator.

I had just settled into Habbaniyah's aircrew quarters when Fane rushed into my room. "Tony. You'll never believe this. I just bumped into Lester Brown. He's an old, old friend from Nassau. I just can't believe it." Grinning, he bubbled on, "Yes, he's a Flying Officer, a pilot in the "raf". I just can't believe it!"

Only a handful of Bahamians were in the RAF. It was an extraordinary coincidence that these two men should meet in an out-of-the-way place in the middle of the Iraqi desert.

We stayed three days at Habbaniyah where we met several other crews like us *en route* to India. Fane spent a lot of the time with his old friend Lester.

On the day we arrived a Corporal offered us an open invitation to drop into the Corporals' Club for a beer. One evening, with nothing better to do, I wandered over to the Club. I opened the door and found myself in the middle of a drunken orgy. Everyone was totally sloshed and two young Corporals, glasses in hand, pranced naked down the centre of the table, dodging glasses and beer bottles and shouting and enacting obscenities. That kind of affair didn't really appeal to me, so I left.

It made me wonder, though, whether there was much homosexuality in the RAF. I'd never noticed any indications. But since a small proportion of society always has been homosexual, I presumed the same proportion probably existed in the services. I certainly hadn't seen such desires amongst the aircrew I knew;

136

most of them spent a lot of their spare time chasing girls; and once in a while they caught one!

After leaving Habbaniyah we continued south, over the barren Iraqi desert to Basra and down the Persian Gulf coast to Bahrain where, on 23 December 1942, we landed at the flat sandy Muhurrak Island airstrip.

Even though there was a war on we weren't exactly rushed along on our way to India.

"It's Christmas," the Sergeant said, "We'll get your aircraft inspected after Christmas and get you out of here."

To improve our Christmas spirit we were each given a bottle of liquor of our choice. On Christmas Eve some of the crew got together and celebrated. I wasn't in a partying mood so I found a good book and stayed up most of the night reading, drinking whiskey and listening to the radio in the small, sparsely furnished reading room. I finished the whole bottle of scotch by myself! This was a new "first experience" and the following morning, with a thundering hangover, I decided it would be the last time I'd try that.

On Christmas Day an oil company executive invited all the transient crews at Muhurrak to a party. A rickety taxi driven by a fat Arab delivered the five of us to the oil company's base, a group of stark, square, white, concrete buildings in the desert miles from anywhere.

Our host's house was spacious. In the middle of a well-appointed dining room, with fine rich carpets on the tiled floor, stood a long table piled with things we hadn't seen since the war started. Dishes filled with delicious black caviar, smoked salmon and every kind

137

of cold-cut imaginable. There were bowls of fruit and fresh salads. I wondered where it all came from in this dry, benighted desert.

The bar, attended by a white-coated, bearded Arab, had enough bottles to more than satisfy this group of thirsty aviators.

This set-up was even better than our first unrationed food binge at Gibraltar. Our oil company hosts were all men. I wondered if any women worked there, or if the staff had wives with them; but I didn't see women that night. Maybe they kept them hidden from wild, young aircrew.

After several drinks, light conversation and eating our fill, we wished everyone a Merry Christmas, thanked our hosts and said our polite goodbyes.

On the way out to our waiting taxi Mac spotted, parked by the front door, a motorbike sitting on its back-wheel stand. He decided he had to ride it.

"Wait for me," he called out swinging his leg over the saddle. "I'm going for a quick spin."

He was so drunk he could hardly stand up let alone ride a powerful machine like that!

Trying to coax him into the taxi, I said, "Come on, Mac. Let's go home." But no amount of cajoling would dissuade him. He was determined to ride that bike. Realizing we would have difficulty getting him to leave without riding it, and if he did ride he'd probably kill himself, I gave the others a quick signal.

While they diverted his attention, I took out a soft pencil and marked a line down the spark plug's ceramic insulation, shorting it — a trick I'd learned riding my motorbike at a rally in England. At these rallies one of the stewards would do something like this to your bike to disable it, but nothing that would harm the machine. You then had to find the fault, correct it and ride the bike over a designated course.

Mac, drunk and unsuspecting, was easy to fool. He pumped the kick-starter repeatedly for about twenty minutes, cursing the machine and turning very red in the face. Finally, he gave up, climbed into the taxi and we left.

I've often wondered if the owner of that bike had difficulty getting it started!

During the taxi ride home we had our first crew altercation. MacNab, sitting in the back, tried to climb out of the window several times — "to walk home" — and Nick Rushworth finally slugged him. When he came to he was slightly bruised and very upset, all the more so because he wasn't really sure who had knocked him out.

First he accused me, and then each crew member in turn. I think he finally decided that Nick had done it. From then on, except when we were flying, the relationship between the two of them was always a bit strained, but their personal feelings over this incident never caused any crew problems. They were always very professional in the aircraft.

I believe this professional relationship and crew discipline were the result of the way we "crewed up" at Chipping Warden at the OTU. As we neared the end of our training there, students from each of the crew trades went around asking "May I fly with you?" or "Will you join my crew?"

Since I didn't know any of the navigators, wireless operators, gunners or bomb aimers well enough to be selective, I left the matter of crew selection to fate; as had my four crew members. After all the crew positions had been allotted, the "leftovers" in each trade became our crew. This meant no one ever felt he'd made a mistake and wished he had chosen to fly with someone else. I don't know how many other RAF bomber crews came together this way, but it worked for us.

While in Bahrain I met the Captain of one the Catalina flying boats anchored offshore in the blue-green Persian Gulf. After we chatted for a while, he said, "I've got to do an air test. Would you like to go for a ride?"

Having never flown in a flying boat, or seaplane, I jumped at the opportunity. Under a hot sun we paddled out to the Catalina in a small boat carrying drums of petrol, boxes and crew flight bags. What a performance, I thought, all that effort just to get out to the aircraft was almost a day's work! On top of that the aircrew, together with the ground crew, had to heave 5-gallon drums of petrol out of the boat and haul them up on the top of the wing to refuel the 'plane. Enough to dampen the enthusiasm of most, I thought.

The wind was very light, barely rippling the water's surface. "Weigh anchor!" the Skipper ordered as he started the engines. We immediately taxied away from the shore. No brakes, of course, just like the Tiger Moths at Cambridge, only a hell of a lot bigger!

He did a quick run-up, tested the mags and headed into what little wind there was for take-off. With a great roar from the two engines and a cloud of spray from the flying boat's hull we skidded across the sparkling aquamarine water and, suddenly, we were airborne. The pilot circled around the island while the flight engineer did some engine tests.

When the engineer finished the pilot turned to me, "Like low flying?"

I'd never been really thrilled flying close to the ground, but what could I say!

He dropped the 'plane down to about 10ft above the water and headed towards the anchored Catalina still being refuelled. He eased the 'plane down, down, down until the hull brushed the water making a strange swishing sound; a breathtaking experience.

Three days after my Catalina flight we boarded our Wellington bound for Karachi. After take-off I stayed below 300ft, circled and headed for the two anchored Catalinas.

"They think they can low fly, wait till they see this!" I called out to the crew over the intercom. I eased the aircraft down lower and lower. "Nick. Look out of your window and tell me how far the tip of the prop is from the water."

"That's low enough, Tony," he yelled, "You've got a rooster tail blowing back from it."

As we shot by the two flying boats one of the crew standing on the Catalina's wing lowered the fuel drum he was holding and waved at us. I heaved back on the stick.

Mac's voice came over the intercom, "What the hell!" he yelled. "I'm drenched."

When I pulled the control column back the aircraft's tail dropped, hitting the water and punching in the fabric along the underside of the aluminium fuselage frame. The rounded aluminium bottom of Mac's turret acted as a scoop and several gallons of sea water shot up into his turret and cascaded down on him. He was justifiably upset because he'd have to clean the salt water off his guns and the turret's control mechanism.

On 28 December, en route to Karachi, we landed at Sharjah. There we spent a couple of days in the lap of luxury, living in a Beau Geste-like desert fort used by British Overseas Airways passengers.

Two days later we took off, heading for India. After a twenty-five minute flight in bright sun under a clear, blue sky, I found the aircraft unserviceable and returned to Sharjah. I taxied to the fort and parked in the desert, a few hundred yards from the compound's huge, wooden gates set in thick, whitewashed stone walls.

British Airways staff gave each of us a nicely furnished room with a ceiling fan and we ate in the passengers' dining room. Considering we were isolated in the desert, the place was really an oasis; comfortable and with very good food.

Late that evening I walked in darkness out of the fort's main gate and across the sandy road to get something from our 'plane. As I reached up to open the forward hatch I caught the glint of metal and I found myself staring down the barrel of an ancient Lee

Enfield rifle, held inches away from my nose. At the other end of the rifle stood a dark-eyed, hook-nosed, elderly Arab. In the faint light I could see the greying stubble of his beard.

Moving very carefully, speaking slowly and softly and using sign language, I tried to explain to him that I belonged to the 'plane and was allowed to go inside. But no amount of pantomiming would persuade the fierce-looking guard to let me open the hatch.

He'd been instructed to guard the aeroplanes and, by Allah, he was going to do just that! Keeping his finger on the trigger he nudged the barrel towards me and grunted. His breath smelt worse than a camel's.

I didn't like the meaningful look in his dark eyes and decided that whatever it was I wanted from the 'plane wasn't that important.

With a parting "*Salaam alikham*" I nervously turned my back and walked slowly across the sand to the fort and returned to my room.

On the next day, on 31 December 1942, we roared down Sharjah's dusty landing strip, climbed away from the desert outpost and headed for the Straits of Hormuz. *En route* once more to India.

In our departure briefing at Cairo we were told, "After leaving Sharjah, for political reasons, you are not to fly over the island Ras Musahdam, which lies off the tip of the cape dividing the Persian Gulf from the Gulf of Oman."

Frank gave me a series of courses to steer and manoeuvred us carefully round the dogleg over the

Straits of Hormuz, avoiding the forbidden island and keeping us clear of the Persian territorial limits off the coast of Biaban. He then gave me a southeast compass course for our non-stop flight of more than 1,000 miles, over the Indian Ocean to Karachi.

The blue-green ocean, with the Persian coast always in view on our left, seemed endless.

To break the monotony I called the crew on the intercom, "I think you should have some gunnery practice."

"Good idea," came Mac's voice from the rear turret.

"Call when ready," I added.

Nick climbed into the forward turret, Fane and Frank positioned themselves at the beam guns. We had never simultaneously fired all of the turret's guns; the four rear-turret, two beam and two forward-turret guns.

"Guns loaded," I called over the intercom. Everyone replied, "Ready."

"Fire!"

The aircraft shook and shuddered and I watched bursts of tracers arc from Nick's forward guns into the deep blue ocean below. When Nick and Mac swung their turrets from side to side it changed the aircraft's trim and I was kept busy holding the 'plane straight and level. A cloud of blue, acrid smoke from the guns soon filled the cockpit and stung my eyes.

"Cease fire. Cease fire," I called out over the intercom.

Nick climbed back into the seat beside me, a smile stretched across his face. "I enjoyed that," he said, "but now I'll have to clean the bloody guns."

144

Our arrival at Karachi, like several of our previous escapades, had a touch of flair; and it got me in hot water again with the "brass".

We made landfall right on course and on Frank's ETA. In spite of the brown haze hanging over the city, we easily found Karachi's aerodrome. Approaching it, I called the tower on the radio. The controller gave me the runway in use, the QFE altimeter setting and landing instructions, adding, "Land as soon as possible."

On the downwind leg I lowered the undercarriage, but didn't get any green lights to indicate the wheels were "down and locked". I raised and lowered the wheels several times. No luck! I called the tower. "Karachi. This is Wellington eight-four-one. I've got undercarriage trouble . . . can't get any green lights . . . I'm leaving the circuit."

I climbed a few thousand feet and, lowered the undercarriage, but no lights!

I put the aeroplane into a steep dive, selected wheels down and pulled the stick back hard, hoping the "G" force would cause the wheels to snap in locked down position. Still no luck.

Meanwhile the tower called and told me to hurry up and land because several Stearmen, single engine training 'planes, flown by Chinese student pilots, were expected to return any minute from a cross-country flight. "Some of them may be short of fuel," the controller added.

Rejoining the circuit I told the tower I still couldn't get green lights, but with the dismal thought that the undercarriage mechanism might be packed full of Cairo sand and might fold up on landing, I lowered the gear again and there they were — three in the green!

I landed and taxied to what was obviously a brand new parking area with its freshly-finished, bright, white concrete.

At the bottom of the aircraft's boarding ladder I stepped down on to the dazzling clean surface and confronted a bristling Wing Commander. Without any form of greeting he burst out, "Sergeant. Why didn't you land when ordered to?"

I had been in the service long enough to learn that some ground crew officers just didn't like aircrew and were unusually bellicose when talking to aircrew Sergeant pilots. I had also learned that the more one talked back in a level, well-modulated voice, the more upset they became!

Before I could tell him I had undercarriage trouble, he turned and pointed at the torn fabric around the front gun turret, sealed before we left England to give increased airspeed. When Nick fired the guns he rotated the turret and tore away this fabric, leaving a gap between the turret and the fuselage.

"How did you tear that?" He then pointed towards the tail. "What happened to that fabric hanging down there under the rear turret. Did you hit something?"

"I ordered practice firing of all guns, Sir." I quickly added, glancing at Nick, "And all eight of them now need cleaning."

Nick and Mac smiled.

I expected a rebuttal for this remark and a follow-up on the damaged tail but, instead, the Wing Commander said, "Because you delayed your landing you could have caused the Chinese student pilots to run out of petrol."

I looked around the aerodrome and asked, "What student pilots, Sir?"

This set him off again. He finally stopped his tirade long enough to ask me to explain about the undercarriage problem. In the middle of my explanation he cut me off in mid-sentence saying, "I don't believe anything you've said, Sergeant," he continued. "You young pilots think you know everything about aeroplanes; we'll probably find out that your 'plane's quite serviceable."

At that moment the old Wimpy, bless her geodesic ribs, cooperated beautifully and disgorged gallons of hot, smelly oil from a vent pipe in the starboard engine. As the dark black puddle slowly spread over the pristine, white concrete the Wing Commander just stood there bug-eyed, open-mouthed. Flabbergasted.

For the first time in my life I realized I was witnessing someone who was actually speechless!

At that moment the flock of Stearmen streamed into the circuit and, one after another, bounced down on the runway.

The Wing Commander turned his back on the five of us and walked away!

For our flight from England to India we were credited with thirty-seven hours and twenty minutes Operational Flying Hours.

I wondered where I'd be when I logged my next Ops hours, but this wasn't to happen right away because I spent the next two months in No 1 British General Hospital in Karachi for treatment of dysentery. I must have picked up the bug in the desert or in Iraq. Dysentery, a common complaint in the Middle and Far East, was sometimes fatal.

The hospital staff were very kind to me, but the place was a bit depressing. It was even more depressing when a patient was taken out of the ward and put into a room with a single bed at the end of the corridor. Patients never walked out of that room. When the cleaning squad arrived and worked behind the closed door a strong smell of disinfectant leaked into the ward and we knew that death had taken another victim.

As well as being a very uncomfortable, embarrassing complaint, dysentery also made it difficult, if not impossible, to fly an aeroplane.

I didn't find out until later that Fane, concerned because he might be posted to another crew, complained of a sore throat and convinced the MO that he should have his tonsils removed. Later he arrived on the squadron at Jessore about the same time as I did.

Weakened by dysentery I convalesced for a couple of weeks at Manora Isle before going to No 4 Hill Depot, Chakrata, a hill station North of Ambala, North of Delhi.

For the next month I shared a bungalow with Sgt Waugh, aircrew and a member of the English literary family, who had a badly infected arm. "I have been told," he said, grinning, "that as soon as I'm fit enough to travel, I'm going back to England." He paused and sighed. "I'll be glad to get out of this God-forsaken country."

Both barely out of school, we talked about our impressions and experiences, which, in the short time we had been in the RAF, were quite extensive; sometimes almost unbelievable and often rather frightening!

On my travels I had concluded that although people from various parts of the world lived differently, and usually with a philosophy unlike ours, they were neither worse, nor better than the rest of us; just different. I liked many of the differences. I thought the food and clothing in India much better suited to their way of living and climatic conditions than ours.

My evaluation of the traditional mores of my upbringing changed as I travelled and saw how other people lived. Through this experience I realized that I could now be selective in adopting any ideas that I liked.

Built on a flat area cut into the side of the mountain our bungalow overlooked a wide valley. Rocks covered the ground and tall trees hung precariously from the side of the hill. One afternoon the stone bungalow walls shook violently.

"Earthquake!" I shouted to Sgt Waugh. "Let's get to hell out of here."

We both rushed outside in time to see a huge portion of the mountain on the other side of the valley, slide down 3 or 4,000ft towards a winding river below. Trees tumbled and disappeared as millions of tons of rock

149

and earth rumbled to the bottom of the valley. The ground shook under our feet. The earthquake's few seconds seemed an eternity.

After the avalanche had stopped, the distant sound of snapping timber continued as large boulders rolled down the hill. Then, as though it had never happened, it became quiet and still and the birds sang again. The other side of the valley looked as if someone had sliced the green mountainside with a huge knife leaving an ugly, brown wound.

We stood in awe, marvelling at the devastation wreaked by nature in a few seconds and we wondered how many times this hillside, with evergreen trees at the top and tropical trees at the bottom, had been torn apart by earthquakes.

In the mountains I had plenty of time to think and ponder about life and my participation in the war. In a matter of a few months I had left England, an island under siege, now being bombed day and night by the Luftwaffe and dependent on convoys to bring in food and supplies.

I had left my mother and father, recently divorced, and travelled thousands of miles, flying myself to another country, another continent; to places I'd only previously read about. I'd left my country with its food shortage, blackouts and air raids. All of this seemed so far away and so long ago. As a bomber pilot, where would I be sent next?

Now, what of India? All I knew up until now was what I had learned at school; that it was part of the British Empire, one of the many countries coloured pink in my atlas. Since my arrival I was impressed by India's railway that rambled across a vast continent, and the huge unwieldy Indian civil service; both built by the British. To me there appeared to be a lack of leadership among Indians; everyone seemed to be a follower. They gave the impression of being resigned to the harsh effects of nature, and they accepted their caste system with apathy.

The country and the people intrigued me. I wanted to travel, to talk to people from all walks of life, to learn as much as I could about India.

I remember strolling along the crowded streets of Karachi. Napier Road with its strange smells, cluttered stores and ragged beggars. A place where time didn't seem very important.

I especially remember the day at Drigh Road, while my crew and I waited for a taxi to go to Karachi, a camel train of six rubber-tyred, flat carts ambled towards us. Each cart was pulled by a camel, with one driver on the leading cart, and he was asleep. I stepped into the road and carefully took hold of the rope hanging down from the lead camel's neck and pulled it, gently steering the beast across the road heading him back in the opposite direction. The camel coughed, gurgled and complained, but it didn't awaken the driver. The rest of the camels dutifully turned and followed and the procession headed back up the road in the wrong direction.

Finally, a taxi came along. As I climbed in I wondered if the driver figured out what had happened to him?

151

While I was convalescing up in the mountains my crew had been posted to No 215 Squadron at Jessore, in Bengal. As soon as I was declared fit for flying I returned to Karachi and caught the train heading east to join them.

While on this long trip across India I recalled my Canadian rail journey from Halifax to Carberry, Manitoba. It was an incredible experience, chugging along day after day with ever-changing scenery. First it was wooded areas. Then, overnight, the flat vast prairies replaced rocks, rivers and lakes. But in comparison the train journey across India was a revelation. The scenery changed from the dry Sind desert of the west to the moist tropical jungle and paddy fields of Bengal in the east.

Each railway station along the way brought a blare of sound with hoards of people coming and going. An explosion of brightly dressed people carrying cloth bundles, earthenware *chatties* with some hustling flocks of little children ahead of them. I saw tall, turbaned Sikhs and scurrying businessmen. Some in dapper suits, others with their dazzling white *dhoti* pulled up between their legs. Indians, I decided, were a handsome race.

At some stations monkeys jumped on the carriage roof and screeched and chattered as they chased back and forth looking for scraps of food on the platform. Vendors pushed carts full of strange, succulent-smelling goods, which I desperately wanted to sample, but my bout of dysentery had made me very cautious of what I ate and where I ate it!

152

Then there were the beggars. One old, grey-haired cripple pressed a tin can towards the open train window, "*Backshees, sahib. Backshees, backshees,*" he pleaded. I shook my head with a disdainful negative nod as I'd seen others do. Little boys, ragamuffins wearing only tattered shirts barely covering their little pointed penises, screamed at me. "*Backshees, sahib.*" Again I twisted my head — no.

The sights and sounds of poverty were hard to take. I soon realized I could help one or two beggars by giving them all of my RAF pay, but I couldn't help all of them. So, like most rich Indians and foreigners in India, I became inured to begging and beggars. They just became a nuisance. I, too, acted like a career colonist and waved them away with a sharp, "Bugger off!"

The train pulled into Calcutta at Howhar Station. I got a porter to carry my kit bag and bedroll and pushed my way through a seething mass of people until I finally located the Movements Officer. He directed me to the platform from where I could catch my train to Jessore.

CHAPTER
NINE

Jessore, Bengal

On 14 June 1943, I arrived by train at Jessore, a small town set in the green jungle of Bengal on the Bhairib River, near the Sunderbunds and 100 miles northeast of Calcutta. Unless I completed my operational tour early, or something unfortunate happened, this would be my home for at least the next year with 215 Squadron.

The unfortunate happened earlier than I thought possible. On the second day at my new post I discovered, to my horror, that my urine was as black as Indian ink. Immediately I was sent back in Calcutta to No 47 British General Hospital and treated for albuminuria. I responded well to the treatment and soon returned to the squadron.

At Jessore the old, thick-walled brick and stone houses, built by the British in the late nineteenth century, were a reminder of the thriving days when a processing plant there turned indigo into dye. When a blight killed the indigo, the British left.

The RAF had taken over the town's courthouse building as the squadron's senior NCOs quarters. The long rectangular bungalow, with a concrete verandah on all sides, had a shallow overhanging corrugated tin roof. The gaol at the end of the building, with its heavy steel-bar enclosures, became the sergeant's bar.

Our sleeping quarters had wooden slatted doors that opened onto the verandah on each side. About ten NCOs shared a room. Each person had a *charpoy*, a bed with rope stretched over a rough wood frame, and a small bedside table around on which we spread our few personal belongings.

When the mosquito net was dropped down around one's *charpoy*, it became a refuge. A place to read, write, sleep, or be left alone. A necessary refuge because fatigue, sickness, heat and humidity brought bouts of depression to some of us.

Once in a while a violent argument erupted. But, after a few heated threats were exchanged, the problem would fizzle away as quickly as it had started. Good humour prevailed most of the time and we hailed one another by Christian names, surnames or nicknames.

One day an irate wireless operator, with a name difficult to spell and even harder to pronounce, jumped up on his *charpoy* and shaking his fist at us, shouted, "You . . . you . . . you call me by my proper name, or bugger all!"

From then on we called him "Bugger All." He loved it.

The squadron's aircrew complement allowed for about two full flying crews for each squadron aircraft. But sickness among crews sometimes made it difficult to find enough aircrew to fly serviceable 'planes. Many times, because of maintenance problems, we didn't

155

even have enough serviceable aeroplanes for crews to fly.

No 215 Squadron shared Jessore's single runway with 99 Squadron. The runway had a black-top surface spread over palm fronds as a stabilizing agent. Both squadron's Wellington Ics were gradually being replaced with Bristol Hercules powered Wellington IIIs.

Supplies, fuel and bombs arrived by rail to a spur line near the airfield. When a trainload of bombs arrived all hands, officers, NCOs and airmen helped to manhandle the heavy, cumbersome bombs from the flatcar to the bomb dump.

Having seen German bombs devastate England, I had an insecure feeling the first time I helped roll 250lb and 500lb bombs off a flatcar onto the ground like firewood. During training I'd been told that TNT wouldn't explode unless it was properly detonated. But that didn't make me feel any easier. Strangely, I never experienced that feeling when sitting on top of 4,000lb of fused, ready to be delivered bombs in my own 'plane's bomb bay.

In the Victorian era the British military in India wore heavy woollen uniforms, solar *topees*, *puttees* and a spinepad for protection from the sun. They may have looked smart, but they must have been miserably uncomfortable, hot and extremely sweaty and smelly. Our dress regulations at Jessore were somewhat lax. Unlike them, we dressed to suit the climate. In the evening we wore long-sleeved shirts, long trousers and shoes to avoid being eaten alive by mosquitoes. I wore suede desert boots and I found that light-coloured socks, instead of the regulation black socks, seemed to discourage mosquitoes from biting my ankles. During the day nearly everyone wore shorts and *chaples* (sandals); shirts were usually removed for work. At the aerodrome, 4 or 5 miles from town, the afternoon temperature might reach 114°F in the shade with the humidity in the high 90s. Work started at dawn because aeroplanes became so hot it was impossible to work on them in the open after midday; our hangar space was limited to a couple of aircraft undergoing major inspections.

At the Operational Training Unit at Chipping Warden, Sergeant pilots of our ilk were scorned by the regular force Sergeants. In the Mess they tolerated us, but didn't invite us into their cliques for a drink, or to discuss the war situation. They resented our suggestions for Mess improvements; especially if it cost them money.

Here, at Jessore, however, aircrew and ground crew worked as a team. On the job, rank rarely made a difference between airmen and NCOs, particularly aircrew NCOs. Many crews had a mixed bag of officers and NCOs; quite often the Captain might be a Sergeant with Flight Sergeants, Flight Officers and Flight Lieutenants as his crew members. They could also be a mixed bag of Canadians, Australians and English. There was one American RAF pilot.

One crew were all Australians. Their aircraft's letter was "Y," so they painted in large letters on the sides of the fuselage "KISWASTE"; Hindoustani for "why?"

With my crew, all NCOs, I usually flew the same aircraft and shared it with another crew. The 'plane was always serviced by the same ground crew who did the daily maintenance as well as special inspections carried out in the hangar. Central maintenance had not yet come to Jessore.

The aircraft I flew when I came to the squadron was, I'm sure, the oldest and most operationally tired Wellington Ic at Jessore, but the pilot of the other crew that flew it did us a favour. After take-off he raised the undercarriage and the knee-action of the mechanism had just opened when the aircraft sank a little. The wheels touched the ground in a "brush take-off", putting a load on the wrong supporting member. This cracked a support and when the aircraft landed the undercarriage collapsed. We then got the next oldest 'plane.

Before an operational flight the ground crew were always out on the flight line and they helped us get our gear aboard. They watched our departure and they'd be at the dispersal, anxiously waiting for our return. Ground crews were badly shaken when their aeroplane did not come back.

When we flew in the circuit around the aerodrome we shared the sky with vultures and kite hawks, birds that years ago mastered flight in a way we'd never be able to. One day someone suggested, "Let's see if we can outsmart a hawk's flying skill."

We tossed a bit of bread into the air and induced several birds to dive for it. Slowly, we moved closer and closer to a building, towards a corner where two walls met. One at a time, the birds continued to swoop on the target, but they now had to take violent evasive action to avoid hitting the walls. The test of the hawk's flying skills was abandoned when a piece of bread thrown too close to the wall caused a bird to experience "pilot error" and bash into the wall.

Fortunately, except for the loss of few feathers, the bird appeared unharmed. After its "prang" it perched at the top of a nearby tree; no doubt recovering its dignity and considering its mistakes while awaiting a "court of inquiry".

Vultures, seen everywhere, ate any and all dead creatures. Their scavenging kept the place clean. One morning, driving with my crew out to the aerodrome, I saw a bloated, dead cow lying beside the road. I stopped and, for a few minutes, we watched as several ungainly vultures hopped around grotesquely on top of the carcass, stabbing at it with their hooked beaks. They directed their slashes at vulnerable body openings. One bird pulled out yards of intestines and the rest of them immediately pounced and squabbled over this choice morsel.

When we returned that afternoon, all that was left of the cow was a pile of bones with several slightly pink ribs sticking up into the air. The bloody, overfed, subdued vultures squatting nearby had done their job well.

As second pilot to Warrant Officer Gillis, I made my first operational flight with the squadron on the night of 21 July 1943. A seven hour operational flight to bomb Taungup, a small town in Burma.

The next day's edition of *The Statesman*, Calcutta's main newspaper, had a front page column that read:

RAF SORTIES OVER BURMA
US Bombers attack key bridges. NEW DELHI. JULY 21.
Command Joint Communiqué — The RAF carried out further attacks yesterday on Japanese transportation and troop positions in Burma, stated today's India Command joint war communiqué. Shortly before dawn this morning, Wellington aircraft bombed Taungup and Akyab. Bursts were seen in both target areas, but heavy cloud prevented observations of the results. From these operations none of our aircraft is missing.

While our crews were not mentioned by name, it was gratifying to know that a few people, at least, knew we were doing something productive towards the war effort!
I wondered why they said heavy clouds prevented observations of the results. I didn't see any clouds!

Several other reports in *The Statesman* corresponded to my logbook entries:

5 Feb 1944 — Wellington LN 369 — Self — Crew Ops Aungban. Aerodrome bombed. Flying Time: 1hr 15mins day; 5hrs 25mins night; 2hrs cloud
The Statesman Sunday 6 February 1944: New

Delhi February 5.

On the nights of February 4-5 medium bombers of the Strategic Airforce bombed the airfields at Hemo and Aungban 90 miles southeast of Mandalay. At both places the majority of bombs were seen to burst in the runway and dispersal areas and fires were started.

---

13 Feb 1944 — Wellington LN369 — Self — Crew — Ops Kyaukpyu bombed. Flying Time: 15 mins day; 4 hrs 50 mins night; 2hrs 30mins cloud

The *Statesman*, Thursday 15 February: New Delhi 14 February: RAF medium bombers of the Strategic Airforce Eastern Asia Command attacked Kyaukyu (on Ramree Island in the Bay of Bengal) on the night of February 12-13.

On my second operational flight the following night, to gain experience I flew as third pilot with a seasoned crew. Bad weather prevented us from reaching our primary target at Taungup so Fg Off Sutton, the Captain, decided to bomb the alternative target of Akyab, a supply dump at the Japanese held island off the Arakan coast. My job was to drop propaganda leaflets.

I had been briefed on how to push the leaflets out of the extended flare chute, located just aft the wing's trailing edge. This 'chute, used to toss out flares and photo flashes, looked like a 3ft-long, 10in-round coal scuttle. A smaller section inside extended so it stuck

161

out of the fuselage into the slipstream and anything dropped down it was supposed to fall clear of the aircraft.

We arrived over Akyab's supply dump as dawn broke with a clear, pale orange sky. I took my position in the astrodome. In the half-light we slowly circled the target area at 4,000ft while the navigator calculated a three-drift wind; a slow laborious procedure I'd often done in an Avro Anson over the Manitoba prairies. I kept wishing the crew would get on with the job before daylight came. I even willed them to drop the bloody bombs so we could go home.

On the first bombing run the bomb aimer, lying in the nose of the 'plane looking through the bomb sight, called out heading changes to the pilot. His voice came quietly and calmly over the intercom. "Left a little . . . Steady . . . Steady . . . Left a little, a little more . . . Steady . . . Left a little . . . Steady . . . Bombs gone!"

I felt the aircraft lurch slightly as the bombs left the bomb racks. Relieved, I waited in the astrodome, listening on the intercom, waiting for my orders to drop the leaflets.

No such luck!

Apparently only two 250lb bombs had been dropped to assess the accuracy of the calculated wind direction.

While the pilot continued circling the target area, the navigator and bomb aimer had a lengthy discussion about wind speed and direction.

Just what some Japanese anti-aircraft gunner's waiting for, I thought — we're a sitting duck, especially as it was now almost fully daylight. I was right. Flak suddenly sprouted around us leaving dirty, grey puffs in the morning sky.

This was the first flak I'd shared the same sky with. I decided I didn't like it!

As it slowly became lighter we started another bombing run towards the target. How cool and calm the rest of the crew seemed; in my mind I tried to emulate them.

When we crabbed over the still dark ocean heading back towards the island I noticed the anti-aircraft gunner's shooting had improved after the little bit of practice we'd given him. He was now shooting dead ahead, and at our altitude.

This bombing run turned out to be another practice; two more 250lb bombs dropped.

On the next run we kept flying through puffs of smoke. Not only could I smell the flak, I could hear it. I stood in the astrodome, like a snake charmer's hypnotized cobra, staring at the orange flashes.

The aircraft lurched viciously. I grabbed a handhold. My God! We've been hit, I thought.

The bomb aimer called out, "Bombs gone."

At that moment Fg Off Sutton suddenly banked the aircraft sharply and the flak trailed past our wing. I watched as the Japanese supply dump below us erupted into a dark-red, boiling mass spewing dense black smoke.

Sutton's voice came over the intercom. "Okay, Leicester, drop 'em."

I leapt into action. It was my moment of truth. The crew were now waiting for me to finish my job.

I shoved out the flare chute extension. Grabbed a bundle of leaflets, slid the rubber band down one-third of the way, as I'd been told, and hurled the package down the open tube.

To my horror the slipstream hurtling up the tube caught the leaflets and sent most of them swirling back into the aircraft. They pounded my face and hands as they twisted their way, like confetti, into the crew compartment.

Not bothering to adjust the rubber bands, I shoved the rest of the bundles down the chute as fast as I could, hoping they would open and spread their good propaganda out over Akyab's countryside. If they didn't, too bad, but maybe a bundle would hit a Japanese soldier on the head.

I pulled the flare chute in, called over the intercom, "Leaflets dropped," and then went forward to the cockpit to receive the accolades due to me.

Instead, I watched as the Captain and co-pilot, with disdainful wrist motions, peeled dozens of leaflets off the perspex canopy, where air leaks had sucked and held them. Carefully, and pointedly, they screwed each leaflet into a ball and dropped it on the floor. Without so much as a word to me, or even acknowledging my presence, the Captain eased the wheel over and we turned and flew home.

I'd heard of that good old RAF expression, "Like a spare prick at a wedding." I now knew how it felt to be just that!

Cows had a habit of wandering across the runway, especially at night, so some of the aircrew were assigned "cow punchers". Scattered along each side of the runway they chased off straying cattle before aircraft landed.

Raising and lowering the flag, or marching a delinquent airman before the CO, called for some semblance of a military parade, but formal squadron or wing parades were unheard of at Jessore. Since I hated parades that was fine with me; I didn't have to look around for an excuse to be absent.

South East Asia Command (SEAC) was formed in June 1943. Weeks later we were told that SEACs Supreme Commander, Lord Louis Mountbatten, was coming to Jessore to inspect us. With this alarming news in mind I watched DROs (Daily Routine Orders) for lists of those required to attend practice parades. If my name came up, I'd have to be ready with an excuse.

I was out of luck. We learned that everybody not flying, or not sick, was listed for the big, formal Wing Parade. Not even I could find a way out of that!

On the day of the parade, officers and men from the two squadrons were formed up. Warrant Officers loved this part of their work; they "organized" everyone into ranks, positioning them correctly according to the Drill Manual. They also got to shout a lot. They even shouted at Officers, which they especially enjoyed.

As we stood at ease, waiting for Lord Louis to arrive, I looked around at the assembled parade of officers and men. It certainly didn't look like the Service Flying Training School parades we had at Carberry,

Manitoba; parades there really had spit and polish, especially the Wings parades.

On Jessore's hot, dank, grass parade ground no two officers, or airmen, were dressed alike. Some wore shorts, leather boots, desert boots, with or without socks. Others had on bush shirts, shirts with long sleeves, or short sleeves. One airman wore a shirt with no sleeves!

Although our dress was casual, our deportment appeared to be the standard expected by the RAF. The parade had been sized; tallest on the right, shortest on the left. As a 6ft 2in airman, I was usually selected as right marker; this meant I had to be on parade on time because the markers were the first to fall in.

Since there were so many of us NCO aircrew, we formed a Flight of our own. We stood, in our odd regalia, waiting in the hot sun.

Once-in-a-while a victim of the heat dropped out of ranks to be dragged away into the shade, fanned and given a cool drink of water, or, in some cases, rushed by ambulance to sick quarters.

Because I disliked parades I'd often contemplated faking heat prostration but, somehow, I couldn't bring myself to do it.

Suddenly Lord Mountbatten's jeep roared into sight.

The parade commander's strident "PARADE" brought us smartly to attention. This exertion caused a couple more casualties to fall.

At attention, I glanced left and right. There certainly was a strange assortment of uniforms, but, notwithstanding, we looked pretty good.

The jeep wheeled across the grass and stopped in front of the parade. Lord Mountbatten, in a crisp, white naval uniform with a splash of colourful medals, stood with one hand resting on top of the windscreen. From under his cap's scrambled-egg visor his steady eyes, in his tanned face, looked us over.

Was he noticing our motley array of uniforms, I wondered, or was he seeing a fine troop of men? His men.

Suddenly breaking the tense silence, his firm, authoritative voice called out, "Everyone over here." With a wave of his arm he beckoned us to gather round him.

No order was given, we just broke ranks and formed a circle around his jeep.

He told us how successful our bombing had been in hindering the Japanese army's advance towards India. Those in front pressed against his jeep while he spoke. He certainly had a leader's charm. He also briefed us on the progress of the war in Europe and the Pacific.

I was quite surprised when he mentioned that in February the Japanese had started their Operation C plan — the invasion of India. During our operations briefing this plan had never been mentioned to the crews, although bombing activity had increased. I never knew, until his talk, that all RAF operational units in northeast India were amalgamated with the American Tenth Air Force.

He left as quickly as he came. One minute he was talking, the next minute he was looking back over his shoulder waving to us as his jeep drove away.

It seemed pointless to line up again just to be dismissed. The warrant officers didn't shout anything so we wandered away to get on with our work.

Even though Lord Mountbatten left us with a kind of "glow" of self-satisfaction for doing a good job, that job had been done only because of our resourcefulness.

A shortage of supplies forced us to do a lot of nonregulation improvisation, all condoned by the "brass". For a long period we couldn't get replacement tyres for the aircraft. The situation became so bad that when a squadron was not scheduled for operations we had to jack up their aircraft, remove the wheels and put them on the aircraft going on "Ops". The next night we reversed the roles.

As I mentioned earlier it was not Air Force regulations, but climate and jungle surroundings that influenced our dress and deportment.

When flying I wore my Mae West and leather jacket over a Beaden survival suit. Created by Squadron Leader Beaden, this long-sleeved overall with pockets and zip fasteners was designed for jungle protection. Made of lightweight cotton-drill it had pockets everywhere. I carried fishhooks, cans of sardines, escape gear, chocolate, rubberized silk maps. The more pessimistic crews even carried a toothbrush!

Because steel in the cans would cause a huge compass error, the pilot had to be careful not to put a tin of sardines in a pocket near the pilot's compass positioned beside his right knee.

I created my own survival *accoutrements*. I'd scrounged a Sam Browne leather belt from an army officer and I had the local *moochi wallah*, who'd made a pair of shoes for me, sew long straps on the right side of my belt to hold the holster for my .38 Smith and Wesson revolver. On the left side he sewed straps for my *kukri*, a foot-long curved knife, and another strap at the back to hold a water bottle. These straps were purposely made very long. When I walked I looked like a caricature from a Hollywood cowboy movie with my holster, *kukri* and water bottle flapping at knee-level; but seated in the cockpit, they all rested on the floor under my seat. For added security I wore a 9mm Berreta automatic in a shoulder holster under my shirt. I figured, if I had to leave the 'plane in a hurry, I had everything I needed.

Most aircrew discarded their issue Rudyard Kipling solar topees because they liked the rakish, waterproof, comfortable and practical Australian bush-hats, sporting khaki cotton *pugrees* and RAF flashes.

While I was with the squadron the Beaden survival suit was never tested for effectiveness because we never had a crew crash land or bail out into the jungle. But the risk was always there.

CHAPTER
TEN

Night flights over Burma

Most of our operations were flights into the night. One evening as I climbed away from the airfield over the black jungle below, Mac's voice came over the intercom. "What the hell's going on up front? Balls of fire and sheets of flame are whizzing past my turret."

I sent Nick aft to see what was happening.

Moments later he leaned into the cockpit and tapped my right arm. "Mac's right," he shouted. "The starboard engine's shooting roman candles out of the exhaust. Looks like we're on fire."

I quickly checked the starboard engine gauges. Everything looked normal. I throttled back, levelled out and called to Mac to let me know if the flames were still there.

"There's no change," he called back.

I'd never had this problem before, nor had I heard of it happening to anyone else. I tried to reason what could have caused it. But I couldn't come up with a solution. Maybe the exhaust was igniting fuel from a broken fuel line? I didn't like contemplating what that could lead to. It was obvious that it was unsafe to continue the flight so I alerted the crew. "We're returning to the aerodrome. We'll jettison the load over the lake."

I wanted to get back on the ground as quickly as possible, but with a full fuel load and bombs we were overweight for landing. I couldn't jettison fuel because the petrol would come out of the jettisoning pipe and spray over the exhaust's flames. I elected to dump the bombs.

A large lake near the aerodrome had been designated for such an emergency. As I flew towards it through the darkness, I spotted fires from native villages scattered around the lake. I wondered what Bengalis sitting around those fires must have thought when Nick plopped the whole load of unfused bombs, with a huge splash into the water.

On my low, final approach to the landing strip I could see the exhaust flames' red glare on the trees a few feet below. Were we on fire?

After landing, Mac called over the intercom. "The flames went out just as we landed."

I taxied over to my dispersal to park. Dispersal areas, scattered around the aerodrome, were designed to protect parked aircraft from a bombing attack. Each bay had a brick wall about 14ft high, banked from behind with earth and wide enough to taxi the 'plane in, but the fuselage and tail were left sticking out.

Greatly relieved to be back on the ground and, apparently not on fire, I eased the 'plane into its dispersal, stopped and an airman shoved chocks under the wheels.

Before I could shut off the engines the CO, Wg Cdr Cross, and the engineering officer who had followed us in a vehicle along the taxi way, climbed the ladder through the forward hatch into the cockpit.

"What happened?" the Wing Commander asked as he clambered up beside my seat.

I described the balls of fire whipping out of the exhaust pipe.

"Shut down the port engine," he ordered gruffly.

I sensed he was perturbed because I'd aborted an operational flight and I knew I'd better have a good reason for doing so.

"Now do a run-up and we'll see if we get those flames."

The two of them watched the engine's instruments as I slowly moved the right throttle lever forward. At half throttle the flames in the exhaust reappeared; I pulled the throttle back and the flames died away.

"It looks as if raw fuel's coming through the engine." The engineering officer called out. "You're bloody lucky it didn't burn the fuselage. Open the throttle again."

I opened the throttle, flames shot out and at the same moment the chock under the starboard wheel slipped. The braked wheel slid on the oily ground and the aircraft swung violently to the left. I snapped the throttle closed, but the wing tip slammed forward and hit the brick wall. A large section of the wall fell inwards, knocking off about 4ft of the wing.

The engine problem turned out to be over-rich mixture, easily corrected by a mechanic. But if I had continued the flight, besides setting the fabric on fire, with an abnormally high fuel consumption we risked running out of petrol. The aircraft would have looked like a flaming brand in the sky — a perfect target for the Japs.

The CO said I'd made the right decision when I aborted the flight, jettisoned the bombs and returned to the aerodrome.

Improvisation was necessary to repair the damage. A section of wing was salvaged from the local dump were there were several wrecked aircraft. No questions were asked, no recriminations, no paperwork; the job was just done. Back in England there would have been an investigation and I might have even qualified for another red endorsement in my logbook!

Once we left our aerodrome at Jessore it was up to the navigator to get us to our target and bring us back home. Most of our flights were made at night and often lasted eight or nine hours. There were no radio navigation aids. No H2S or airborne radar as used by Bomber Command in Europe. South East Asia Command (SEAC) had no radar-equipped night-fighters so our aircraft had no need for IFF (Identification Friend or Foe) equipment.

At night the navigator might have to wait for hours for a glimpse of a star to get an astro shot with his sextant. At other times, along with his meticulous dead reckoning he would apply a guess or two, locally known as the "buggery factor." But dead reckoning got us to a target in the jungle in the middle of nowhere and, better still, got us home night after night. Approaching Jessore our navigator, Frank Prescott, had memorized the exact position of places, little villages, within a 20 mile radius of the aerodrome with unpronounceable names such as Naral, Sridhapur, Sallikha, Chaugacha, Jhingeracha, Dhopakola and Ruddim. All he needed was a glimpse of the ground and he'd steer us to the runway.

On our flight of the night of 9 March 1944, the crew had settled into their routine, they probably wondered, as I did, what our target would be.

We had been briefed for a round-robin flight and assigned Wellington HF 578, the aircraft we often flew. The Briefing Officer had given us a choice of three targets to bomb. If we saw nothing of importance on the first, or second target, we had to bomb the third. We were to look for Japanese troops, gun positions (usually found when they shot at you) and convoys on the roads.

That night several aircraft took off at widely separated departure times. Some of the aircraft went round the triangular course clockwise; others flew it the other way round. The idea was to harass the enemy by having aircraft appear all through the night at different times and from different directions.

We crossed the Chin hills, heading east and approached our first turning point at Mogaung in Burma, about 50 miles from the Chinese border and 650 miles from Jessore. Flying at about 4,000ft a few scattered clouds broke the monotony of the tropical, black sky. The intercom's long silence suddenly ended with Nick's excited voice. "Skipper. Look! Up ahead. Aren't those lights? Looks like a Jap convoy."

Along the road that stood from the darkness like a faint grey band, I could just pick out a row of moving dim lights.

"Quick, Nick," I shouted across to him. "Get down there and select a couple of two-fifties."

Nick scrambled out of his folding seat and lay down in the bomb aimer's position below me.

"Fane. You there?"

"Yep, Skipper. What's up?"

"A convoy. We're going to have a crack at it. Load a photo flash," I called over the intercom. "Bomb doors open."

Frank leaned into the cockpit and looked out of the windshield at the convoy, now in front of us and quite close.

"Flash loaded, Skipper," Fane called in from the flare chute.

"Left a bit, Tony." Nick paused. "A bit more. That's it. Steady, steady."

The vehicle's lights had disappeared below the nose of the aircraft when Nick called over the intercom. "Oh, for Christ sake. They heard us. All the lights have gone out."

I closed the bomb doors.

About five minutes later Mac's Scottish brogue came over the intercom. "They're moving again, Skipper. Their lights are on, must be at least fifty vehicles down there."

I turned starboard, grabbed the bomb bay operating handle with my left hand and opened the bomb doors while the 'plane headed back to the convoy lights. I could now see clearly the twinkling lights ahead.

"Nick. Select a couple of two-fifties and drop 'em when you're ready."

Fane's voice broke into the intercom. "Flash still ready."

The aircraft lurched slightly as the bombs fell away. The photo flash automatically dropped down the flare chute when the bombs were released and went off below us, lighting up the cockpit for a split second.

"Good shot, Nick," Mac came on the intercom. "You hit the leading vehicle. There's a hell of fire. Just look at that black smoke."

I turned again to cross the convoy at about 45 degrees. "Drop the rest in a long stick, Nick."

He called back. "Left a bit. That's good. Hey they're shooting at us with rifles, or a machine gun, tracers are whizzing up at us. Bombs gone."

I swung the aircraft around in time to see part of the stick of bombs bursting on the ground in long line of big orange blobs, plop, plop, plop about a second apart. But they were nowhere near the road. They hadn't cut across the convoy as planned.

Nick climbed into his seat beside me. "Messed that up, didn't I?"

"Don't feel bad about it, Nick, you really hit something important with the first drop. Maybe another kite coming along will see the fire and drop their load on them."

176

Nick grinned at me. "Yeah, you're right. Those lorries really burned."

I called over the intercom to the crew, "Since we've no bombs left, let's go home. Give me a course Frank."

Fane called in to let me know he was back at his radio, and the crew settled down for a routine flight home. After a six and a half hour night flight, we landed back at Jessore.

Many times when returning from an operational flight over Burma, navigation was often forgotten as we dodged and weaved for miles through a solid line of monsoon thunderstorms over the Chin hills.

The monsoon came to the southern part of India as regular as clockwork on the first of June, and then gradually moved north. The monsoon, or *chagara*, lasted three months. While it brought life-giving rains to farmers, to aircrew it was a nightmare of horrendous thunderstorms, teeming rain and crackling lightning; a far cry from the Indian poets, "Earth and cloud love making."

Flying in this stuff it was every man for himself, each of my crew had to find something strong to hang on to as we bounced and pitched through heavy turbulence like riding in a square-wheeled cart.

Lightning flashes stabbed the clouds like flames from a Pittsburg steel foundry. We had no choice but to fly through it. Each flash filled the cockpit with dazzling, blue light and froze all movement for a split second. The only place for me to hide was behind the instrument panel, which bounced and trembled as though trying to throw off all the flight instruments.

Drops of rain that tattooed against the windscreen would suddenly change into a wall of solid water. I wondered why the engine's air intakes weren't drowned, but in spite of the deluge the engines kept running.

In this kind of turbulence I would look at the wet, shiny wing tip and watch the wing flex. As we lurched and dropped, a wave moved out across the fabric to the wing tip and I wondered how much bending the wing's geodetic structure could stand; like the little tabs on a child's metal toy, how many bends were allowed before it broke?

The doped, stitched fabric covering the wings, pulled by the turbulence, stood up in little bulges like muscles on a strongman's back. On nights like this I hoped Vicker's factory workers in Weybridge who made *this* Wellington had been happy in their work and had put in all the parts they were supposed to!

A few weeks after we had bombed the convoy, the squadron intelligence office showed me the photo we took when the photo flash went off. I could see a bomb bursting right at the head of the convoy.

"Our army's moved in there now. Look at this," he said. He then showed me another photo of mangled vehicles shoved off to the side of a jungle road. "Photos of those Jap vehicles you bombed."

I thought about that incident and wondered what it must be have been like on the ground driving, along a jungle road in a convoy of Japanese vehicles. Did they hear us approach, or did a soldier spot us and give the signal to douse their lights? The Wellington's Hercules engines were called "whispering death" because they were so silent. Used in Beaufighters, pilots on low level ground sweeps in Africa caught a lot of Germans unaware of their presence.

When we turned back were they hit by the first or second bomb? What did the driver think as he saw a bomb go off a few hundred feet away and seconds later another right in front of him. He would have seen trucks fly to pieces in great orange flames. Senior officers would likely be in those vehicles. I imagined the confusion on the ground would have been terrific, especially when we came back again. Was there panic, or did military discipline prevail? What did they think when a whole stick, about 3,250lb, of high-explosive bombs suddenly dropped beside them. I'd had the frightening experience of being bombed in England, so I thought I had some idea how the soldiers in that convoy must have felt.

One of squadron's crew flying a FIRPO (a coastal patrol along the Arakan and Burma coast looking for enemy shipping) crashed into the Bay of Bengal. Apparently having lost an engine and being unable to maintain altitude on one engine, they ditched into the sea. One crew member was killed in the crash but the rest managed to get into the dinghy.

In case we didn't come back from an operational flight, most of us had an understanding about the disposal of our personal effects, to be divided between designated recipients.

After several days, the Bay of Bengal wind and currents pushed the downed crew ashore in the

Sunderbunds. They staggered on to the beach and were nearly shot by an elderly Bengali wielding an ancient muzzle-loading blunderbuss. He thought the Japanese invasion had started.

When we heard news of this crew's survival their personal gear was quickly rounded up from the inheritors and put back before they returned. I was in line for a pair of leather boots, but I was glad I never had to wear them!

While I was on the squadron at Jessore an aircraft crashed on take-off with a full bomb load. This messy incident upset everyone on the squadron. The large hole in the ground was a constant reminder when taxiing out for take-off.

I was a pall-bearer at the funeral and the coffin leaked blood! (To this day I avoid attending funerals.) Heavy monsoon rains floated the coffins out of the ground. A guard had to be placed in the cemetery to keep starving pi-dogs away.

At the end of November amoebic dysentery struck again and I went to No 47 British General Hospital in Calcutta. Dysentery is a depleting disease: you lie on your bed, get very depressed and don't want to eat or drink.

No matter how sick we felt, we all perked up when a pretty Royal Navy Nursing Sister did her rounds. She was stunningly beautiful with dark hair and an English peaches and cream complexion. She looked so cool and efficient in her crisp, white, well-fitting uniform and she had a smile and a few words of encouragement for each of us. We speculated that perhaps she had been planted in the hospital just to raise morale! On the first Sunday of December 1943 hospital patients and staff were stunned to hear bombs exploding in broad daylight. The Japanese had bombed the Calcutta docks.

Later I heard that the Japanese bomber had dropped antipersonnel bombs, the kind that go off as soon as they strike the ground, spreading shrapnel around close to the surface without digging a hole.

Word went around that, during this raid, fighter pilot Flight Sergeant Pring was killed when his Hurricane was shot down. Pring piloted one of the three Beaufighters that had arrived in India in January 1943 and had shot down three of the four Japanese aircraft attacking Calcutta on the night of 13 January. That attack was the last Japanese night raid on Calcutta.

The air raid on the docks just about emptied the city. The roads to the countryside were jammed with people fleeing. We noticed several hospital sweepers were missing for a few days and we kidded them when they came back with, "Did you have a nice holiday in the country?"

In December 1943, officers and men of 99 and 215 Squadrons were told we now were a part of Eastern Air Command, a united force of British, Indian and American air forces under the command of American General Stratmeyer. Our Wellingtons would operate as part of the Strategic Air Force.

Even though we had a new boss, it didn't change our day-to-day living and, as far I could tell, we flew the same kind of operational flights.

When I heard the following story I wondered if it could possibly be true.

Before Wellington bombers were stationed at Jessore, Hurricane fighters operated from the aerodrome. The squadron had a rash of accidents when wing-mounted cannons repeatedly blew up when fired, bursting the barrels.

Two Warrant Officers were sure it was sabotage. Since they couldn't convince the official hard-liners, who didn't agree with them, they decided to carry out their own investigation.

They hid in the bush and watched as a long line of coolies returned from their day's work on the aerodrome. As they passed by the parked Hurricanes several of them picked up handfuls of mud and slapped them against the open end of the gun barrels. The coolies repeated this act for several days while the Warrant Officers tried to spot the ringleaders.

A few days later, as the line of coolies moved towards the Hurricanes, the two Warrant Officers stepped out of their hiding place and beckoned to the two ringleaders to step forward.

Without waiting for a reply to their accusations, the Warrant Officers pulled out their service revolvers and shot both natives in the head. Then they made the rest of the terrified coolies dig a hole and bury the two dead men.

When 215 and 99 Wellington Squadrons arrived at Jessore they needed additional administration office space on the aerodrome. A site was chosen for a small basha hut, a building with a concrete floor, brick and bamboo walls with a thick thatched roof.

As coolies dug the foundation they unearthed two skeletons. Each skull had a bullet hole!

Some aircrew had a tendency to be loud and boisterous, especially after a drink, or two; others oozed an aura of being totally carefree without a responsibility in the world. I also noticed the quietest were often the ones with the greatest staying power — the unsung heroes. Once in a while the subject of heroism would come up in one of our long, "putting the world in order" conversations.

We discussed topics such as what made the "Five Hundred" ride into the "Valley of Death". Was it heroism, or was it outright stupidity mistaken as heroism? We wondered what made people do the heroic deeds that won them the Victoria Cross? Sitting on our *charpoys* in India swatting mosquitoes, we pondered why people took unbelievable risks to save a life, capture a military position, bomb a target and, possibly, get killed while doing it?

Were they trying to be brave, out to win that gong? Was it part of their nature, or was it something in their background that made them do it? What makes a man overcome the strong force of fear? Could it be that heroism is really imprudence?

If a person isn't born a hero, can they be trained to become one? I never felt I was in the hero league because I was more interested in survival.

Although flying over Burma could be exciting it could also be harrowing but we certainly didn't think we were heroes for doing it. Actually there were times when I wished I were somewhere else and doing something other than sitting in a drafty, noisy aeroplane at night dropping bombs, worrying . . . Would we find the target? . . . Would we lose an engine and have to crash land in the jungle? . . . How much turbulence could the 'plane take before it would fall apart?

We didn't get shot at very often by the Japanese, but when they did shoot it became top of the worrying list!

Aircrew Sergeants, other than their flying and associated flying duties, had few station administrative jobs so they had plenty of leisure time. Reading was a favourite occupation, propped up on one's *charpoy*, cigarettes handy — what more could a Sergeant ask for except a little light entertainment?

Entertainment came to the door when "Do-Anna Dekko" — loosely translated as "two annas a look" — wandered by the Sergeants' quarters. Do-Anna Dekko was a small-boned, dark young Bengali girl, with a beguiling pixie-like face, probably in her late teens. Wearing a rather grubby, dull-coloured sari she announced her arrival by calling out in her singsong voice, "*Sahibs, sahibs.*"

In the mad scramble to get the best position at the verandah railing everything was tossed aside as eager young studs jumped to attention. When Do-Anna considered her audience large enough she would bare her small, well-formed breasts and raise her sari with one hand. Without any seductive preamble she

184

masturbated with her other hand, gyrating and twisting her body as though dancing. The audience cheered, stamped their feet, and shouted "More! More!"

After a few minutes into her dance she'd drop her sari and out would go her right hand, palm raised, "*Backshees, sahibs.*"

Coins were tossed. She'd pick them up and tuck them away somewhere in her sari before continuing. To get her audience warmed up her act might include a little more masturbation. When the cries of "more" were loud enough, she'd produce a banana from the folds of the sari, show her breasts and the show would get more raucous. She'd writhe and twist and then suddenly stop. Out would go the hand for *backshees.* She really knew how to work her audience.

We might not see Do-Anna for a few days, but we knew she'd be back.

Boredom by day and lack of sleep at night frayed tempers. As darkness closed in, the eerie piercing howls of jackals jangled nerves already on edge because of the heat and humidity. On some nights an aircrew sergeant would stand up, stretch, and say, "Let's go and shoot up a few jackals. Who's coming?"

The chase was on. Bodies tumbled off *charpoys* and hands grabbed revolvers. Shooting wailing jackals was an alternative to reading, swatting mosquitoes, or drinking warm beer. In the black tropical darkness armed figures, some alone, others in pairs, crept around the buildings. Suddenly a barrage of pistol shots would shatter the night's silence and the howling would stop.

When a jackal's howl was cut short, score one for the marksman. A clang of metal following a shot meant one of the rubbish bins at the back of the Mess had another hole in it and another jackal was out there, somewhere, thumbing its nose.

The nightly shooting went on for several weeks until one day at a briefing, the CO told us, "I appreciate your efforts in trying to deter those annoying jackals, but the shooting has got to stop before one of us or, worse still, one of the locals, gets shot."

From then on howling jackals again became part of the Bengal night.

One evening I went over to see Lieutenant Sanders of the Signal Corps for a chat and a drink. Michael Sanders had been with me at Bradfield College in "D" House. He lived in a bungalow down the road several hundred yards from the sergeants' quarters.

As I walked along the road, waving my torch from side-to-side I saw reflections glinting from several pairs of eyes and got a glimpse of several grey and brown jackals as they slid away into darkness.

Suddenly, up ahead, my light picked up a pack of animals standing motionless in the middle of the road. I stopped, not moving a muscle. Then, swinging the beam back and forth I counted at least seven jackals and, in the middle of the pack, a large hyena.

The jackal is a cowardly, skulking animal like the fox that raids the barn. The ones I'd seen usually ran in packs of five or six. Scavenging hyenas usually foraged alone.

186

I shone my light directly at the ungainly, misproportioned hyena to scare him away. But he didn't move. He never wavered; he bared his small sharp white teeth at me as his round, staring eyes reflected my torch's beam.

I'd heard that if a hyena joins up with a pack of jackals it will give the jackals "Dutch courage". A pack, like the one that was facing me, has been known to be aggressive enough to attack a lone intruder.

I backtracked slowly, keeping my torch pointing at the hyena, then turned and ran like hell, keeping an eye over my shoulder hoping I wasn't being followed!

Another night I lay awake under the mosquito net cursing the humidity and the buzzing mosquitoes when a tiger's roar from the nearby jungle rumbled in through the open windows.

The next morning I asked my bearer, "Do tigers ever came near Jessore?"

"Sometimes, *sahib*," he said, "But they usually stay in the jungle, away from people. But," he continued, his eyes getting wider, "The game warden's looking for a tiger that killed a man in a nearby village the other night."

I wondered if that was the tiger I'd heard.

Several days later on a hot afternoon, ambling home in the shade along the dusty tree-lined road from Jessore's bazaar, I noticed a crowd of natives walking down the road towards me carrying a dead tiger. Trussed by its legs to a long bamboo pole, it took three men on each side to carry the huge beast.

I stopped and watched. As they moved past me the tiger's head lolled from side-to-side, its long, thick, white whiskers like stiff wire. Its unstaring eyes seemed to be looking for a way to escape. The afternoon sun, shining on its beautifully marked body, brought out the colour of its orange and black stripes.

I was saddened to see such a magnificent beast being carried in this ignominious way. The noble animal was a far cry from those I'd seen crouching on wooden stools in the ring at Olympia's, Bertram Mills circus or London Zoo.

Apparently it was the man-eater they'd been looking for. I wondered how many men it had killed? Was it sick and unable to stalk its normal prey?

Periodically all station personnel were given a security briefing and reminded that there were probably a few Bengalis among the villagers spying for the Japanese by watching and reporting on our operations and listening for information about our sorties.

We used to buy fruit from a fruit "wallah", a friendly little man with a bright smile full of white teeth, who used to do business out at the aerodrome. With his tea pot and charcoal burner he sat under a banyan tree near the parked aircraft with his legs tucked up under his *dhoti*. Depending on the season he'd sell us bananas, mangoes and oranges from his cotton, muslin-covered wicker basket. He had a little can filled with an (Air Force approved) solution of water and potassium permanganate, into which he dipped the fruit before selling it.

I heard that two army service policemen called on him one day. They walked straight up to him and dragged him to his feet. They ripped the muslin cover from his basket and spilled his fruit on to the ground. At the bottom of the basket were a radio transmitter and a Morse sending key.

We learned that he was a Japanese spy and had probably been transmitting the take-off times of our 'planes, giving tail numbers, and maybe even supplying the name of intended targets. Spy or not, we missed his fruit!

CHAPTER
ELEVEN

Seeing India
— Supply dropping into Burma

Although Jessore was "home", most aircrew, when they had the opportunity, headed for somewhere else. Anywhere else!

I often went to Calcutta for the weekend because I had friends there. Barbara Gibson, the eldest daughter of our next-door neighbour in Weybridge, married a civil engineer before the war and went to live in far away, mythical India.

In their large three-storey house not far from Chowringhee, Calcutta's main street, the ground floor was mostly used for storage, but one of the rooms had been reinforced and made into a bomb shelter. This became my room.

Compared to Jessore's sergeants' quarter I was in the lap of luxury. A house full of servants attended to my every need. My gracious host and hostess took care to see I was entertained, often at the Bengal Club.

They put at my disposal a small motorbike — nothing like the BSA Blue Star 500 I had left with the local BSA dealer in Weybridge, but it was transportation. I'd ride along crowded Chowringhee to the downtown area for lunch at Firpos, a fashionable restaurant and social meeting spot, or I'd meet someone for drinks and *tiffen* at the Great Eastern Hotel.

Sometimes, on my way to town, I'd stop and watch an unusual sight; a snarling Hawker Hurricane taking off from the airstrip on Palam, a street running through the park in the middle of the city.

One day as I entered the lobby at Firpos, I noticed several pretty Anglo-Indian girls in their bright dresses sitting side-by-side in a row of chairs along the wall. Probably waiting for their escorts, I thought. Their heads were motionless and their eyes seemed transfixed; none of the usual bright smiles, chatter and fidgeting of young girls. I glanced across the lobby and saw the reason. A burly young Scots officer, wearing a brightly polished Sam Browne and a kilt sat sprawled in his chair with his long legs wide apart reading the 'paper.

If I had ever had any doubt what a Scotsman wore under his kilt, along with the young Anglo-Indian girls, I now knew! For a Scotsman, I suppose he was very well proportioned!

Day and night Calcutta's hot dusty streets were crowded with service personnel, mostly Americans. They shuffled along the packed pavements, looked in shop windows and stood around in groups talking. I'll never forget a burly black GI saying, as he waved his arms and pushed a small, slight *dhoti*-clad Bengali off the pavement, "Get out of my way, you black bastard."

One day on Chowringhee while waiting in a queue for the afternoon cinema show there was a scuffle just ahead of me. A large, black American soldier stumbled out of line, fell face down and lay on the pavement with a knife stuck in his back.

I decided I didn't want to go to the cinema after all and slipped away.

To make myself presentable for my busy social life I bought some civilian clothes, including a fancy white sharkskin jacket. One night, returning to my friend's house rather late, I took a rickshaw. In my best, fractured Hindi I gave the driver the address, climbed aboard and promptly fell asleep. Some time later I awoke and noticed trees instead of buildings. The rickshaw driver padded on. He's lost, I thought. "*Idar roko,*" I called to get him to stop.

I climbed out of the rickshaw and asked the driver where we were. From our stilted conversation I gathered he'd misunderstood the address I'd given him and we'd headed out to the city's outskirts. As always seemed to happen in India, a small crowd of dark-eyed, *dhoti*-clad men quickly gathered.

One of the spectators spoke a little English; he asked me what address I'd given the rickshaw driver. He then spoke to the driver and I assumed he was trying to straighten out the problem, but the situation got worse. The driver, with allies in the crowd, demanded more money to take me to my destination.

Enough was enough, I thought. I wasn't about to loose face and pay more; he was the one who'd got lost, not me. We argued. The crowd joined in. We all argued some more.

The situation was getting a little uncomfortable and I began to feel hostility. I also realized, since I was outnumbered, that I'd better stop being pompous and either get the situation under control quickly, or get the hell out of there.

To give myself a little time to think I reached for my cigarette case in the inner pocket of my white jacket. As I carefully selected a cigarette the whole situation, to my surprise, suddenly changed. The English-speaking Indian turned and told the driver he was wrong, "*Tumko karna chaheeye,*" — which translates as "you must do what the sahib says and take him home right away, for no extra charge."

I climbed back into my seat and looked out at the sullen, dark faces. The skinny driver with his orange turban spun the rickshaw around and trotted back towards the city.

As I smoked my cigarette I wondered what had caused such an abrupt change in attitude of the crowd. There'd been a lot of arguing, but I couldn't understand what anyone was saying. Then it struck me — of course! When I'd reached for my cigarette case I'd opened my coat enough for the crowd to see the chest strap and my 9mm Berreta's shoulder holster.

Even though the rickshaw driver had misunderstood me, I felt sorry for the little guy after he'd hauled me halfway across Calcutta, so I gave him a fat tip. He smiled a pink betel-juice smile and bowed, "Thankya, *salaam sahib*."

When they had time off, most aircrew went no farther from Jessore than Calcutta. I wanted to see as many places in India as I possibly could. If I had the time I'd board a train and head into central India. A mysterious country, India fascinated me. Its intriguing history with a civilization over 5000 years old; a country full of interesting people, strange sights, sounds and smells. There was much to see and learn.

I liked Lahore with the Mall's wide street and fancy stores. I stayed a couple of times at Filleti's hotel. I enjoyed the luxurious amenities; the food was good too. On my second visit I was ushered into a large comfortable room that had a white linen ceiling.

After an enjoyable dinner and a drink with some of the other guests, I went to bed. In the middle of the night I woke up to a strange scuffling noise. I turned on the light and spotted a bulge moving across the linen ceiling. That's got to be healthy sized rat, I figured, scurrying about up there.

I reached under the pillow for my 9mm Berreta, aimed carefully and fired. The one shot echoed through the room and, no doubt, throughout the whole hotel. I waited. There were no yells, no footsteps running down the hall.

Much to my amazement I'd scored a direct hit on the unfortunate rat, it wiggled for a moment and then lay still, a lump in the ceiling. Then a small crimson circle of blood slowly spread across the white cloth and dripped to the floor.

The following morning when I went to the dining room for breakfast I fully expected to hear the hotel guests discussing the gun shot. No one mentioned it. I also expected a tactful question from the young man at the front desk, or even the hotel's manager, but nothing was said.

After a long leisurely breakfast I sauntered down the hall back to my room. When I opened the door I immediately noticed the cleaning staff had been there. The bed was made, clothes hung in the cupboard and, to my amazement, the bloodstained linen ceiling had been replaced.

When I paid my bill I again expected some comment about my shot in the night. Nothing!

Where, but in India, would hotel staff be so discreet?

During one short leave I visited Darjeeling, a hill station in the Himalayan foothills. Over the years English families built English-looking houses with English gardens and tried to lead English lives. A pretty little place, but now overcrowded with service people.

I looked around for somewhere more remote and someone suggested Kalimpong, about 20 miles from Darjeeling near the Sikkim border. A trading place for Tibetans.

Taking the suggestion I went to Kalimpong with some of my crew. We stayed at a hotel owned by a forest ranger and had a good time there. It was quiet, the food was good; any food eaten outside of Jessore was good.

We discovered a very potent drink. The owner of the hotel, an Englishman, called it "Jungle Juice". To make

195

this drink, he poured hot water over a mixture of grains and rice in a cup-like piece of hollowed bamboo. I presume it immediately fermented. After drinking some of the brew, more hot water was added, but it never seemed to dilute the potency of the mash.

One morning a member of the hotel staff came to my room and handed me a telegram. I knew it was bad news; that's all telegrams brought people these days. I was right; it was from my stepmother telling me my father had died on 18 December in England. I'd received a letter from him written in August, from the Royal London Ophthalmic Hospital, telling me he was having trouble with an eye infection.

Several weeks later I got the last letter he wrote to me; it was dated 7 December. He said he hadn't been feeling too well, he also mentioned a family matter he'd wanted to talk to me about, but could never get around to it. He ended his letter with, "I hope this reaches you early in January — to wish at least a successful and happy new year — the last of this blasted war we all hope."

My crew rallied and expressed their sympathy. Although deeply saddened there was nothing they, or I, could do. My parents had divorced when I was sixteen. My brother, an RAF pilot, had been killed two years ago at El Alamein, and now my father was dead at the age of 52.

His death was a very sad experience for me; one of many. Lots of my school friends and fellow RAF comrades died during the war.

A few days later the hotel owner told me he had to leave on an inspection tour and asked me to try and kill a few of the crows that hung around the hotel. "They're a bloody nuisance," he said. "Use my shotgun. See how many you can hit."

One morning, shotgun in hand, I stalked some of the wily crows. I stalked slowly around the hotel, trying to catch them in the trees. But as soon as they saw me they flew across the roof and landed in trees on the other side of the hotel and cawed insults at me.

Creeping back around the building I suddenly came face-to-face with Captain Scattergood, another guest, sitting on a wooden picnic-table table in the sun admiring the view of distant snow capped mountains.

I lowered the shotgun and with my thumb eased one of the hammers forward. The second hammer slipped and the gun fired, hitting the ground a few feet ahead of the Captain.

When he told the story about the incident he embellished it by saying. "We all know there is inter-service rivalry between the RAF and the Army, but I really don't think it's necessary to go that far to put a point across!"

During my visit to Kalimpong I had another gun incident. Late one afternoon the sun was low, almost touching the top of the nearby mountain and it was getting cool, when a frantic, red-faced English woman, wearing a tan-coloured mackintosh, rushed into the hotel looking for the owner. I happened to be near the front door and told her he was away.

The little, mousey-looking woman was hysterical. "A cow's been hit by a car," she blurted out. "It's got a broken leg and somebody's got to do something about it."

I tried to calm her, but she fixed me with her pale-blue eyes and kept saying. "You've got to do something. Please, somebody's got to do something."

I became that somebody. From the gun-case in the hotel I grabbed a powerful looking rifle and a handful of bullets, and called out to Nick, my bomb aimer, to join me. We followed the frantic woman on foot down the hill.

She led us to a rather small, light brown cow lying half on the paved road and half on the grass edge of a vertical drop off. Several hundred feet below the road twisted down the hill in a series of hairpin bends.

A small group of brightly-clothed Nepalese had gathered; when we arrived they stopped talking and gazed, wide-eyed, at every move I made.

The cow lay quietly chewing the cud. "How do you know the cow's leg is broken?" I asked the woman. "It looks okay to me."

"I did it," she said, sheepishly. "It stepped into the road in front of me. I couldn't stop. I hit it and it stumbled away on three legs and dropped down over there."

Without getting too close I examined the animal carefully, trying not to disturb it. Its left back leg stuck out at a grotesque, unnatural angle.

"You must shoot the poor beast," the woman implored. "There is no one else around here to do it."

"Well," I mumbled to her, "Isn't it sort of frowned on to go around killing sacred cows?"

"This is an emergency," she said. "You must do it."

I turned to Nick. "Ever shot a cow?"

"No," he answered. "Have you?"

"I've seen a horse shot, in a steeple-chase in England. It fell at a jump and broke a leg."

The crowd drew away from me as I snapped a bullet about the size of an aircraft's cannon shell, into the breech. I moved around and stood about 10ft in front of the injured animal's head holding the rifle at the ready. The cow just lay there chewing the cud gazing at me with big brown eyes.

I really didn't want to do this. But since Frank hadn't exactly volunteered for the job, it was up to me. As far as these natives were concerned, in their eyes I was the *sahib* and had to live up to their expectations.

"Frank. Sacred cow, or not, I don't know how this event is going to turn out. You'd better move everyone further away."

I leaned closer to him and whispered, "For God's sake take that woman even further away."

In my mind I could see, after I fired, a wounded, maddened cow suddenly leaping to its feet, charging into the crowd and galloping down the road on three legs as cars swerved to avoid her.

I remembered my riding instructor telling me that to shoot a horse you took an imaginary line from the base of one ear to the opposite eye, where the lines crossed was the aiming point. I hoped it worked for cows too.

I raised the long, thick barrel and took careful aim at the magic spot. Trying to avoid looking into the cow's soulful brown eyes. I squeezed the trigger.

The recoil of the rifle surprised me as it slammed against my shoulder. Slightly dazed, I lowered the rifle and looked at the cow. Enveloped in a cloud of blue smoke, it slowly chewed the cud.

As the smoke swirled away I looked harder. Had I missed? No, there was a small black spot in the middle of the broad forehead right where it should be.

God! The bullet looked big enough to stop a tank, but it didn't kill a cow? What now? While I was trying to make up my mind whether to reload and take a second shot, the cow cooperated beautifully. She slowly lay down on her side and stopped chewing. She was dead.

The woman, now calm, broke away from the awed crowd and came over to me to thank me for my act of mercy. I suggested rather pointedly, "You should find the cow's owner and pay him the going price for cows around here."

She was about to leave, so I continued my lecture. "Arrange to have the body removed immediately to the slaughter house. It seems a pity to waste the meat."

The Burders, who owned a house in Kalimpong called TashiDing, invited me to stay with them the next time I came to Kalimpong. Their very English-looking house overlooked the distant Himalayas with a wonderful view of Mount Katchenjunga. I enjoyed staying there with Betty Burders, her two young daughters Susan and Caroline and a house full of servants.

When Betty Burder found out I liked to ride, she said, "Good. We have a horse, but he hasn't been ridden for a long time."

Likewise, I hadn't ridden for a long time. The next morning the syce produced a magnificent beast. I soon discovered he really did need exercising and I got quite an exciting work-out. Cantering down narrow steep trails in the Himalayas was somewhat different to a sedate ride in the Surrey countryside.

Fortunately, the animal was surefooted and knew the paths. Shaking his head and grabbing at the bit he gave me a wild ride.

We had many family picnics where there were always lots of interesting guests, among them many influential people. At one of the outdoor lunches I met Corporal Ian Parks, son of Air Marshal Parks.

Kalimpong boasted a cinema, which was barely better than no cinema. Seated in the raised gallery at the back, on sofas draped in white cloth, we knew we were in the "box seats". On benches in front of us sat Tibetans, ardent film fans. I looked at the wall-to-wall wire fence dividing us and wondered, could they be that unruly?

When it rained on the corrugated tin roof during a performance the actors' voices were literally drowned out. To follow the story it helped if you could lip-read. Adding to the discomfort, occasionally you felt a rat brush over your foot.

As pleasant as it was to go up to a hill station, I had to return to Jessore. There was a war on.

General Orde C. Wingate conceived the idea of using small, mobile army units to fight the highly elusive Japanese forces in the Burma jungle. RAF Dakotas, or DCs dropped food and ammunition to his Chindits and light, single-engined Austers, called "Angles", airlifted the wounded from jungle airstrips to base hospitals.

In the Burma theatre RAF transport squadron crews flew such a large number of operational hours they became tour-expired before replacements could reach India. I was one of the tour-expired crews from other squadrons in India assigned to fill this gap.

In May I received my commission and moved into the Officers' Mess. On 29 May 1944, as I neared the end of my operational tour with 215 Squadron, I was attached to 62 Squadron in Chandina to fly Dakotas. Chandina, near Comilla on the Bengal/Assam railway line, was east of the Ganges and about 160 miles northeast of Calcutta.

The day after I arrived on the squadron I flew as co-pilot to Flt Lt Graham, and logged eight hours and fifteen minutes on two supply trips into Imphal, near the Burma border 300 miles northeast of Chandina. The following day I made three flights to Imphal and logged another eight hours and forty-five minutes. I found out firsthand by flying this number of hours, day after day, why aircrew quickly completed operational tours. The pace was exhausting.

One flight to Imphal, in the saucer-shaped Manipur valley ringed by 2,000ft high mountains, stands out in my memory. Ten-tenths of overcast cloud at about

1,500ft covered the mountain rim surrounding the valley. As we approached, below cloud, the Captain, Sqn Ldr Harries, pointed out a dip in the mountain ridge, "That vee in the hill top is where we cross into the valley."

As we neared the gap, which looked wide enough for about two aircraft flying side by side, the ground rose sharply up towards us. I held my breath as we skimmed the tops of thick, jungle trees.

Below I spotted uniformed men scurrying around on the ground. "Who are they?" I asked.

"Japs," Harries shouted back. "They'll probably take pot shots at us; they usually do."

No sooner had he finished the sentence than the Japanese soldiers stopped running, raised their rifles and puffs of smoke dotted the area. We were so close I could see their faces as they swung their rifles keeping us in their sights. The next moment we roared over their heads and out into the valley. This was the first time I had actually seen the enemy in the flesh. My operational bombing flights with 215 Squadron were mostly at night, and seldom below 4,000ft.

The British army, it seemed to me, managed to get cut off in the most inaccessible places in the jungle and then called for a supply airdrop.

On one of these supply flights I was co-pilot, again, to Sqn Ldr Harries, the Captain. We were flying one of several Dakotas arriving independently at the drop zone (DZ). The pilots positioned their 'planes in single file and flew in a large circle skirting the hill tops. One by one the 'planes descended towards the drop zone, located on a small treeless bend in a river, and tossed out their cargo.

On the downwind leg to the drop zone we flew over hills held by the Japanese. As each Dakota swooped by them at eye level they fired at the 'planes with light machine guns and rifles. Turning towards the bend in the river, Harries reached over and pulled back on the throttles letting the 'plane slide down over the side of a hill. Skimming the trees, we were so close I could pick out individual leaves.

We neared the flat, sandy bulge in the river bend, levelled out and "WHAM"! The aircraft hit turbulence coming up from the hot ground. Radios, behind us in the crew's cabin, rattled in their racks and maps spilled off the navigator's table. Harries, with both hands on the wheel, fought the control column to hold the aircraft level.

A few hundred feet ahead, over the drop zone, another 'plane suddenly spewed a brightly coloured stream of parachutes from its left side.

In seconds we were over the drop zone.

"Now!" Harries shouted.

I reached over to the left-hand upper switch panel, just above Harries's head, and pressed the spring-loaded caution-jump switch, ringing the bell in the cabin. On this signal the two-man drop-crew, moving as fast as they could, heaved bales and sacks out through the open door. Caught in the slipstream each bundle whisked out of sight as if snatched away by a giant hand. The rope parachute tethers snapped tight jerking the parachutes open. As they drifted down, the tethers slapped against the side of the fuselage.

We were so low the parachutes barely had time to open before the cargo thumped the ground.

"That's it," Harries shouted.

I let go of the bell switch and shoved both throttles forward to 48in, maximum take-off power. The 'plane shuddered as we crawled up the side of the hill with the airspeed wavering around 110mph. Heavy turbulence shook the instrument panel; I could hardly read the gauges. Trees underneath us seemed even closer than before.

Harries, sweating, wrestled the control column while pumping the rudder pedals, struggling to stay clear of the slipstream of the aircraft ahead of us. If we got caught in that slipstream, this close to the ground, a wing might suddenly drop and we'd be pushed downwards into the trees below.

At the top of the hill I pulled the throttles back to 40in and adjusted the revs to 2,550rpm. I quickly scanned the engine instruments, looking for a drop in oil pressure, or engine overheating. Sure signs of a possible engine failure.

Following the aircraft ahead we circled the hill to the left for another run past the waiting Japanese marksmen. Would they get us this time? I could almost feel a bullet smack against the fuselage.

Nothing happened.

One by one, in the few seconds available, parachutes floated down to the beleaguered soldiers as several Dakotas, in line-astern, trailed across the drop zone.

Instead of dropping supplies they were sometimes delivered by Dakotas landing on a rough runway scratched out in the jungle. On one such flight we carried a load of mules, tethered down one side of the cabin under the care of an army Corporal.

We'd reached cruising altitude when suddenly the aircraft's nose pitched up, then dropped throwing us into a steep dive. The pilot pulled the control column back and shouted, "Full power!"

I slammed the throttles fully forward and the twin Wasp R-1830 engines roared.

"I can't hold it. We're losing height!" the Skipper shouted.

The altimeter's needle was unwinding at a frightening rate. The next second the aircraft reared again and pointed up at the clouds.

"Power off," the Skipper yelled as he shoved the column forward. "For God's sake! Get those f★★★★★★ mules tied up before we stall and the buggers kill us."

I turned and shouted his message to the navigator. He whipped opened the cabin door, letting a stench of manure fill the cockpit, and yelled the message to the army Corporal.

When the seesawing finally stopped, a sweaty Corporal in a straw-speckled, khaki battle dress, smelling of mules, appeared in the cockpit.

"Sorry about that, Skipper," he said. "A couple of them got excited, I think they were trying to get out." A grin spread across his weather-beaten face. "Good thing they can't make love isn't it?" He went back to his charges chuckling to himself.

206

Once a Dak had carried mules it became known as a "muler" and from then on, no matter how many times the aircraft was cleaned, the smell of mule manure and urine never went away.

On another flight with Flt Lt Burrows as Captain, we'd had a busy morning landing at several strips. We were getting ready to leave when Burrows said, "Okay, Tony, I think it's time. Get in the left seat and fly it." I made my first left seat Dakota landing on a *kutcha* strip, barely wider than the Dakota's wheels, hacked out in the jungle. I flew straight towards the brown area between the trees, no circuit to assess distance, and lined up with runway. But I underestimated my rate of descent.

"Watch your height," Burrows called across to me.

I eased the throttles forward, keeping my airspeed at 112mph. A moment later I called out to him, "Full flaps."

The Dak slid closer and closer to the treetops. Suddenly we were over the strip and the wheels thumped the ground.

"Flaps coming up. Nice landing, Tony," the Skipper said, pointing ahead. "They're waiting for us over there."

As I taxied towards a group of men standing in the shade of the trees, I felt the same feeling of elation I had experienced when I made my first solo landing in a Tiger Moth at Marshalls Flying in Cambridge.

I liked flying Dakotas. They were so new, crisp and clean compared to the old, bedraggled, oil-stained Wellingtons I'd flown during my year's operational tour at Jessore. The "clapped out" Wimpys on our squadron had probably done several operational tours in Europe before being ferried out to India. At Jessore I never saw the one I ferried from Cairo to Karachi; I often wondered where it finished up.

On 13 June we had just finished a flight bringing supplies from Comilla to Imphal when our wireless operator received a recall for all squadron aircraft to rendezvous at Argetala.

The Argetala briefing officer told us a supply drop would be made that night to an army unit in the jungle desperately needing food and ammunition. Flt Lt Burrows, who had never done a night drop, was to fly with Squadron Leader Harries.

When the briefing ended the Wing Commander announced to the assembled aircrew, "One aircraft is not going on the drop tonight, who's not flying?"

Together with the rest of Flt Lt Burrow's crew I raised a hand.

"Leicester, you take 643 and Burrow's crew back to Comilla."

Crews prepared their aircraft for the night operations and I climbed into Dak 643. Flt Lt Sinclair, the navigator, settled beside me in the co-pilot's seat. He knew I hadn't flown a Dakota solo and he kept a watchful eye on everything I did. Generally, navigators had a tendency to be extremely methodical. To inspire his confidence, I went through the pre-start checklist meticulously, calling out each check as I made it. He seemed satisfied.

I managed the twenty minute routine flight back to Comilla without making the crew, Warrant Officers Wood and Hall, any more nervous than I was.

For this flight I made a unique entry in my logbook — *"Operational flight and first solo on type!"*

On another flight to the Manipur valley — we called it Imphal valley — I landed at Kanglataungbi, one of the valley's six landing strips, to airlift equipment from an army brigade being replaced.

The operation's officer briefing us said we were to pick up a load of tents. This seemed illogical. Another batch of tents, belonging to the new unit, were to be flown in. But, as pilots, it wasn't our place to question those who were running the war!

While waiting for the 'plane to be loaded I stood under a wing in the shade, drinking tea and talking to some aircrew.

An Indian army Corporal, wearing shorts two sizes to large for him, came towards me. "Your aeroplane's loaded, *sahib*," he said.

As I made the external inspection I noticed the tyres seemed a little flat and made a mental note to write it up in the F700. Satisfied with my 'plane's readiness I climbed the portable steps, stuck my head in the cabin and stopped — dumbfounded.

Folded canvas tents, stacked from floor to ceiling, filled the cabin leaving only a narrow gangway to the cockpit.

Stupid buggers! I muttered.

I stormed back down the steps, found the Indian army Subaldar in charge of loading, and asked him for the weight and balance sheet. The figures showed that the aircraft was way over the maximum all-up weight of 31,000lb. It was miracle that the aircraft's back hadn't broken just sitting on the ground!

With great patience I explained to the young Indian officer, "An aeroplane's not like a train's box car, you don't load it up until it's full."

With his swagger cane tucked under his left arm he apologized. "Sorry, *sahib*. I'll get my men to unload it right away."

Tents were unloaded and piled on the ground, leaving only one layer on the cabin floor. The Subaldar looked at all the wasted space and shook his head.

On another operational flight I took a load of freight to Palel, a landing strip at the southeast end of Imphal valley. After landing I taxied to the end of the wet runway and shut down the engines. There wasn't a soul around.

As I climbed out of the back door a voice bellowed, "Quick! Over here." I turned towards the sound and saw an arm waving from a foxhole.

Without waiting for a further invitation I jumped to the ground and with my crew right behind me, ran full tilt to the narrow, shallow hole and dived in; practically on top of three crouched airmen.

The next moment a mortar shell exploded on the far side of the runway and shot mud over us. I could hear small stones and blobs of mud rattling off the wings of our Dak. Peeping out over the edge of the foxhole, I saw a small puff of smoke drifting out of the trees on the nearby hillside.

Moments later a Hurricane "Hurri-bomber", from 221 Group, roared across the valley at 200ft towards the telltale smoke. It pulled up into a sharp climb and a couple of bombs streaked from under its wings and exploded among the trees.

The tan-coloured camouflage-painted Hurricane then turned and zoomed at low-level back across the valley. Its Merlin engines' throaty roar echoed from the hills. I don't know if the bombs hit the Japanese mortar crew, but no more shells were lobbed at us.

All at once a bunch of airmen scrambled out of several foxholes and quickly unloaded the freight.

Before I flew Dakotas, I had ferried bombs to Imphal in a Wellington; bombs for Hurricane and Vultee Vengance dive-bomber sorties, like the one I had experienced. On one of these bomb ferry flights on 25 May 1944, I nearly "bought it."

On this particular flight my crew was Shaw, Munton, Gough and Nash. They were all experienced 215 Squadron Flight Sergeants, but I'd never flown with any of them before. On that day we made two flights from Khimbergram into Imphal carrying 4,000lb of bombs. Sixteen 250lb bombs, without their tail fins, hung from the bomb racks.

After landing at Kangla, Imphal's landing strip, I taxied off the runway, stopped and opened the bomb doors. The bomb aimer pulled the bomb-toggle and all the bombs clunked to the ground.

The Wellington is low-slung and its opened bomb bay doors came very close to the ground. Before closing the doors, I waited for the airman's signal that they would clear the bombs lying on the ground. He stooped, peered under the belly of the fuselage and then gave me a thumbs up. I taxied slowly forward, swinging the tail to miss the pile of bombs, while a couple of the crew shoved the bomb tail fins out of the fuselage's aft-end emergency hatch. We flew back to Khimbergram, picked up another load and returned to Kangla.

Kangla's landing strip ended at the foot of an almost vertical range of hills about 1,000ft high. In this precarious situation, traffic control landed incoming 'planes towards the hill for about fifteen minutes, or until the parking area was full. A red Aldis lamp signal then stopped the landings and allowed waiting 'planes to take off for the next fifteen minutes, heading away from the hill.

I slowed my 'plane to circuit speed and followed another aircraft circling in the traffic pattern. When my turn came to land I turned, lined up with the runway and put down the undercarriage and some flap. At the right moment I dropped full flap and opened the throttle to control my rate of sink.

I planned to put the wheels smack on the end of the runway and then turn off the strip as quickly as possible.

My airspeed was as slow as I dared keep it for the weight of the heavy bomb load.

Suddenly, out of the corner of my eye, I saw another 'plane, a Mitchell (B-25) with US markings, coming up alongside from the left. Abruptly it cut in front of me and I caught its slipstream. The old Wimpy rolled violently from left to right, sinking like a wounded whale. I rammed open the throttles to full climbing power and frantically worked the control column to regain control. Luck was with me; I managed to hold my height at about 200ft.

Flying over the end of the runway I caught a glimpse of the offending Mitchell below as it flared out for landing.

From then on I was too busy to worry about anything except the huge brown, rocky wall dead ahead looming closer and closer. My airspeed was too slow, but I dared not raise flaps.

"Undercarriage up!" I yelled to Flt Sgt Shaw, my co-pilot.

As the wheels drew into the engine nacelles, I got a little more airspeed and started a slow, gentle turn to the right. I hoped the turn was fast enough to get me around before I careened into the hill.

The intercom was silent.

I glanced at Shaw. He was staring straight ahead, fear etched on his face.

Fast approaching the rocky hill ahead, still at 200ft, I gripped the wheel. My palms were wet — Christ! I'm going to hit before I finish the turn!

Relying on experience of several hundred hours flying Wellingtons, I increased the turn as much as I dared and held my breath as the hill slowly slid by on my port side.

Sweat rolled down my face and back. I continued the turn. Trees at the foothill were getting bloody close. Would I clear them?

I now had a little more airspeed with engines still screaming at full throttle. Not a good time, I thought, to lose an engine.

I didn't want to think about it. I'd seen a bomb-loaded Wimpy crash in a ball of fire at Jessore.

Moments later, with the hill and trees drifting behind me, I was flying almost parallel to the runway where I'd intended to land.

My airspeed looked healthier. I throttled back the engines and glanced out of the side window. No aircraft were landing or taking off. A Jap mortar attack on the field?

I'd lost about 50ft getting the aircraft turned around but I was now flying straight and level.

At this moment keeping controllable speed was more important than height. I eased the stick forward and lost a little more height. My airspeed increased a notch, but to get the safe speed I needed I'd have to raise the flaps.

With both hands on the wheel I called to Shaw, "Take off a bit of flap." The aircraft's trim changed. "Bit more." It changed again and our airspeed increased.

With airspeed building I felt a lot easier so I eased back the throttles and the engines' snarl changed to a comfortable roar.

Finally, almost relaxed, I wiped my right palm on my trouser leg and called out, "Flaps up," turning my hard-gained airspeed into extra height above the ground.

Five hundred feet looked much better than 150ft with flaps down and a dangerously slow airspeed!

Back over the approach end of the runway, with a great sigh of relief, I joined the circling aircraft and took my turn to land.

"Nice work, Skipper," a voice called over the intercom.

I looked across at Flt Sgt Shaw. All the anxiety in his face had gone. He grinned back at me. "Nice work. Bit dicey there for a while, wasn't it?"

After a normal landing I taxied to the parking area. In seconds I was out of the forward hatch, down the ladder and heading on the double towards the parked Mitchell.

The American pilot, a Captain wearing an obviously freshly-ironed khaki shirt, saw me coming and I think he immediately knew who I was.

Rage replaced the anxiety and tension of the landing incident. I was furious. I didn't get angry very often, but now I was really mad.

Forgetting my Flight Sergeant rank for the moment, I told that Captain things he didn't want to hear. A crowd of aircrew gathered and I sensed everyone was on my side. I berated the American pilot for nearly killing us, made allusions to his parentage and finished up telling him, "Your obvious lack of flying ability is only exceeded by your marked stupidity!"

The Captain looked everywhere except at me and he didn't say a word. Completely cowered he made no attempt to defend his actions.

I turned my back on him and walked away.

A voice from the crowd called out to the Captain, "Yeah, stupid clot. Who's bloody side are you on anyway?"

An airman turned to me and said, "We knew you were carrying bombs and when that Yank cut you off we didn't think you'd make it, Sarge."

Another airman called out. "Landings and take-offs stopped. When you started that low turn away from the hill we all cheered like hell."

Jessore also had an effective "bush telegraph". While I was attached to 62 Squadron flying Dakotas, another 215 Squadron crew was killed when turbulence in a violent monsoon broke their 'plane apart. I flew back to Jessore carrying the confidential papers concerning the crash and handed them over to the squadron adjutant.

The next morning I went into Jessore's general store to be greeted by the owner, a jolly, fat Bengali *babu*.

"So sorry to hear about the accident." He then named all the crew of the crashed 'plane and how much money they owed him!

How did he know?

There was very little crime at Jessore, but we had an occasional theft of small, personal items from the crews' quarters. One night, someone bumped into the mosquito net over Fane's bed. He woke suddenly and saw a "*loose wallah*," hunched beside his bed, going through the pockets of his clothes hanging over the mosquito netting.

"What the hell are you doing?" he yelled.

In seconds several fellows shot out from their *charpoys* and grabbed at the thief. One of the grabbers said, "I had my hands around the little bastard's arm, but he slipped away."

Within seconds he fled over the verandah's railing into the night.

A *loose wallah*, or native burglar, covered his naked body with grease making him too slippery to hold on to.

Nothing was stolen; but we set alarms using bottles precariously balanced on edges of books and string stretched from bed to bed to catch any future night visitors. The alarms didn't catch a thief, but sleepy aircrew staggering out in the early hours for a leak set them off! Because there was always the possibility of sudden death in a crash, or going missing over the jungle, most aircrew had a cavalier approach to life. They were young and invincible and rarely showed their true feelings. Yet some were a little superstitious.

One ritual, performed to ward off evil spirits, was the "pre-operational rite" developed by our group. Crew members going on Ops would ask Larry Pyman to play their favourite gramophone record on his wind-up player. For me, they played Helen O'Connell's "*Embraceable You*". Even those who were not superstitious knew better than not play their favourite record; one couldn't trust to luck.

After dinner most of the officers in the Mess gathered at the bar in the corner of the anteroom and got down to some serious drinking. The anteroom, on the ground floor, was furnished with several sofas and easy chairs. Large Indian carpets covered the concrete floor giving the room a comfortable, warm look. Not that we needed the warmth because even though there was a *punka*, the Mess was usually unbearably hot.

The *punka* consisted of several strips of heavy carpet-like fabric hanging down about 4ft, attached to a sturdy pole spanning the width of the room. The horizontal poles were suspended by ropes from metal rings in the ceiling, connected together by a long rope that went outside through a hole in the wall near the ceiling.

The *punka wallah* sat outside under the rope, with his back to the wall, and pulled the rope to make the *punka* swing slowly back and forth. A little movement just stirring the air gave the illusion of coolness and made the room more comfortable.

When the *punka wallah* stopped pulling there was a cry from the bar crowd, "*Punka wallah!*" The *punka* would jerk a few times and then settle into a smooth, slow rhythm — until he nodded off again.

One evening, after we'd woken the *punka wallah* several times, a few of us decided to make sure he stayed alert in the future. The next time the *punka* stopped, two officers went outside the Mess and quietly worked their way around to the sleeping *punka wallah*. With great care, so as not awaken him, they tied the end of the rope around his feet and then crept back into the Mess.

We piled several chairs up under the *punka* and two of us, the tallest, reached up and gently took hold of the rope now connected to *punka wallah's* feet. Then, at a

218

given signal, we jumped off the chairs, pulling the rope down sharply. A shrill yell of surprise came from outside. We had jerked the unfortunate *punka wallah*, feet first, up the side of the wall. When he reached the end of our pull, we let go of the rope. Then another yell as he fell head first to the ground.

Forever after the *punkas* maintained their rhythmical swaying.

Because we were young and, I'm sure, foolish, we sometimes behaved very badly. No wonder the Indians wanted to get the British troops out of India.

RAF aircrew found an excuse for a party on the slightest pretext, so when someone was posted, what better excuse? When I received my posting to 322 Maintenance Unit in Cawnpore I knew a party in the Officers' Mess was in the offing.

The party had been in full swing for a couple of hours when the CO, Wing Commander Cross, tall and stern-looking, rapped the bar with his glass.

"We've two officers posted," he announced. "Pilot Officer Brown and Pilot Officer Leicester." He then gave a little speech praising the two of us. "You've done a damned good job." He held out his empty glass for a refill. "We'll miss you." The former, I agreed with; the latter, I didn't. The barman poured a fresh round of drinks and everyone raised their glasses in a toast.

The "Wingco" rapped the bar again. "Off with Brown's trousers!"

Brown, an ex-policeman, about 6ft 4in and solidly-built, was no match for the gaggle of officers that pounced on him. He fought well, but lost both the struggle and his trousers.

I was next for a debagging so I prepared myself for the onslaught by working my way around to the end of the L-shaped bar. When the call went out, "Off with Leicester's trousers!" I darted across the anteroom with the pack following me. Nearing the front door I brushed off a couple of hands grabbing at my waist. I thought I had it made when a rugger tackle around my knees brought me crashing down on the carpeted floor. Then, flat on my face and hopelessly outnumbered, I was quickly and ceremoniously debagged.

About a half an hour later, back at the bar, I turned to Frank and asked, "Where's the CO?"

Frank looked towards the bar, then turned and looked round the room. "I'm sure he was here a few moments ago. But maybe it was quite a while ago."

We commented on his absence because we had an uneasy feeling that all was not well. Since no one remembered seeing him leave we decided to investigate. We hurried to his bungalow and knocked on the door. No answer. The silence disturbed us. I led the way in and headed for the light shining from the bedroom.

Wing Commander Cross lay on his bed under the mosquito netting in the glare of the bedside lamp. His eyes were closed and his face white. He reminded me of the painting of Nelson dying on the deck of the *Victory*.

"Are you all right, Sir?" I asked, peering down at him.

He opened his eyes and, obviously in pain, mumbled, "Get the MO, I think I've broken something," he groaned, "Hurts like hell."

Frank said he'd stay with the CO while I got the Medical Officer. I climbed into the CO's jeep and headed to the 99 Squadron's MO's living quarters. Our squadron doctor was away, recovering from a bout of the DTs, at least that's what most of us suspected.

I banged on the bungalow door until the doctor, bleary-eyed, opened it. "Wg Cdr Cross has been hurt. He needs you."

"Go away. You're drunk."

Again, I tried to convince him I was telling the truth, but he wouldn't believe me.

"I've heard your excuses before, anything to get me to join your lousy parties." He started to close the door, "For God's sake go away."

I stuck my foot in the door. "Look, Doc, I'm serious. There really has been an accident."

Finally, he agreed to come, but he said he'd drive his own jeep. "You're too drunk and you stink of rum."

Off to one side in the CO's bedroom, Frank and I watched as the MO bandaged and taped the "Wingco" and gave him a pain pill. "You've broken your collar bone. How did it happen, Sir?" the MO asked.

"We were trying to debag Leicester. He was getting away. I took a flying tackle and hit the floor pretty hard," the CO said, grimacing in pain.

A few days later I left Jessore. My crew, until now, had stayed together from August 1942, when we met at Chipping Warden's OTU, to our break up on 5 July 1944. We had tried to get a posting as a crew, to become instructors at the Wellington OTU in Palestine, but the "powers that be" had other things in store for us.

Several weeks later, at Risalpur on the northwest frontier, I received a letter from Wg Cdr Cross. He told me he had been posted to Staff College at Quetta. Because his arm was still in a sling and he couldn't take notes, he had an easy time, he said, and passed the course; this led to his promotion to Group Captain.

While at Jessore's 215 Squadron I had shared a bearer with several other officers. He was a young Bengali, Ram, about eighteen years old, slightly on the stocky side, with dark, pockmarked skin. He took care of our needs, picked up our dirty clothes and took them to the *dhobi*, brought us tea several times a day, shopped for us in the bazaar and generally kept us organized and presentable enough to go out in public.

When he smiled, which he did most of time, his white teeth glittered against his dark skin. He was completely honest, loved us all and asked question after question about everything. I'm sure, short of murder, Ram would have done anything we asked.

When the time came to leave Jessore for my posting to 322 Maintenance Unit in Cawnpore, Ram begged to go with me as my personal bearer.

"*Sahib*, I like working for you. Please let me stay with you," he pleaded.

222

I sat him down and talked to him like a Dutch uncle. I explained that I was going hundreds and hundreds of miles away where people spoke another language, ate different food and where the climate was quite different to what he was used to. I put it to him, as best as I could, that where I was going the people had a different religion, they weren't Hindus and he would have a very, very difficult time. But it didn't work.

With a downcast look on his dark, young face, he pleaded. "Please, *Sahib*, please take me with you."

Because he'd never gone far from Jessore it was difficult to make him understand the size of India, and how different the rest of the country was to his Bengal with its lush, green jungles and rivers. His loyalty touched me, but there was nothing I could say to cheer him up.

When the day came for me to leave for Jessore railway station, Ram loaded my stuff into the back of the aircrew 1,500-weight. We shook hands and I climbed in beside the driver. As we pulled away he stepped back, smiled that wonderful smile, and saluted me.

CHAPTER
TWELVE

Cawnpore's maintenance unit

I arrived at 322 Maintenance Unit (MU) Cawnpore, with its sprawling red-brick buildings, on a hot, dry and dusty 16 July 1944. Two days later, in spite of a logbook bulging with Dakota experience, Flt Lt Howard, the Flight Commander, took me up in a Dakota to prove to him I could fly it.

Compared to squadron life I found this maintenance unit pretty dull. Several pilots sat around in the crew room at the front of one of the hangars, reading, smoking too much and playing cards, waiting to air test Wellingtons and Dakotas when they came off maintenance inspection.

In spite of the heat I played played tennis on the concrete court. Very hard on the feet.

During the hottest months at Jessore, little or no maintenance could be done outside in the afternoon. As Cawnpore was a maintenance depot however, airmen worked all day thanks to the enterprising person who designed an aircraft "cooling machine". This was based on the principle of the *chatty*, a porous, clay drinking water container that oozed a slight amount of water and cooled the jug by evaporation. This elaborate, sheet-metal, Heath Robinson-looking contraption was about 5ft square. A hand-driven fan blew air into the front of the box and across hemp-fibre mats hanging inside the machine. The mats soaked up water from a trough below and evaporation cooled the air blown out of the back, through a canvas tube suspended to a 'plane's doorway. During the stifling afternoon heat, the cool, albeit damp, air enabled mechanics to work inside an aeroplane.

I hadn't flown for several days when Flt Lt Rabb, Indian Air Force, asked me if I would like to go up with him in a Tiger Moth and be a "student pilot" while he practiced his "instructor's patter." I jumped at the opportunity. Anything to get away from the smoky crew room; besides, I hadn't seen a Tiger Moth since my Cambridge days.

Back in 1941 the Tiger Moth biplane seemed big with its two open cockpits and wire rigging but, after flying Wellingtons and Dakotas with wingspans of about 90ft, it looked like a toy.

I climbed into the back cockpit. Flt Lt Rabb, short and stocky, snapped on his parachute harness, stepped on the wing and quickly swung himself into the cockpit in front of me.

After he adjusted the instructor's mirror I could see his dark-moustached face and white teeth as he called out, "Contact," to the ground crew swinging the propeller.

From the moment we taxied out Flt Lt Rabb started his instructor's patter in his singsong English putting me through a training exercise. After taking off and levelling out he gave me detailed instructions through the Gosport intercom tube; then he made me fly the exercise as though I were a student pilot.

"Now I want you to make a three hundred and sixty degree banked turn to the left, maintain your altitude, open up to twenty-one hundred, keep your airspeed at seventy and I expect you to fly back into your slipstream." His high-pitched voice was firm, full of authority.

I thoroughly enjoyed wheeling the little Tiger Moth about the sky, sensing the wind whistling round the open cockpit. Feeling the Gypsy Major engine's vibrations run through the frail fabric-covered fuselage took me back to Elementary Flying School, back to fond memories of flying over the Fens and looking for Ely Cathedral, my landmark when I got twisted around doing aerobatics.

Over the engine noise Flt Lt Rabb called, "Now I'm going to demonstrate a forced landing."

Like a wound up machine, he started his "patter" again.

"See that nice, flat, green area ahead." He raised his hand and pointed. "That's where I'll make my approach."

He did everything right, he checked the wind and set up his circuit pattern. On final approach he closed the throttle for a glide approach at 55mph, keeping his "patter" going like a running commentary of a football game.

"Oh my God!" he suddenly called out in his high-pitched voice. I could hear him laughing as he pushed the throttle forward. "Look up ahead. It's a bloody paddy field, let's go home."

I'd hardly got settled at 322 MU when I was moved to No 308 MU at Ambala, 100 miles north of Delhi. Some boffin had the bright idea of using a Wellington as a freighter to fly fresh fruit and vegetables to RAF Stations at Willingdon, Delhi and Chakeri.

The idea was good, but why use a clapped out Wellington? The Wimpy's canvas-covered geodetic frame had proved reliable in many incidents when hit by "ack-ack", and many a 'plane had struggled home with large holes knocked in wings, tail or fuselage; but it was designed as a bomber, not a freighter. There was no place for cargo. Vegetables were loaded into an almost inaccessible storage container built into the bomb bay. It was a fiasco and the idea didn't last very long. Four days later I was back at Cawnpore!

One morning Flt Lt Howard, the Flight Commander, stuck his head round the door of the crew room and called out, "Leicester. Let's go and air test the Liberator."

I climbed aboard the large four-engined 'plane. I'd never been inside a cavernous Liberator so Flt Lt Howard briefed me on emergency procedures and showed me how the fuel system worked, with its miles of fuel pipes and glass bottles.

Sitting in the cockpit high above the ground he explained the turbo-charging system and briefed me on how I should handle the engine controls for take-off. He started the engines, taxied to the end of the runway and did the runup. He went through the pre-takeoff check and called across to me, "Let's go. Take-off power."

I eased the throttles forward, as instructed, and we rolled down the runway gathering speed. The four-engined aircraft accelerated smoothly and quicker than either a Wellington or Dakota. I was impressed.

Suddenly we swung slightly to the left and drifted off the runway and the wheels thumped on the grass infield. We were now moving really fast. I expected Flt Lt Howard to reach out, close the throttles and abandon the take-off. He didn't. Instead he heaved on the nose-wheel control and we swung, still accelerating, back on to the runway. Moments later he pulled back on the control column and the wheels left the ground.

"Undercarriage up, climbing power," he called out. Then looking across at me he grinned, "First time I've flown one these, too!"

After an hour flying around Flt Lt Howard "greased" that Liberator back on to the runway as if he had thousands of hours flying them; being a Farnborough test pilot must have made a difference!

At the Maintenance Unit, in addition to air testing Wellingtons and Dakotas, I occasionally taxied a Hawker Hurricane from the parking area to the hangar for inspection. Before doing so I had to read the Hurricane's Pilot's Notes on starting and stopping the engine, and how to taxi the 'plane. The Hurricane's long engine stuck out at an angle preventing the pilot from seeing directly ahead when taxiing. To see where he's going he has to kick the rudder to swing the nose from side to side.

I enjoyed taxiing Hurricanes to and from the dispersal area. Sitting behind the throbbing in-line Rolls-Royce Merlin engine, with its stubby exhaust stacks just ahead and on either side of the cockpit, I remembered how I had desperately wanted to be a fighter pilot when I had joined the RAF.

One day I asked Plt Off Gebbles, another Wellington pilot, "Do you think there's a chance we could get "checked out" on a Hurricane?"

"Let's find out," he said.

When we asked Flt Lt Howard if this was possible, he agreed. "But," he said, "I won't authorize the flight unless conditions are ideal. There's got to be a clear sky and a light wind down the runway."

Flt Lt Howard told us to learn all about the Hurricane's systems and the pilot's procedures. "I'll go over them with each of you before you fly. It's not like getting checked out in a twin." He added, "In a single seater you'd better get it right first time." Gebbles and I tossed to see who'd make the first flight. I lost.

To prepare ourselves for this big event we would choose a Hurricane on the flight line. I would climb into the cockpit, while Gebbles would stand on the wing with the Pilot's Notes. As I went over the cockpit procedures he followed them in the book. I simulated hand movements for raising the wheels and operating the flaps. Blindfolded I could touch and point to any lever, or instrument in the cockpit. I also memorized the speed and power settings needed for any manoeuvre. I repeated them again and again until I knew them by heart. Then he would climb into the cockpit and I would monitor him. After doing this several hours we felt we were ready to tackle a Hurricane.

When the time came for Plt Off Gebbles's solo flight, I joined several other aircrew to watch. I must say I was a little envious because he got to go first.

He swung into the cockpit like a veteran Hurricane pilot, buckled his parachute and safety harness and taxied to the end of the runway. After a short run-up he closed the canopy, turned and lined up for take-off.

I was sure he must have been surprised at the acceleration from the roaring Merlin engine, it was far greater than any 'plane he'd flown. The powerful engine produced a lot of propeller torque making it difficult for him, until the tail came up, to hold the 'plane straight as it tore down the runway. The rudder sawed from side to side as Gebbles tried to hold the machine on the runway's centre line, but he made it, and the next moment he was in the air, climbing rapidly.

I watched as the aircraft rose straight ahead with the undercarriage down. Suddenly the 'plane pitched forward into a dive. My God! He's lost control! I thought. But he hadn't.

As he explained later he'd looked down for the undercarriage lever and inadvertently pushed the stick forward slightly.

With a clear, blue sky above him, within a few seconds, he was circling the aerodrome at about 4,000ft. I shielded my eyes and watched as he slowed

230

the 'plane, lowered the undercarriage and flaps and simulated a landing approach. He did this several times, and a couple of practice stalls, before dropping down for a landing. On the downwind leg the wheels popped out from under the 'plane's wing. In my mind, I followed his every move in the cockpit.

As he made a slow descending turn to line up with the runway I could tell he was in trouble by the way he yawed the aircraft. I just knew he couldn't see the runway with that big engine sticking up in front. We had talked about not being able to make a straight-in final approach as a pilot does in a twin-engined 'plane.

Finally, making a series of gentle "S" turns, he arrived over the end of the runway and landed.

"What was it like?" I asked, feeling him out for any bits of information that would make it easier when my turn came.

"I was so busy, and so surprised at how responsive that 'plane is, I was on the ground before I knew it." He added, "Then I had a hell of time staying on the runway."

My turn to fly a Hurricane never came. I was posted again. This time to 350 Maintenance Unit at Risalpur.

Risalpur, near Peshawar, was once the capital of India's northwest frontier province. The station had a nostalgic air of peacetime RAF of the 1930s. I imagined pilots in their Wapitis taking off in formation, heading for the Khyber Pass to keep an eye on overaggressive Afghan tribesmen who would take pot-shots at them with stolen rifles

From Sqn Ldr Sinclair, the CO, I learned that my job was Officer Commanding Flying Control. A heady position for a newly commissioned Pilot Officer; certainly a notch above my first administrative job. As a brand new Pilot Officer at Jessore I became "OC Latrines". But, fortunately, I didn't hold this position for long; not because of incompetence, or lack of job appreciation, but a recently promoted, junior-to-me Pilot Officer got the job and I was promoted to "OC Parachute Section."

Sqn Ldr Sinclair introduced me to my Indian Air Force assistant tower controllers, two young Sikh Provisional Pilot Officers. I outranked them — just. They were both pilots about my age, twenty-one, each with a wing on their chests, but they didn't seem keen on flying. I could see they regarded me with considerable awe because I'd flown Wellingtons and Dakotas and had completed a tour of operations over Burma. Their dark complexions blanched when I suggested they should ask for a posting and get some operational time.

As OC Flying Control I was in charge of the station's operational codebooks and I had to encode and decode outgoing and incoming classified signals. There weren't many; most of them were aircraft movement messages.

Each evening when I left the control tower I dutifully locked every piece of paper, including my codebooks, in the large, solid, metal safe bolted to the floor. On my third day I discovered that the massive iron Victorian safe wouldn't stay locked. A little jiggling with the huge, round combination lock and "presto"; it was open.

When I told Sqn Ldr Sinclair about this potential breech of security, he said, "It's probably been like that for the last thirty years and no one's ever noticed it. I'll get it repaired."

"Repaired" meant a padlock and large metal hasp bolted to the safe.

Station life was very quiet, even quieter than Cawnpore. Maybe a little daily tennis on the Mess courts, and swimming now and then in the Mess pool. Work was from "about" nine to five. Only a handful of flights were made in and out of the station, and most of these were test flights, and, thank goodness, no night flying to interfere with one's evening activities.

And there was a war on?

One day a voice over the radio shattered the control tower's serenity. "I can't get my wheels down," called a test pilot flying a Hurricane.

I took the microphone from the Sikh on duty and gave him instructions. "Circle the field and burn off fuel, I'll alert the emergency crews." I turned and called across to my assistant, "Get the crash crew."

The first vehicle to appear on the scene was the dark grey ambulance, the box-like "blood-wagon" with its red crosses. Right behind it came the crash truck festooned with tools and ladders and, finally, the wheezing, old fire engine crawled into position. They lined up in front of the control tower, ready for action. A crowd of curious spectators gathered.

After he'd burned off enough fuel the pilot turned on final approach, heading towards the grass infield as I'd instructed. I watched anxiously as he descended in a full tail-down attitude, flying as slowly as possible with full flaps down.

The crash truck and ambulance started their engines in readiness. I hope he doesn't catch fire, I thought.

As the pilot came over the aerodrome boundary he cut the engine, rounded out about 10ft above the ground and eased the 'plane slowly down. He landed it on its belly and slid across the grass infield in a cloud of dust and gravel. A beautiful landing!

The emergency vehicles bounced across the grass, but before they reached the crash the pilot slid back the canopy and jumped to the ground, unharmed. But two days later he "pranged" another Hurricane because he couldn't get the wheels down. I often wondered if that could have happened to me on my first Hurricane flight. The one I never made.

The investigations indicated that both accidents were "pilot error." When they jacked up each 'plane, the undercarriage flopped down and operated normally; the pilot mishandled the undercarriage controls. I never heard what happened to him.

My quarters at Risalpur reflected peacetime prosperity. I had a beautiful brick bungalow complete with a living room and a large bedroom furnished with heavy, old dark wooden furniture. Next to the bedroom, a huge bathroom, and in the middle of the tiled floor sat a high-backed zinc bathtub.

My bearer, Ahmad, an elderly, angular, hawk-nosed Pathan came with the bungalow. He had real presence.

My day began with a bath in my big zinc tub which Ahmad had filled with hot water. While I bathed he stood by, ready to hand me my towel. By the time I'd dried and got my shorts on, he'd be ready with my shirt. Ahmad then held my trousers by the crease for me to slide my legs in, first one then the other. I then sat while he put on each sock and shoe. After he'd tied the laces he left for the Mess to prepare my breakfast. Is this how the peacetime RAF officers lived, I wondered?

In the early morning sun I sauntered from the bungalow, through the garden with its jasmine bushes and buzzing bees, along the path by the swimming pool, then cut across the lawn, entered the Mess through palatial front doors and into the dining room.

The deserted dining room had one long table that could seat at least forty people. Behind an empty chair, ready to seat me, stood Ahmed, elegant in his Mess clothes with green-trimmed white turban and cummerbund.

During my three weeks at Risalpur I never did find out how he changed uniforms without my seeing him, and still got to the Mess ahead of me.

To keep Ahmed gainfully employed each day I assigned him odd jobs. One morning I told him to clean my tunic buttons. I was very proud of these buttons. I'd taken them off my Sergeant's uniform and had the *durzi* sew them on my brand new officer's tunic, with its thin Pilot Officer's ring. I explained, in detail, how he should clean these buttons I had worn smooth, polishing them from my airman's days.

"You must use only Silvo polish and a soft cloth." I instructed, "And," I added, "You must pick out the dried white polish with a wooden match stick." I pointed to a button's embossed crown and eagle. "You must never," I stressed, "Clean them with a brush."

Ahmed drew himself up to his full 6ft 6in, looked at me with unblinking, green eyes for a moment and then said, "*Sahib*. I have been cleaning officers' buttons for forty years."

Risalpur's runways were built to fly aeroplanes of the 1930s. With the expansion of the RAF and IAF to tackle the Japanese knocking on India's eastern frontier, a new 2,000ft landing strip had been built several hundred yards away, connected by a long taxi strip to the old field.

Captains of all departing aircraft were supposed to report to the control tower, file a flight plan and complete their departure signal prior to leaving.

One morning I noticed a Liberator taxiing out to the new strip. The pilot hadn't reported to the control tower. I jumped into my 1,500-weight, raced down the taxi way and intercepted the 'plane at the end of the long runway. I got out and strode over to the 'plane. The pilot opened his side window. Determined to be heard over the noise of the four engines I cupped my hands and shouted, "Where are you going?"

At that moment the Squadron Leader in charge of the test flight arrived in his vehicle and pulled up beside me. "What the hell are you doing delaying one my 'planes?"

"No departure signal sent, Sir," I replied. "I was trying to find out from the pilot where he's going so I can send the signal off."

"That's none of your bloody business, get your bloody truck out of the way," he said, glaring at me with piggy eyes.

"Sir, as O/C Flying Control, I was doing my duty to send departure signals, as instructed by Sqn Ldr Sinclair."

His face contorted with rage.

I realized, as a very junior Pilot Officer I'd perhaps said the wrong thing. I knew I was right to stand my ground, but now I needed support and I needed it quickly.

I ran over to my vehicle, jumped in, slammed it into gear and headed for the administration building. The Squadron Leader followed and tried to pass. I'd learned to drive on Brooklands Racetrack and managed to hold the lead and out-drive him as we roared down the taxi ways.

I got to the administration building first. With a quick knock on the door I burst into Sqn Ldr Sinclair's office. He stood up quickly with a surprised look on his face. I could tell he knew from my agitated state that something serious had happened.

"Sir," I blurted out. "Do I report to you, or to OC Flying?"

"You report to me, and whatever's happened I'll support you." He looked at me incredulously. "What happened?"

I started to tell him, when he cut in. "I saw two vehicles arrive. I have a feeling someone else is waiting to see me. You'd better go, we'll talk about it later."

As I left Sinclair's office the Squadron Leader OC Flying gave me a cold look and went in.

I paused outside the door long enough to hear raised voices. The two Squadron Leaders were really going at it. Sqn Ldr Sinclair was not aircrew and he wasn't going to be told how to run his station by anyone, least of all by an aircrew officer.

After whatever happened in that office all pilots, even those on test flights, dutifully called the control tower from then on.

Risalpur was a small station. This incident, I realized, could have made it pretty unpleasant for me; I really didn't want to stay there much longer.

I needn't have worried; I was posted back to Cawnpore.

Three days later, on 20 September 1944, I left Cawnpore bound for No 9 PRD Worli. I was off to Bombay and, hopefully, home by ship to England!

CHAPTER
THIRTEEN

Cairo revisited
— Back to England

*Leaving No 9 PRD in Bombay on 25 September
1944, I boarded HMT Otranto for an uneventful
trip to Cairo.*

I can't say that I was unhappy to leave India. Although
I found the country and people fascinating, I'd had
several bouts of dysentery and my health could have
been better. Through heat, stress and a tour of "Ops"
I'd also lost a lot of weight. Only twenty-one, but I was
exhausted, tour expired and ready for a change.

My Wellington crew had been posted to various
places in India and I'd lost touch with them, but I'd
hoped to find them in Cairo. Before we split up we had
discussed the possibility of getting sent to the
Wellington OTU in Palestine.

On my way to India in December 1942, I had stopped
at 22 PTC (Personnel Transit Camp) in Cairo. Now,
two years later, I was back there waiting for a posting.

Bored, after sitting around in a hot dusty tent day
after day, with a couple of fellow aircrew also waiting

239

for a posting, I suggested that we go into Cairo and have a drink at the famous Shepherd Hotel.

We hitched a ride into Cairo and were dropped off right in front of the hotel. I had heard that it was a luxurious meeting place where people came to see and to be seen. Elegantly dressed women sat in the foyer, obviously waiting for their escorts. The three of us sauntered through the lounge, with its painted columns, and found the bar.

We chose a marble-topped table and ordered a round of beer. Our aircrew wings and striped rank epaulettes on our khaki bush shirts were the only giveaway that the three of us were RAF, and not some of the many army officers there.

We were nursing our second beers when I noticed an aloof man enter the bar. He wore a monocle on his right eye and had slicked-back black hair. His riding boots and tweed jacket looked very Austin Reedish. In his right hand he carried a riding crop and slapped it absentmindedly against his boot as he glanced around the room. Spotting the empty table next to ours, he headed in our direction.

I nodded to my partners, drawing their attention to him. The three of us eyed him cynically while he settled in a chair facing us and placing his riding crop on the table.

"He looks just like old Captain Reilly Ffoul," one of my mates remarked in rather a loud voice. "You know, that debauched *Daily Mirror* cartoon character."

The man with the monocle heard the remark and glared at us.

240

We ignored him and went about the serious business of enjoying Shepherd Hotel's beer. Each round brought to our table tasted better than the last one as we talked about the experiences that had brought us to Cairo. We discussed serious topics such as reorganizing the Air Force, ways to win the war and what we'd do when it ended. By this time we'd had enough to drink to solve these, and any other, major international problems.

Most of the people who were in the bar when we arrived were probably having a drink before lunch and had now left, including the man with a monocle. A few stragglers came and went, but we were still sitting at our table when the late afternoon cocktail crowd arrived. Most of them were army officers from nearby headquarters.

By this time we had switched from beer to a hotel specialty, the Suffering Bastard; one jigger of brandy, one jigger of gin, filled up with ginger ale and garnished with cucumber, celery, etc. Delicious!

In the middle of making a profound statement I stopped and stared in disbelief — just about to sit down at the table between us and the bar was our Capt Reilly Ffoul! But now he looked very dapper, dressed as a Colonel complete with red tabs, monocle and swagger cane.

I leaned across the table and said in a stage whisper, "Look! The old boy's back."

My two companions had their backs to him. As they each took a discreet glance in his direction, I added, "He really is the spitting image of old Reilly Ffoul, isn't he?"

The Colonel, now seated, scowled at us and went a little red in the face.

After a few minutes of conversation, I stood up and waved my arm to hail the huge, black Sudanese barman behind the ornate mahogany bar looking splendid in a yellow turban.

"George," I called out to him, holding up two fingers, "Two Suffering Bastards."

As he leapt to his feet the Colonel's chair scraped the marble floor, he took two steps and stood by our table glaring down at us.

Conversation in the bar ceased. Talk about a pregnant silence, it had arrived with a crash!

"I'll not stand your insolence," the Colonel sputtered. "You damned aircrew officers are a disgrace to the service. You're all under arrest!"

"Why?" I asked, remaining seated. "What have we done?" hastily adding, "Sir."

The Colonel didn't answer. He turned abruptly, grabbed his hat and swagger cane off the table and marched, with determined strides, out of the door into the lounge.

Our fellow bar patrons gave us a rousing round of applause, and someone sent drinks over.

A short time later the Colonel returned, with two Corporal army redcaps in tow, and headed straight to our table.

Everyone in the bar stopped talking and watched the three new arrivals.

"Arrest these officers," the Colonel commanded the two military policemen.

"Wait a minute," I struggled to my feet. "Sir, I don't think you can do that. Only an officer of equal rank or above can arrest us." I'd heard that remark from a barrack room lawyer somewhere, and right now it sounded like a good idea.

The Colonel frowned at us for a moment, motioned to the two policemen with a flick of his swagger cane and said something that sounded like "whipper-snappers."

With the Colonel leading, the three of them filed out the door.

As they left thunderous clapping and cheers broke out from the bar's patrons. Another round of drinks, which we really didn't need, appeared at our table.

We were well into this new round when the Colonel returned. This time he had two army officers with him. I counted three cloth shoulder pips on each uniform — Captains!

"Arrest these officers!" The now red-faced Colonel snapped, pointing his swagger cane at us. "Take them away."

Without getting up, I said, "Can't we at least finish our drinks?"

The Captain standing beside me leaned over and whispered in my ear, "You'd better leave now, and come with us."

The Colonel snapped his swagger cane under his arm and strutted out of the bar.

The three of us stood, raised our glasses, drained them with a big gulp and slammed them back on the table. We grabbed our hats and followed the two

Captains to the door. The bar patrons gave us a standing ovation. Stopping in the doorway we turned, bowed to our audience and left.

In the subdued silence of Shepherds' elegant lounge I leaned against an ornate painted column. "Who is that Colonel blimp?" I asked one of the Captains. "What's wrong with him and why the hell are we under arrest?"

"The Colonel, for some reason," the Captain replied, "Hates RAF aircrew officers and on the slightest pretext he has them arrested." Grinning at me he continued, "He's always doing it. But in your case he said that you not only called him a bastard, but a *suffering bastard!*"

The Captain went on to say that the Colonel never pressed charges and suggested we'd better quickly leave the hotel and forget the incident. "No. I've got a better idea," he added. "There's a little club around the corner. Mostly army types. Come and have a drink with us."

We did.

I stayed at No 39 PTC at Kasfarit for another two weeks and left Egypt on 14 November 1944, on board HMT *Queen of Bermuda* bound for England.

What next, I wondered. Bomber Command? Lancasters? Stirlings?

One day, when the sea was very rough, I took my turn as Duty Officer. In addition to inspection rounds I had to visit the other ranks' deck and ask the airmen and soldiers a routine question, "Any complaints about the food?" I knew there would be grumbling and the NCO with me dutifully recorded them in his notebook. I doubt if anything was done to improve the food. In the Officers' Mess the food was not very good, and we didn't even get a chance to complain!

After a thirty day voyage the *Queen of Bermuda* arrived at Liverpool. I went to nearby West Kirby, where I received an extensive medical check-up. A couple of weeks later I was posted to No 105 (Transport) OTU at Bramcote, about 5 miles southwest of Nottingham.

After I arrived at the OTU, I thought their arrangement for training Transport Command pilots seemed rather odd. I was slated for a Dakota Transport Squadron, but I was told I'd do my Transport training flying in a Wellington! Apparently they were short of Daks but had plenty of Wimpys.

I enjoyed flying the Wellington around the English countryside. After Bengal's jungles and rivers, it looked so tidy with its winding roads and neatly-fenced fields. Being back in England was a wonderful feeling. I didn't even mind the cold compared to Egypt's sandy desert and Bengal's hot, steamy jungle. Even the smoky, industrial air smelt good, and the rows of houses no longer looked drab.

Most of the training consisted of cross-country flights. When my instructor Flt Lt Williams discovered I had more Wellington flying time than he had, he told me to take a couple of weeks off while he instructed pilots who had never flown a Wellington.

At the end of the course I was given a form to fill out showing where I'd like to be posted. I talked this over with my new crew. My navigator was Fg Off E. Moore ("Roary"), aged twenty-five. He was two years older than me, had flown in Mosquitoes, and served with 201, 109 and 105 Squadrons, Bomber Command 2 Group. Fg Off Ted Veal, the wireless operator, aged twenty-three, had flown in Blenheims in the desert (DAF) with 13 Squadron and then in Baltimores in Italy. He had also flown in Whitleys and had been with 297 Squadron.

Despite our youth, between us we had accumulated a fair amount of wartime operational flying. For this reason I put down as my first posting preferences 110 Wing, 147 Squadron at Croydon , flying Dakotas, or 167 Squadron (reformed 21 October 1944 and flying transport Warwicks, Ansons, Dakotas and Lancasters). My second choice was 271 Squadron and in third place was the Metropolitan Communication Squadron.

We were posted to 48 Squadron. So much for preferential postings!

On 7 May 1945, my crew and I joined 48 Squadron at Down Ampney, a little village in Gloucester. After a couple of flights with a "screen" (squadron check pilot), I was flying Transport Command Dakotas flights. These carried passengers and freight to and from Europe.

On several trips from Europe to England I carried returning prisoners of war. Some of these soldiers and airmen had been in prison camps since Dunkirk; others were aircrew who had bailed out and been picked up by the Germans and taken to one of the Stalags.

On one of these POW flights we crossed the Channel near Kent. I told the co-pilot to bring the passengers — mostly soldiers — up to the cockpit, a few at a time for their first glimpse of the English coast. Seeing the white cliffs of Dover brought tears to the eyes of most of them. Watching them point, wave and cheer the crew were hardly dry-eyed either.

In many of these flights we'd carry stretcher cases. If conditions permitted, I'd go back into the cabin to talk to the wounded. The majority of them, still in their twenties, were obviously hurting, but they were thrilled to be going home. I knew they needed all the support we could give them. I tried to give them a smooth ride and an especially smooth landing.

The squadron kept us very busy. Many pilots flew two, sometimes three, trips into and out of Europe in one day, but it was interesting flying. In addition to the scheduled flights, which flew over a fixed route, many of our operations took us to unusual places.

In Europe the ground support for our transport flights was a bit shaky. On one flight into Eindhoven, to pick up a load of passengers, I taxied onto the grass to get around some 'planes, parked on the tarmac, and promptly got stuck in soft ground from a filled-in bomb hole. Someone could have stuck a warning flag, marking a soft sand bunker. Fortunately I got the engine stopped before the prop sank to ground level. A tractor and a few men with shovels soon got us out; the 'plane was undamaged.

On 8 May 1945, VE Day, the war in Europe was over.

Preparations for celebrations in the Officers' Mess at Down Ampney started and kegs of beer were rolled into the Mess lounge, propped up and broached. A lot of thirsty mouths waited to be filled.

In a short time the normally serene Mess had become a shambles. The spigots ran almost constantly and gallons of beer swamped the floor and carpets; and it wasn't long before a lot of people were very drunk.

Trouble started when someone brought a large carthorse into the Mess. At first this noble beast entered into the spirit of the occasion as she clopped slowly from room to room, even taking the odd sip from a proffered glass, but she became very upset when a drunken officer tried to climb on her back.

First, she let go with a swift kick that caught a passerby in the crotch, doubling him over in pain. She then tried to leave the Mess by the quickest, most direct route. At a fast trot she headed towards the front door pushing aside furniture and knocking over several drunken officers. But before she reached the door the excitement became too much for her. She paused, lifted her docked tail, dropped her load on the beer-sodden floor and, contented, left the Mess.

Later that night a thinned-out crowd gathered in front of the Mess in the dark. Officers sat on the 5ft high air raid blast-wall, glass in hand, waiting for the fireworks display to start. Flying control had promised a show using the only things available — signal pyrotechnics.

After several white signal rockets streaked across the sky someone lit the fuse to a bunch of Very cartridges stuffed into a metal pipe. Nothing happened.

The station Commanding Officer, Colonel Joubert, South African Air Force, climbed on top of the blast wall to investigate the failed fireworks. From then on no one really knows what happened; perhaps he picked up the pipe and relit the fuse, or the pipe exploded just as he arrived. The blast killed him instantly and took out most of the Mess windows.

This, needless to say, ended the maffick and put a damper on the rest of the VE Day celebrations.

We were reminded of the incident when the Sunday newspaper described the events in detail under its bold black headline, "Drunken Orgy In Officers' Mess Kills CO."

One day in June Wg Cdr Squires, the CO of 48 Squadron, sent for me for to come to his office. After formalities he said, "The squadron's going out to India. I've looked over your record and see you flew a Wellington out to India in '42, did a tour of Ops on them and flew Daks on supply operations in Burma." He beamed at me. "With that kind of experience I need you as a Flight Commander."

I left his office feeling quite depressed. Just when I had regained my health they wanted to send me back to India and face the possibility of getting dysentery again. Even the thought of becoming a Squadron Leader didn't cheer me up.

The Station Medical Officer Flt Lt Peter Ransford, a fellow old Bradfieldian (though he had left Bradfield

249

before I arrived), joined me for a drink in the Mess and listened as I moaned about being posted back to India.

A couple of days later I was told to report to the MO. Flt Lt Ransford pulled a chair to the front of his desk. "Sit down," he said. "This may come as a bit of shock to you, but I've gone over your medical records and I'm afraid I've some bad news for you."

What now, I wondered? Was I going to be grounded for harbouring some strange Asiatic disease?

Leaning back in his chair, Ransford said, "Yes, Leicester, your medical records indicate that you are not fit enough to go to India with 48 Squadron. I've boarded you and I've changed your flying category from A1H to A1HBH. This means," he continued, "You have your full flying medical category, but you must be based in England. You may, of course, fly out of the country, but you must be based in England."

I jumped up, leaned over the desk and shook his hand. "Thanks, Peter."

When my posting from 48 Squadron to 271 Squadron, also based at Down Ampney, came through, Wg Cdr Squires called me into his office. He said he didn't know how I'd pulled strings to get myself posted to 271 Squadron. From his clipped, strained voice I could tell he was angry because I'd got out of going to India with the squadron.

My transition to 271 Squadron was quick and uneventful; one day I was flying for 48 Squadron, the next day for 271 Squadron.

On my first flight with the new squadron my aircraft landed, along with several other 'planes, at Celle in

Lower Saxony, Germany, about 30 miles from the horror slave-camp at Bergen-Belsen. We'd been told that we would be carrying Belsen victims back to Brussels.

We waited by the 'plane for a long time. Finally, a line of trucks, cars and buses appeared on the road leading to the aerodrome. I was shocked when I saw our passengers; about fifty scarecrow-like men, and a few women, being helped into the back of the Dakota. Most were so emaciated they had to be lifted from the bus into the 'plane. Those that could walk shuffled to the boarding ladder where they had to be lifted into the back of the Dakota.

The poor wretches, with white skin stretched tightly over their bones, looked like walking skeletons and smelt strongly of carbolic soap and, I hoped, were free of typhus. The back of the aircraft was crowded. I don't remember how many we actually carried; I know we had many more passengers than seatbelts, but we were still well below our maximum all-up weight.

I'd been told that when British troops found this concentration camp there were over 10,000 unburied corpses. Of the remaining 40,000 victims, 28,000 died of typhus. The British burned the camp to the ground.

It was a heartbreaking experience for me and my crew. I had seen the bodies of people killed in bombed buildings and wrecked aircraft, but never had I seen a sight like this. We, who had fought a war by dropping bombs on enemy targets, had returned home to reasonable comfort without ever really seeing the devastation we had caused. Now we were seeing man's inhumanity to man even more clearly.

After this experience, and after seeing devastated cities and piles of rubble, I wondered if Europe would, or could, ever recover from all of the horror of this conflict? Would this war, like The Great War my father fought, be the war to finally end all wars? I hoped so.

On another flight to Germany my crew and I saw the other side of life; the way the German military had lived. At Wunstorf, near Hannover, where we were billeted overnight, a staff car drove us up a winding, tree-lined road through the middle of a forest, to a building that had once been a Luftwaffe Mess. Large pine trees stood inches away from the wall; this natural camouflage must have been a nightmare for the contractor who had probably had to build the place without knocking down trees.

The Mess inside was clean and modern, but the windows in the bedroom where I was to sleep were the first thing I really noticed. In Canada I'd been in houses with removable storm-windows — some houses even had double-glass windows to keep out the cold — but these German windows had triple layers of glass built right into the hinged window.

Another intriguing feature of this once German Air Force Mess were the toilets in the basement. There, in the clinically white-tiled room against the wall under bright overhead lights sat a splendid Teutonic "honk bowl". A white, vitreous china bowl, like a regular wash basin, but deeper. Above it a flat chromium plated bar was placed strategically so that when a wretched

Luftwaffe wretch retched and leaned forward to throw up, his head would hit the bar and on came running water. What a civilized device, I thought; even if it didn't win the war for the Luftwaffe, it should have been adopted by all RAF Messes and English pubs!

On many of our flights over Europe my navigator, Fg Off "Roary" Moore, often routed us over the burned-out shells of German cities. He had flown in Pathfinder Mosquitoes for two tours of Ops, and knew details of German cities he had bombed. He'd come up into the cockpit and point, "See that building, that's where we dropped our markers. No not there. By the doors at the back. Over there."

I circled the devastated area with its broken walls and acres of roofless buildings and wondered, what happened to all the people?

One of our scheduled flights took us to an allied landing strip beside a German fuel dump where acres of Jerry cans full of petrol were piled high. They were guarded by a handful of RAF airmen and a Sergeant who were totally isolated in the countryside and we had to bring in their rations. They requested books, newspapers. I was glad to do anything to ease their boredom. I even managed to scrounge a few boxes of chocolate bars for them.

"Do you drive a car?" the Sergeant asked me one day.

I said I did. From then on, every time I landed there, he would put three or four full Jerry cans in the back of the 'plane. The ersatz fuel made from coal had a strange smell, quite different from our petrol, but it worked fine in my old Morris!

RAF Form 1256, a passenger list, was prepared in several copies for each Transport Command flight. This form showed each passenger's nationality, religion and weight, voluntarily given, and the number of items and the weight of the baggage.

I could never understand why a passenger's religion was needed. We certainly didn't hold any religious ceremonies during flight and if we crashed who'd be around to provide the appropriate religious rites? They even asked for the crew's religion. Defying the wrath, or whatever's supposed to happen, I always put down — "none".

On many flights to Europe I often landed at Brussels, Belgium, a stopover point for many of our scheduled flights. On one flight we almost didn't make it. A high pressure weather system sat over Europe making it hot, dry, cloudless and very windy. On the weather maps, isobars were drawn as neat round circles, as if someone had drawn them with a compass.

My navigator, Fg Off Moore, gave me a course to steer for Brussels Evere. We discussed our head wind, slow ground speed and fuel consumption, but he didn't appear to be as concerned as I was. As we neared our destination I ran each of the auxiliary fuel tanks down until the red warning light came on before switching back to the main tanks, but I knew our fuel problem was going to be touch and go.

Still many miles from the aerodrome, Moore came into the cockpit. "What's our ground speed, Roary?" I asked.

Pulling at his scraggly, blond moustache he said, "It's slower than I expected, start a gradual descent. It'll build up airspeed. That'll help." He then disappeared back to his desk.

I ran the engines on each auxiliary tank again, waiting until the fuel pressure fell and then switched back to the main tank. I now knew those tanks were really dry.

When the aerodrome came into sight, still miles away, I called the tower and told them I had a fuel emergency and asked for a straight-in approach. I still didn't think we would make it to the field before running out of fuel. But we did.

When the ground crew brought out the petrol bowser to refill the 'plane's tanks they were shocked when they measured the small amount of fuel remaining in the tanks. So was I!

"I knew we'd make it," Roary said, smiling, as we left the 'plane.

Roary Moore was a loner. It wasn't that he was unsociable, but he seldom joined in general bar gatherings and conversations. In a pub, or in the Mess, he was quite happy to just sit, smoke and drink alone and watch others make fools of themselves. If this was a failing he certainly made up for it with his brilliant navigating ability as a member of the élite Pathfinder Force.

One day I wormed this story out of him. Returning from an operational flight he helped his wounded pilot bring their badly shot-up Mosquito back to the aerodrome and make a crash landing. Apparently he reached over and flew the 'plane while the semi-conscious pilot told him what to do. He got it down on the ground but the aircraft broke apart on the runway. The rescue crew pulled the two of them out of the fuselage where the tail broke off. The AOC was at the aerodrome at the time and for this extraordinarily brave and skilful act awarded him an immediate DFM.

When we returned to Down Ampney from Europe, before we reached the Cotswold Hills, we usually had a quick discussion about whether we'd descend below the clouds or we'd stay in them, or above them, and make a GEE instrument approach at the aerodrome.

One day, while in cloud, I asked Roary which approach we should make. He came into the cockpit and stood between the two pilots' seats and gave me a course to steer, along with a rate of descent at so many feet per minute.

After a few minutes he said harshly, "I said two hundred feet per minute, not two hundred and fifty."

Okay, I thought, if he wants to call the numbers I can fly them. In the slight turbulence I worked the instrument panel as hard as I could and watched the altimeter with concern because I knew hills were right below us and there was no room for error!

One minute we were in swirling grey cloud, the next moment we popped out below them, over water. Hills reached up into the clouds on either side. Moore, using GEE, had brought us down right into the valley over the River Thames.

On another occasion, heading for Holland, we crossed the east coast of England and I asked Moore for our ETA to the Dutch coast. There were no charts on the table, the GEE set was turned off while he read a book and smoked a cigarette.

I reached up to the GEE master switch on the bulkhead behind my head, and turned it off. From the navigator's position he couldn't see me do this and I thought, "I'll fix him." He might know the GEE chains like the back of his hand but he can't do much if it's turned off.

"Where are we, Roary?" I called over the intercom. Nothing happened. Got him! I thought. He's going to have to admit he doesn't know where we are and navigators never like to even hint that they're lost!

A few moments later he came into the cockpit, stuck a torn open empty cigarette pack in front of me and pointed at some scribbled figures. "That's our ETA to the coast, and that's our ETA to our destination." He went back to his seat. Later, the Dutch coastline slid underneath us, right to the second!

From then on I was never concerned about being lost with him on board.

My Flight Commander, Sqn Ldr Pearson, with his ruddy complexion, long, twisted, blond moustache and jovial manner, was the apotheosis of an RAF Squadron Leader. A good leader, he kept us sometimes belligerent Flight Lieutenants in line; but he did it such a nice way no one really minded.

When he went away for a few days I was the only one he trusted with his jeep. He gave me permission to use it, but each time he handed me the key he'd say, "For

God's sake don't wreck it. They won't give me another one!"

Having the use of this jeep increased my capability to explore the English countryside, and meant I might find a few new pubs too. Sqn Ldr Pearson had built up quite a collection of movement orders, all properly signed, stamped with the right dates. If stopped by the military police he could produce a piece of paper stating he was on his way to a satellite aerodrome, visiting another squadron or visiting the local military hospital. His excuses were authentic and endless, and when I drove his jeep his excuses were my excuses!

CHAPTER
FOURTEEN

Transport Command — Berlin

On 8th August, as Captain of RAF Air Transport Command's Schedule Flight M5, my first stop in Germany was Buckeburg and the next stop Gatow, the British-operated aerodrome at Berlin, where the flight remained overnight.

Pilots flying on operations often spoke of a feeling of apprehension when they crossed into enemy territory. "Engines always seem to run rough as soon as you cross a coastline," some said. Even though the war was over, flying into Berlin gave me a strange, uneasy feeling. Was it because this place had been Nazi headquarters, the centre of all the horror of Europe's destruction?

The following day, as scheduled, I took off from Gatow heading for Buckeburg, but bad weather forced me to return to Gatow. I crept back to the aerodrome under a solid, grey cloud ceiling and landed in heavy rain. A miserable flight, but this time I had reason for a tremendous feeling of relief and elation — we'd just heard the news. The war was over! It was VJ Day!

The next day low stratus clouds, with drizzling rain, hung across the sky and the duty forecaster said the weather over England was worse. Since we couldn't fly, my crew — navigator Roy Stevens and radio operator Ted Veal — and I, decided we'd go sight-seeing and hitched a ride into Berlin.

The British army driver dropped us off at the Brandenburg Gate and the three of us strolled along Unten den Linden in a light drizzle, overawed by the extent of the bomb damage.

Trees had no leaves; many had no boughs, or branches. Everything in sight was torn and shredded from the shelling and bombing, and wet with rain. Buildings not completely destroyed were just jagged walls, blackened shells piled high inside with rubble.

An aura of death and decay filled the air.

When we came to Hitler's shell-pockmarked Chancellery, it had stopped raining.

We stood on the pavement and looked at the ominous, grey stone building. "Let's see if we can get inside," I suggested. "You game?"

Roy and Ted nodded.

At the top of the long flight of impressive steps — the kind that force you to break your stride as you climb them — stood a Russian guard wearing an ill-fitting, baggy, khaki uniform. He looked about sixteen years old, with slanted eyes and prominent Mongolian features.

As we approached the door he stepped in front of us barring our way with his rifle held at the ready across his chest. I moved to step closer. He swung the rifle down pointing it at me and muttered something which, from the look on his face, meant, "Stop!" or "I'll shoot you."

I fumbled in my pocket and pulled out my unpaid Mess bill, a long sheaf of paper covering everything from my laundry to my bar expenses, and held it in front of the young Soviet guard.

Keeping the rifle aimed at my chest, with his finger on the trigger, he snatched the paper with his other hand and glanced at it, all the time keeping a wary eye on me. Although the mess bill was upside down, it must have met the required security needs because he handed it back, saluted, lowered the rifle and waved us through the door.

As we set off down a long dim corridor, Ted called out, "I didn't like the glint in his eyes. We're damned lucky you don't pay your bills."

We roamed through the Chancellery's impressive marbled passageways and peered into offices. Overturned, smashed furniture covered the floor, papers were strewn everywhere and the walls were dotted with bullet holes. Obviously we weren't the first visitors. All the rooms had been looted. We rummaged around thinking we might find a souvenir, a typewriter, or some other useful trinket.

Wandering down the hallway we came to the door of an office blocked with fallen debris. With our bare hands we pushed and pulled at broken slabs of concrete and finally got into the room. A mistake. Inside three very dead uniformed Germans lay spread-eagled on the floor. God, did they stink.

In one of the big reception rooms I found an enormous red wall tapestry lying on the floor. About 10ft long and 4ft wide it looked like a piece of thick carpet with a large black swastika in a white circle in its centre. I tried cutting out the swastika with my penknife, but the fabric was too tough. I couldn't even stick the blade into it.

Making our way down another dimly lit hallway we stumbled into Hitler's office. The chandelier had been lowered to the floor, but the Führer's desk and chair were still there, just like I'd seen it in newspaper pictures and on the newsreels. From a table in an adjacent office, I pocketed a couple of hefty 5in square solid glass ashtrays.

Next, we found the Führer's storage room for medals. It was about 100ft long with floor-to-ceiling wooden cupboards on either side. The shelves had been stripped and small paper packets of medals covered the floor several inches deep. Ted, Roy and I each took an area and sitting on the medals piled on the floor we dug down tearing at the packets looking for an Iron Cross. I found several Iron Cross ribbons but no medals. Holding up a newly discovered medal we'd call out, "Look for one of these." Before leaving the room I grabbed a handful of packets and stuffed them in my battle dress pockets. I also picked up a certificate, embossed with a swastika seal and Hitler's printed signature, awarding a medal, Das Kriegsverdienstkreuz 1 Klasse, to a Kesselmeister Engelbert Kuster. Whatever the medal was awarded for, Herr Kuster didn't get his!

Descending a short flight of stairs into a darkened area just below ground level, I heard a strange shuffling sound. "What's that noise?" Ted whispered. We stood still, listening.

"Look." He pointed towards down the corridor.

Several gaunt German civilians, dressed in tattered clothes, stumbled towards us into the light. They were as surprised as we were. I took a step forward and they backed away, fear in their eyes. Of course, I reasoned, we're the enemy. Our RAF uniforms and wings terrify them. We're the dreaded night-bombers of their city; they probably hate our guts.

They turned and scuttled down nearby steps into what looked like a dark cellar. Curious, we followed, but they'd disappeared. Closed doors were everywhere and the place was honeycombed with unlit passageways.

"We must be in Hitler's bunker," I said. "Let's get the hell out of here."

We climbed some steps and followed a passageway that finally led us outside into what was once a garden. Now ploughed up by shellfire and covered with bomb and grenade holes, it looked like a muddy First World War battlefield. Rifles, helmets and spent cartridges lay everywhere.

It started to rain.

Ted, ahead of me, suddenly called out, "Look!" He pointed to a large hole in the ground. "Isn't that the place where Hitler and Eva Braun were burned?" In the mud, beside the hole, lay the Jerry can I'd seen in photos. It still reeked of petrol.

With our battle dress pockets bulging with loot we left Hitler's Chancellery and stood in the rain on Unter den Linden, trying to thumb a ride. Luck was with us and we quickly got a lift that took us straight to Gatow.

That night, at the VJ Day party in the Mess, everyone was obviously determined to get very drunk as quickly as possible, and to stay drunk. As the evening progressed boisterous singing filled the room and the party got noisier and noisier.

In a room off the main lounge two Russian officers, guests of the Mess, sang Russian songs and one of them played a balalaika. Their music was good.

The party wasn't as bad as the drunken orgy at Down Ampney on VE Day where they had brought the farm horse into the mess, although someone did take a few pot shots at the overhead lights with a revolver.

I'd had a few drinks and, like everyone else, was elated that the war was finally over. If the weather cleared up I would be flying in the morning. I didn't like flying with a hangover. I'd tried it! So I decided to call it a night.

On my way through the lobby the 'phone on a table near the front door rang. I paused, no one could hear it with the ruckus coming from the bar, so I picked it up. "Officers' Mess," I said, cupping the mouthpiece to cut out noise.

On the other end an excited voice blurted, "There's a Russian officer here in the Airmen's Mess. He's tearing the place apart. We can't get him to leave. What should we do?"

264

At that point I should have looked for the Senior Duty Officer, but since I was going in the direction of the Airmen's Mess, I thought I might as well stop and try to straighten out the problem.

Waiting for me at the front door of the Airmen's Mess a couple of young airmen greeted me. "In here, Sir." They steered me to the bar.

In front of the fireplace a stocky Russian in uniform was kicking at a wooden chair. His closely-cropped brown hair made his head look a like a fuzzy ball, his weather-beaten face was almost as red as the star on his epaulettes. I also noticed a pistol stuck in a holster at the middle of his back.

He stopped kicking the chair and glared at me with extraordinarily clear china-blue eyes. I beckoned to him and pointed to the door. He raised his foot and kicked the chair again.

What the hell can I do now, I wondered? Should I tell the two airmen to grab him and throw him out of the Mess. What then?

"Hey, you," I called to the Russian, and again pointed to the door.

He shook his head. "Nyet!" and gave the chair another kick. Bits of the shattered chair shot across the room.

I took a couple of strides, grabbed him by the back of his tunic at the neck and the seat of his pants and frog-marched him to the door before he realized what was happening. He was at least a head shorter than me. I let go of him with one hand long enough to pull my 9mm Berreta out of my shoulder holster. I rammed it into his back as hard as I could. I felt him flinch as if to turn on me. He heard me cock the pistol, put a round in the chamber, and he stood completely still. He's heard that noise before, I thought.

"Okay, you Russian bastard, move!"

Holding on to his collar I prodded him again in the back, and at the same time I slipped his pistol out of its holster and shoved it in my trouser pocket.

"Move, you sawn off little red runt."

The two airmen edged back to let me by and they grinned as I marched the Russian out the door and back along the road to the Officers' Mess.

By the front door in the lobby, I met an agitated Flight Lieutenant, one of the RAF interpreters. I put my automatic away and quickly told him what had happened.

"The other two Russians just left and we wondered where this fellow was," he said. He then turned and spoke in Russian to my captive.

I slipped into the bar and went straight to the CO and gave him a quick run-down on what had happened. "Here's his pistol."

Conversation in the bar stopped.

The CO took the Russian's automatic, pulled out the clip, removed the bullets, dropped them into his tunic pocket and went out into the lobby. "Thanks," he said, giving me a quick glance. "I'll take care of this matter."

The Russian officer and the interpreter were now having a heated argument in Russian. A small crowd collected. I stayed in the background.

The CO handed the pistol to the interpreter and said, "Tell the sod he dropped his pistol, then take him out front, shove him in the jeep and tell the driver to take him home."

The Russian grabbed his pistol, whipped out the clip, examined it and realized it had been disarmed. He looked around the crowd of officers, glaring, and I knew he knew who had done it.

I discreetly left the Mess and went to bed.

Like most of Transport Command aircrew my wireless operator, Fg Off Ted Veal, had flown a tour of operations. His tour was in Italy before joining 271 Squadron.

One evening I persuaded him to tell the story he'd told me once before — how he had bailed out over Italy.

"I was on Ops at night," Ted began. "As we neared the target over Italy our Baltimore lost an engine. We were just starting our bombing run so the skipper decided to press on and get the job done. We dropped our bombs, hit the target, turned and headed home. Flying around some heavy thunderstorms, the other engine acted up and the skipper gave the order, 'Standby to bail out.'

"I went to my bailout position and clipped on my parachute pack. The next thing I remember is floating through the air in total darkness. I pulled the ripcord, when the 'chute popped open I realized I was in cloud. Swinging back and forth in the dark I didn't have a clue where I was, or how far above the ground.

"I drifted down, down, down, with the wind whistling past my ears in swirling mist. Just as I broke out the cloud I saw a huge explosion on the side of the mountain where our kite hit the ground.

"I landed hard, on the side of an almost vertical hill. It was so steep I had to grab a small bush to stop myself from sliding down the wet, grassy slope to the road a few hundred feet below.

"I wasn't hurt, just shaken up, but I had to dig my heels well into the ground to stop sliding down that hill. I sat still to catch my breath. Then I heard engines, lots of lorries on the road below. Peering over a rock I nearly s★★★ myself, the place was crawling with Germans just a few hundred feet away.

"I didn't stop to gather up my 'chute and hide it, like you're supposed to. I staggered up the hill away from the road as fast as I could and walked all night. When it started to get light I discovered I was on flat ground among trees. Exhausted, I sat down to rest and fell asleep.

" 'Come over here.' A gruff voice with a heavy Italian accent woke me.

"I looked round and saw three stocky middle-aged men wearing coloured shirts and baggy trousers. They beckoned to me to get up. 'Follow me,' one of the men said. I followed, the other two trailed behind.

"We walked for a couple of miles to an old, dilapidated farmhouse. Inside the sparsely furnished house one of the men pointed to a chair at a bare wooden table and told me to sit down.

"Then the man who'd first spoken to me said in halting English, 'We are with the Underground. We've helped many Royal Air Force flying crews escape. We will help you, but you must do exactly as we say. Okay?'

"I nodded. I couldn't believe I'd not been found by the Germans. I'd do anything they said. They gave me food and wine and told me 'When it's dark we will take you and hide you, okay?'

"That night one of the men escorted me across several fields. When we reached the middle of a cornfield covered in stubble he pointed to a corn shock and said, 'You hide here. Okay?'

"I wormed my way into the prickly, dry corn stalks and the Italian handed me a wine bottle full of water and a small packet of food. "Do not come out until someone comes to tell you to leave. Okay?'

"It was August, and I tell you, it was bloody uncomfortable in that shock. I was hot and sweaty and bugs crawled all over me. Some of them took a bite here and there. My only consolation was to think of the alternatives if the Germans had found me."

"It got dark and a muffled voice called, "You can come out now.'

"I was allowed to walk around for about fifteen minutes, and then told to go back into the shock. I was given more food and water. I learned to practice self-control trying to see how long I could stay motionless while bugs bit me. This went on for five nights. On the sixth morning a voice called out, "You can come out. You're free. The Americans are here.'

"I crawled out of the corn shock, blinking in the bright sunlight, to be greeted by four other escapers who, like me, were hiding in the same field. "How long have you been here? one of them asked. Turning to an American officer, he continued, 'Am I glad to see you . . . I've been here two bloody weeks!'

"An American army officer told us to climb into the back of his truck and he would take all of us to a processing centre."

"When I found out where we were I realized I was not too far away from my squadron's airstrip, so I walked out to the road and hitched a ride.

"That night, in bright moonlight, I found the squadron's tent camp. I was looking for my tent when a figure staggered from one of the tents and headed towards the urinal, a funnel stuck in the sand.

"He suddenly spotted me in the moonlight and gave a shrill yell at the top of his voice. 'Holy s**t! A ghost! Oh my God! Help! Help!'

"Aircrew rushed out of the tents and there was a hell of a reunion. "We thought you were dead,' they said. "We'd heard your 'plane had crashed, burned and all the crew had been killed.'"

After returning from India I bought a car. A 1929, or early 1930s, Morris touring model with a folding roof. Painted an ugly, dirty brown and with cracked leather seats, she was no beauty. But, in spite of her age, and the somewhat marginal condition of the tyres, she was solidly built and mechanically reliable. According to the milometer she hadn't done that many miles. With a limited number of moving parts, the old Morris was also easy to work on.

Having a car at Down Ampney allowed me to travel further afield than the local bus routes. It meant I could explore the countryside.

Flt Sgt Burns approached me one day and asked if I would like to make a deal. For use of my car one, or two, nights a week he would make sure it was kept clean and in good running order. "Don't worry about petrol," he added, "I'll see to it that the tank is always full."

It was a good arrangement. Maybe a little larcenous, but I didn't ask questions.

Before leaving London, where I'd bought the car, I discovered a bad slit on the inside of the left front tyre. Buying a new tyre was impossible so I had it repaired by the garage where I parked the car in a South Kensington mews. Their idea of repairing a tyre was pretty crude. They just sewed up the slit with catgut using a sail maker's stitch.

Although I had put quite a lot of miles on that tyre Burns said he thought it was unsafe and he would replace it. With a fresh tyre on the wheel I must say I drove around with a lot more confidence.

One morning I got a message that the engineering officer wanted to see me, right away, in his office. Before I could close the door behind me, he asked. "Leicester, do you by any chance own a car, a Morris with licence number AG 8699?"

I said I did, thinking perhaps he was interested in buying it.

Seated behind his desk he pressed his fingers together as though he was about to pray. "I'd like to hear your explanation as to why your car's left front wheel has one of His Majesty's tyres. A tyre that's believed to have been stolen from one His Majesty's battery carts?"

For a moment I was stunned, but it dawned on me pretty quickly that Burns had a hand in this somewhere. I didn't want to accuse him, nor did I want to leave myself open to a Court Martial if someone got serious about this incident.

I told the engineering officer I'd shared the car with someone on the station and, before he took any action, I'd like time to speak to that "someone" and find out what was going on.

He looked at me for a long time and then surprised me with, "You'd better speak to Flight Sergeant Burns. He might know something about it."

He finished praying and rested his hands on the desk. "I'm pretty sure Burns may know something. The stolen tyre's from one of his battery carts!"

The clot, I thought, at least he could have pinched a tyre from another flight!

"I'll tell you what," said the Squadron Leader, breaking into a smile. "You tell Burns you've spoken to me, and I said that he's to put that tyre back where it belongs. It'll keep him on his toes, thinking I'll have the battery cart watched to try and catch him red-handed."

It sounded like a fair deal to me, but now I had to find a new tyre from somewhere else.

This car incident reminded me of the little mews, behind Melton Court in South Kensington, where I'd kept the car.

I had noticed a Mercedes there, a magnificent black touring car with lots of heavy chromium fixtures, like the model Hitler and his cronies drove around in. One day I met its owner, an army officer who, after a little prodding, told me how he got the car. He said that in the big push through Germany, during a lull in the fighting, he had found the car abandoned in a field near a barn. He had his men dig a deep trench in the floor of the barn and they buried it.

Many months later he was back in the area and, much to his surprise, the barn was standing and the car was still there. He dug it up, had it sprayed with camouflage paint, stuck on a few military flashes and a white Max Speed sign, and shipped it back to England along with his unit's vehicles.

He had the car cleaned up and repainted, put on a fresh set of identification numbers taken from a wrecked Mercedes, and licenced it. He now had a truly elegant car.

Troops stationed in Germany liked to get their hands on English pounds, because they could buy more with the pound than they could with Allied German marks; to get pounds our troops would gladly pay twice the official exchange.

Aircrew returning from Europe and landing at Northolt could exchange foreign money in one of the hangars. You just went up to a little window, handed over whatever foreign money you had, and received pounds in exchange. I'd take pounds to Germany and make a little spending money by changing marks back into pounds.

My stepfather, Lt Col Veysie Curran, OC Canadian Pay Corps in Europe, advised me that the Russians were printing more Allied marks and flooding the market. He told me the financial authorities were going to replace the Allied marks with a new issue. The only difference in the Russian printed mark was a minus sign in front of the serial number.

Following his tip, on every trip to Europe I took lots of pounds; I bought up all the Allied marks I could lay my hands on and cashed them before the rate dropped with the new issue.

After all, there's a little larceny in all of us!

In August 1945 I moved again, this time to 271 Squadron's detachment at Croydon. We kept our Dakota aircraft about 4 miles south of Croydon at Kenley, one of the famous Battle of Britain aerodromes.

I was billeted in Croydon, sharing a small semidetached house with six other aircrew. I had brought my motorbike with me in the 'plane from Down Ampney. There was no safe place to park it outside the house so I wheeled it into the hallway.

Once in a while one of the officers, returning late, would start the machine and race the engine, waking everyone up and filling the place with oily blue smoke! It was my bike so I got the blame.

Croydon had been a landmark as far back as I can remember. At home in Weybridge before the war, my family listened to the BBC and we often heard that some eminent person had "arrived today at Croydon aerodrome".

In those days this small grass airfield was London's only aerodrome. The control tower, with its radio masts sticking out from the four corners of the building, was a world-famous landmark. I remember the control tower when, as a small boy, I had taken my first aeroplane ride in that three-engined Armstrong Whitworth Argosy. Now, about fourteen years later, I was flying in and out of the aerodrome.

Croydon's traffic pattern took the pilot over streets full of rows of little houses, but one of the final approaches was the tricky part. Nearing the aerodrome for a landing, the pilot found that he had a tall, red brick chimney-stack almost on centre line to the flight-path then, continuing his descent, the last part of the approach took him between two hangars. Pilots used this awkward approach so that they could touchdown on a short stretch of runway extending out from the tarmac in front of the hangars.

Pilots were supposed to stay well above the stack and then descend rapidly and touchdown on the short, so-called runway and finish the landing run on the inner grass field. The aerodrome gradually sloped away from the hangars and a steep landing approach often led to a rough landing. If you didn't make the runway you landed on the grass where the braking action, especially when it was wet, was practically non-existent.

275

Aircraft sometimes finished up sliding gently sideways out of control, down the grass slope on an aerodrome not meant for modern 'planes.

To avoid the steep final approach some pilots curved around the chimney while others, to the horror of their passengers, lifted a wing over the chimney and continued descending!

Returning one afternoon from a flight to Europe I taxied back to the tarmac and parked. While waiting in the Customs Office I got a 'phone call from the tower traffic controller, he gave me a tail number and asked me if I was the Captain of that aircraft.

"Yes. What's the problem?"

"Your trailing antenna hit a house on the circuit and knocked a hole in the roof," came the monotone voice over the 'phone. "When you've cleared Customs, please report to the tower."

Ironically, when my 'plane taxied in it had no trailing antenna and I'd made a note to that effect in the F700. Over the North Sea the wireless operator let the wire antenna trail out too fast and the antenna wire, with a large lead weight on the end of it, broke and dropped into the ocean.

When I arrived at the control tower a large policeman sat at a table writing on a small pad with a very short pencil. He looked up at me, laid his pad and pencil down and reached into a sack. "This yours?"

I examined the large lead weight and length of tangled wire. "Sorry, Constable. That's not mine. What's more, it's not even from a Dakota." The policeman looked surprised, so I continued. "The lead weight's too big and it's the wrong shape."

I learned later that the control tower rechecked their records and discovered a United States Army Aircorps Liberator had landed a few minutes ahead of me; its antenna was the one that had damaged the house.

While I was at Croydon quite a lot of aircrew were fiddling around on the black market; a few were caught, which tended to discourage the others.

Before leaving Kenley for a flight to Europe, one of our squadron pilots would load his 'plane with black-market items such as coffee, chocolate bars and soap which he exchanged for wine. One time he carried a kit bag full of condoms. He said he made a killing on that shipment.

When he returned to Croydon, carrying smuggled wine, he had a simple but effective way of avoiding Customs. After crossing the English coast he would call Croydon tower and give a false position and arrival time. He would then land at Kenley, which was almost in Croydon's circuit, unload the contraband and take off. Moments later he would call Croydon's tower saying he was in their circuit. He would then clear Customs.

One day I followed another 'plane for a landing at Kenley and I heard its radio call to Croydon. I knew immediately who the pilot was. Taxiing in, I watched as a little blue HM Customs van trundled down the runway behind his 'plane and followed him to the parking area.

I never found out what happened, but after this incident this officer was never seen again on the squadron!

One day I got a surprise 'phone call from our family solicitor asking me to drop in and see him at his West End office. Ushered in by his secretary he greeted me effusively, offered me a chair beside his large mahogany desk and poured a Scotch for both of us. I sat down, looked around the room and noticed it was well appointed with several good-looking oil paintings on the walls and fine Persian carpets on the floor.

"I say, old boy, do you ever fly to Paris, or could you arrange to go there?" he asked, handing me the heavy cutglass tumbler. I thought this was a strange question, but I didn't interrupt hoping he'd come to the point. He went on, "I've got a flat in Paris and there's a suitcase full of French francs under the bed." He looked at me sheepishly. "If you'd bring that suitcase to me, half the money is yours."

As if to convince me he was telling the truth he told me how he had made a lot of money when he was an officer with the Judge Advocate General's branch during the operation in Narvik, Norway. "You know," he said, "I shipped a lot of valuable furs home in a diplomatic mail bag and sold them for a lot of money."

I left his office hoping our family affairs were in good order. I didn't go to Paris but, I must confess, I gave it a little thought!

Family solicitors and aircrew weren't the only ones dealing on the black market. We had a Corporal in the

Squadron's Orderly Room, one of those people you occasionally encountered in the service who was a misfit. This chap was obviously extremely well educated, but with his *savoir faire*, fine aristocratic features and proper accent he was quite out of place doing a clerk's job.

The squadron had a small detachment at Brussels Evere aerodrome: a few ground crew to service the aircraft, and some passenger and freight people to supervise aircraft loading and unloading. The out-of-place Corporal joined this detachment.

One day, while I waited for my aircraft to be loaded, he told me he did a few "special" deals with a contact he had at Brussels, and sometimes he had squadron aircrew fly stuff in for him.

"Perhaps, one day you would do me a favour?" he asked, looking me straight in the eye.

"I'll think about it," I replied.

Another time at Brussels, he took me aside and told me he had a good thing going; buying gold and selling it back in England. He told me how it was done. "Are you interested?"

The risk seemed minimal and the price seemed right, so I said, "Maybe."

He gave me the address of his contact in London and suggested I meet him. I made the appointment and late one afternoon I took a taxi to the East End docks. Before the taxi reached the address, which was in a very dowdy neighbourhood, I told the driver to stop. I got out, paid him and when he'd driven away I headed for the address on foot. The street I was looking for was lined with small shops. Many had been badly damaged in the Luftwaffe 1940 bomber blitz on the docks.

I found the right shop and noticed a hole in the roof had been patched with red instead of grey slate tiles. One upstairs window was still boarded up. I was about to pull the unpolished brass bell handle when a little voice inside my head asked me first, "Do you really know what you're getting into? Are you sure you want to do this?"

I stood for a moment with my hand poised. Let's face it, I thought, I'm no con man. I knew I could easily be outwitted by any low grade con artist, and with my luck I would probably be caught and court martialled. The unknown fate of our black marketeer who'd been picked up at Kenley made up my mind for me.

To hell with it, I reasoned, life's too short and I was having too much fun flying around Europe to get into this kind of trouble.

I turned away and walked to the corner of the dark, dirty street and hailed a taxi.

CHAPTER FIFTEEN

Prestwick — Transport conversion flying

My next posting, after leaving 271 Squadron at Down Ampney, sent me north to 1680 (Transport) Flight at Prestwick. This small unit, a branch of Air Transport Command, had a mixed bag of aeroplanes. Some Dakotas, a Walrus, a few Airspeed Oxfords and a couple of de Havilland Dragon Rapides. The unit flew Special and Emergency Rescue Flights, operations that did not fall into Transport Command's regular squadrons' roles.

One of the Special Flights was the Prestwick/Blackbushe shuttle. A Dakota flew every day for a whole year; one flight south from Prestwick to Blackbushe and another flight north from Blackbushe to Prestwick. These flights sometimes carried passengers or freight, but if the weather was marginal, and it often was, they just carried the crew.

We had been briefed that the flight must get through regardless of the weather! We were also told that, in spite of landings in zero-zero conditions in fog, snow or rain and on icy runways, we mustn't bend the

281

aeroplane. (After one year the nature of the flight was publicized to show that, despite the English weather, aircraft could be flown all year round using wartime-developed navigational aids and instrument landing systems.)

Because of this special role we did a lot of Dakota instrument training flights using GCA, radio beacons and the Adcock Radio Range. Aircraft used on these flights had the new SCS51 instrumentation, the prototype of ILS (Instrument Landing System) which gave direction and glide slope to the runway.

The crews flying on flights became very proficient. I had full confidence in the landing system and made many landings in almost zero conditions. I don't remember anyone having an accident, but I do recall some exciting moments landing at Blackbushe in fog with ice on the runway.

In India I had entered one flight in a Dakota in my logbook as "First Solo on Type, Operational Flight". At Prestwick I tried another "first". During an air test in a Dakota I discussed an idea with my co-pilot Flt Lt White, "I wonder what happens when you feather both engines?"

"I've often wondered that too," he replied.

"Do you think we should try it?" I asked.

"Yeah. Let's try it," he said, grinning.

I circled the aerodrome and climbed to 9,000ft. There were no clouds so we were able to keep the aerodrome in sight.

Satisfied with everything I called to Flt Lt White, "Okay. Feather the starboard engine."

He closed the throttle reached up and pressed the red feathering button. We often had to make training flights on one engine so this was quite normal. I kept my speed at 105mph as the propeller windmilled and stopped with the blades fully feathered.

"Now the other one," I said.

He pulled the throttle back and hit the other feathering button.

I wasn't sure how the 'plane would fly with no power. Would it have a high rate of sink? Would I have to shove the stick forward to maintain airspeed? I kept an eye on the aerodrome just in case I had to make a no-engine landing!

We were both pleasantly surprised that the old DC-3 made a pretty good glider. The silence was eerie, just the sound of wind whistling by the fuselage. We could talk in a normal voice and it seemed strange to look out of the cockpit windows and see, on both sides, the sun glinting on propellers stopped in the fully-feathered position.

After a few seconds of flying as a glider, I called out, "That's enough. Better not push our luck. Unfeather the starboard."

I set the throttles open, the pitch lever fully back and the mixture control to Auto-Rich.

White pushed the starboard feathering button and held it in until the revs built to 1000.

I think we were both relieved when the propeller unfeathered and started to slowly windmill before picking up cruising revs.

He started the port engine and we headed home. Needless to say I did not record this experiment in my logbook!

In spite of Transport Command's methodical training, pilots made mistakes. In most situations the pilot was able to get out of trouble, chalk up his folly to experience, and try not to repeat the mistake.

Many of the pilots had hair-raising stories to tell about things that had happened to them flying on operations. They had tales about mechanical failures when they hadn't been really sure what to do to overcome the problems. As pilots we tried to be as professional, careful and exacting as we possibly could to avoid that ominous and degrading remark: PILOT ERROR. We talked about our mistakes and learned a lot from them. But pilots did make mistakes!

One day, for example, one of the pilots at Prestwick took off in a Dakota with the aileron control-locks in position. (The lock was a wooden wedge, held in place with a bungee cord. Shoved into the edge of the aileron it stopped the wind blowing the control surface up and down.) He should have checked the controls for freedom of movement before take-off, but he was airborne before he realized what had happened.

With great skill, and a lot of luck, he struggled around the circuit and finished up landing on the tarmac, between a line of parked 'planes facing the hangars. He nonchalantly climbed out, took off the locks, climbed back aboard and went on about his flight!

284

Wt Off Evans, one of our navigators with whom I had flown quite often, told me he'd never been up in an Oxford.

"I'll show you," I said. "Let's go flying." I signed out a 'plane for GCA (Ground Control Approach) practice.

I hadn't flown an Oxford since May 1942 at No 3 Advanced Flying Training unit at South Cerney. I started the engines, taxied out and flew it for a few practice Ground Control approaches using Dakota speeds. My final approach for landing was a little erratic; I tended to over-correct because the Oxford is more nimble than the Dak. After landing I parked on the flight line and suddenly my mind went blank. I couldn't remember the procedures to shut the engines down.

In the Dakota you pull the mixture lever right back to Idle Cut-Off, but I knew you didn't do that in the Oxford and, of course, it's one of the seven deadly sins to stop an engine by switching off the magnetos! I sat still with the engines idling until I had a memory recall then, with a reflex action, I reached my hand behind the pilot's seat, found the toggle for engine shut-down and pulled it!

In March an order came in for a special operation — two Dakotas to go to Geneva. They carried an unusual cargo: gun barrels and ammunition assigned to the Swiss Army for avalanche control.

One of the 'planes landed in Geneva, but the second aircraft got lost in the foothills of the Alps in a blizzard and crashed into the side of a snow-covered hill. The

Dakota slid in on its belly in the snow but came to a stop almost undamaged. No one was injured.

As the next Captain on the duty roster I got a 'phone call telling me to get ready to go to Geneva. In Dakota F2670, loaded with about 4,000lb of gun barrels, ammo and the crew — Wt Off Evans and Fg Off Goodings — we took off for Northolt to pick up our passports.

Two days later we left for Switzerland.

Radio navigation aids were sparse in Europe. After a long haul across France, Evans, my navigator, came into the cockpit and said, "We're about five minutes away from Geneva's aerodrome; it's somewhere below all that fluffy, white cloud."

"Doesn't look too good," I said, looking out at the cloud below. "That's solid stuff."

Evans, leaning into the cockpit with a map in his hand, looked at his watch and said, "We're right over Geneva . . . NOW!"

A solid layer of cloud covered Europe. The only airfield where it was clear enough for us to land was Istres at Marseille. Transport Command 'planes were forbidden to land there if they had to stay overnight. As aircraft Captain I couldn't authorize a landing but, fortunately, my second pilot, who'd joined us at Northolt, was Group Captain Nicholls from Transport Command headquarters.

I turned to the Group Captain. "Looks like we've had it for today, Sir. Can you authorize us to go to Istres, or shall we go back to Northolt?"

"We'll go to Istres," he said. "Perhaps the weather over Switzerland will be better tomorrow, and we'll try again."

We stayed overnight at Istres. The next morning the weather forecaster was dubious about whether the cloud conditions would be clear enough for us to land in Switzerland, but I decided to try anyway. If we couldn't land in Geneva we'd return to Northolt, drop off the Group Captain and return to Prestwick.

Wt Off Evans stood between the two pilots' seats and looked out at the solid cloud below. "Doesn't look any better than yesterday, does it?"

I'd never flown near the Alps before, but I knew there were some high spots. "Mont Blanc's about twenty thousand feet. How far away is it?" I asked Evans.

"Don't worry, Skipper. It's nearly a hundred miles off to the southeast."

Flt Lt Martin, who had joined us at Northolt, was assigned to the crew because he knew the layout of Geneva's aerodrome. As we neared the Alps, hidden in the clouds below, I put him in the right-hand seat.

Evans gave me a countdown on our ETA. "That's it" he said, "Geneva's below — NOW." I circled in the bright sun, clear blue sky above and nothing below us but solid white stratocumulus with tops at 7,000ft. Just like yesterday, I thought.

"Look!" Martin called out, pointing. "Water."

The navigator craned to look through the side window.

"That's got to be Lake Geneva," he said.

Through a small hole in the clouds below I could see a patch of ink-black water. Evans continued, "But I can't tell you which part of the lake it is. It's about forty miles long, shaped like a banana, the aerodrome's at the southwest end."

"I'm going to try and get down," I told the crew. "I'll make a circling descent. Keep your eyes on that water. The moment you loose sight of it, yell and I'll circle back up."

I reduced airspeed to 110mph, lowered the undercarriage, put down a little flap and started a spiral descent flying on instruments. Scanning the blind-flying instruments we slipped into the tops of the clouds and shadows and patches of light flickered across my instrument panel. Lower down the cloud changed to a solid mass, but we managed to stay in the hole we'd seen from above. I waited, fully expecting the warning that we had lost sight of the lake. It didn't come. I levelled out about 300ft above dark forbidding water, in light rain, and turned on the windshield wipers.

"Follow the shore. Keep it on your right," Martin called across to me.

Keeping an eye on the flat, almost glassy water below, I glanced off to my right at the steep hill climbing out of the water up into the misty clouds. Through the haze and drizzling rain, I could make out chalets with tall, pointed roofs tucked in the trees. Blue smoke from chimneys hung in the top of the evergreens.

288

"As we get near Geneva you'll see a big yellow building off to our right. That's the League of Nations. Then turn right a bit and the aerodrome should be dead ahead," Martin said. I peered through the windshield, streaked by the clanking wipers.

Suddenly, a large building loomed out of the mist.

"That's it," Martin called out, pointing. "Turn."

I turned.

Visibility was barely half a mile when I spotted a shiny, wet runway dead ahead. I didn't have time to call the tower. There was little or no wind, no chatter on the radio and no 'planes on the runway, so I landed!

A "Follow Me" van zipped out towards us, pulled in front and led us to the terminal building. We climbed down the ladder and were greeted by a representative from the British Embassy.

The Group Captain said he had business to attend to, but he'd be in touch with me and he left. Our Embassy host drove us to an hotel in Geneva.

After we cleaned up and had dinner, he came back and he took us in tow for the night. He arranged it so that we arrived at each nightclub just as the floor show started. His timing was perfect. Having been stuck in Switzerland for "the duration" he had obviously had a lot of experience of the local nightlife.

After drab old England, the Swiss cabarets with their sparkling white tablecloths, soft lighting, fine wines and scantily clad girls looked pretty good to us!

I'd been told I could stay two nights in Geneva and the crew looked forward to a second day of entertainment. It didn't happen.

The next morning, under a clear blue sky, another Transport Command aeroplane landed with the AOC Transport Command on board. The AOC told Gp Cpt Nicholls he'd better go home and mind the office. That meant I would be flying him back to England.

Getting ready to leave Geneva I checked my freight manifest. It listed only several wooden boxes weighing 3,700lb. "What's in the boxes?" I asked.

Our embassy host of the previous night became evasive and gave me a non-committal answer.

I explained to him. "As aircraft captain I'm responsible for turning in my paperwork and cargo to Customs in England. If the load doesn't match the manifest I'll be hauled over the coals."

He hesitated for a moment. "Here," he said, pulling out an envelope from his coat pocket. "This'll cover you. It lists clocks, watches and watch parts. You'll be carrying one of the first shipments to leave Switzerland since the war."

I reasoned that even if two-thirds of the weight was packing cases, that was a lot of watches!

From Prestwick I was on the move once again. This time south to 1382 Transport Conversion Unit at Wymeswold, another Transport Command 'drome tucked away in the English countryside, about 10 miles north of my namesake, Leicester. There, I received my promotion to Flight Lieutenant, but after thirty-five days I moved again further south to Syerston, as an instructor.

Ten miles northeast of Nottingham, the 1333 Transport Supply Conversion Unit instructed pilots in the art of transport supply flying. This included pannier dropping and paratroop dropping, formation flying and glider towing.

Most pilots sent on this course were from Transport, or Bomber Command. The majority of them had quite a lot of flying hours. Some had never flown a Dakota and one or two had never flown a twin-engined 'plane. The latter we had to teach how to handle two engines as well as introducing them to the art of transport supply flying.

As instructors we tried to make our students enjoy the flying, to stay relaxed and become as good as we were, or thought we were! I enjoyed this type of flying because I'd done it operationally in Burma and I knew a lot of wrinkles that weren't in the handbook.

When I first learned to fly I thought everything the instructor demonstrated was an adventure. Going solo and practicing the exercise was exciting. When the unusual happened, because of lack of experience, the situation sometimes became frightening.

Most pilots, if asked, would say that after flying several different types of aeroplanes, in various situations, fear of flying diminished. I think this is true; after a few thousand hours I no longer expected an engine to stop at any minute. I'd been shot at by ack-ack, crash landed, had a midair collision and had flown in some of the worst weather a pilot could experience — the monsoons over Bengal and Burma. I now felt quite at home and relaxed in the cockpit.

After we'd made the student pilot comfortable handling the Dakota and they could land and take off, we tried to impart some of our wisdom, keeping them relaxed and putting them through their paces. Before starting an exercise we gave them a detailed briefing on the flight manoeuvres and how to use each of the controls and equipment. Most of the pilots adapted well, but a few tended to be overconfident.

One area in which student overconfidence could lead to serious trouble was formation flying. On two-aircraft low level formation flying exercises we roared around and over the Pennines at about 50ft. We started the formation exercise with two students and an instructor at the controls in each 'plane. After a demonstration flight the instructors put one of the student pilots in the left seat and coached him in low-level formation flying. Instructors stressed the absolute need to stay "ahead of the aircraft" — to be in complete control at all times. The two instructors kept in touch by radio and could alert one another if a problem arose. We let the students fly close together in the formation flying, but never close enough to overlap wings.

Formation flying keeps a pilot very busy. The lead aircraft's pilot must concentrate on where he's going and watch out for ground clearance. The pilot following the lead aircraft must constantly keep his eye on that aircraft while working flight and engine controls to hold his aircraft exactly in position. Even in May there was enough heat buildup to cause turbulence and wrestling with the controls made flying a hot, sweaty business.

After the students got the hang of formation flying, the instructors took the left seat again. This time we really flew close together.

The trick was to get your wing tip close to the back door of the lead aircraft. This meant that the wing was between the other 'plane's wing and the tail 'plane. The slightest error could cause both aircraft to lose control. By this time some students turned pale, some actually clutched the arm rests. This was the idea, scare the hell out of the students! It scared the hell out of me too!

After landing we sent the students off to practice formation flying and told them to keep their distance. I think our little demonstrations had the desired effect; we never had an accident during student formation flying.

Glider-towing called for careful flying by both the pilot flying the towing aircraft, called the "tug", and the glider pilot; especially during take-off. To do this type of flying the "tug" Dakota taxied to within a few hundred yards from the take-off end of the runway. A thick nylon rope is then attached to the retaining hook at the tail of the aircraft. With the glider securely attached the Dakota pilot opens the throttles slowly to take up the slack. Since he can't see what is happening he relies on the glider pilot to tell him over the intercom if there is a problem.

As the two 'planes move down the runway for take-off with the weight of the glider dragging the Dakota's tail, the pilot may have to use coarse rudder and brakes to keep his 'plane lined up with the runway. The glider quickly becomes airborne and then it is critical that the glider pilot stays in position directly behind the tug, especially in a crosswind take-off. If he yaws and pulls the Dak's tail to the side it can cause the 'plane to run off the runway before it has enough speed to get airborne.

On the take-off roll, as soon as the glider becomes airborne, the pilot has to position the glider just slightly above the "tug" to get out of its slipstream. If he gets too high the Dakota's tail is lifted and it can't get airborne! To be correctly positioned the glider pilot must keep the leading edge of the Dak's tail 'plane so that it appears to be touching the main wing's trailing edge. If there is a problem on take off the Dakota pilot can cast off the tow rope and release the glider by pulling the emergency release lever on the bulkhead behind him.

We used to tell glider pilots that if they fouled up the take-off, we'd pull the release and the metal end on the stretched nylon tow rope would hurl back and go right through the glider's windscreen, through them and out of the tail of the glider!

When doing circuits and bumps while towing gliders, usually there were several aircraft and gliders in the circuit at the same time. After take-off the Dak climbs straight ahead to 1,000ft and then makes a slow turn left, to the downwind leg. At that moment the glider pilot pulls his cable-release and casts-off.

The Dakota, staying clear of other aircraft, flies low over the field and drops the tow rope beside the runway, joins the circuit and lands.

The glider, with its low sink rate, remains almost at circuit height until it is downwind of the aerodrome, ready for a landing approach. Flaps are then fully lowered and the glider makes a steep, but slow approach to the grass infield. After it lands a tractor tows it back to the end of the runway for another circuit.

I decided I'd like to fly a glider and asked Captain Waldron, one of the glider instructors, if he would take me for ride.

Sitting in the left seat of glider FL197, a lumbering black Horsa II, I waited at the end of the runway as the ground crew hooked-up the nylon tow rope. The glider's windshield, like the rest of the craft, looked very fragile and I imagined what would happen if the tow rope coupling whipped back and smashed into it!

As the glider climbed away from the field the silence intrigued me, no roaring engines, just the rush of air.

On the downwind leg Capt. Waldron, in the right seat, called across to me, "I'm going to pull the tow rope release. You'll slow down. Push the stick forward to keep the right speed and watch your rate-of-sink indicator." When the left wing tip lined up with the downwind end of the runway Waldron said, "Okay, turn crosswind."

A few moments later it was a strange sensation to be over the end of the runway still at nearly 1,000ft.

"Full flap," he called out.

"What's my airspeed?" I replied.

"Don't bother about airspeed," he said, "With the control column's wheel pushed up against the instrument panel it'll be the right speed."

As the barn door-like flaps went down the glider tilted forward to an alarming 45 degrees and at 40mph headed downhill, aimed at the grass infield. Floating down to the ground, I eased the stick back to round out for a landing.

Waldron nudged the wheel fully forward again. "Hold it there a bit longer. Wait 'till you can see the blades of grass."

As he spoke we hung, nose down, heading for what seemed to me as certain destruction. Down, down, down. When we seemed almost sure to smash into the ground Waldron called out, "Now!"

I heaved the wheel back into my stomach. There was a gentle thud as we hit the ground followed by a grating sound as we rolled a few yards across the grass and stopped.

"Not bad for a first try," Waldron called across to me grinning as the yellow tractor trundled towards us.

"Let's change seats and I'll show you how it's really done."

We lifted into the air, turned downwind, cast-off and turned over the edge of the 'drome. Waldron put down flaps and once again we floated down towards the grass infield.

Waldron pointed. "See that tractor. Watch this."

He headed the glider down towards the tractor. Nearing the ground he made a slight turn and eased the wheel back. We crunched gently onto the ground, slid across the grass and stopped. The tractor driver backed up a couple of feet and, with a slight click, hooked on to the glider.

"That's how we do it," he said. "On Ops you might have to dodge trees, put your glider into the corner of a field. We talk feet, not yards, when we give the glider pilot a landing point."

I was impressed, but still preferred two engines!

I thanked him for the glider ride and asked for another favour. "I'd like to take a photo of you doing a landing." Capt. Waldron agreed.

I stood at the end of the runway and watched as he took off.

Syerston aerodrome is on top of a hill and Capt. Waldron, on final approach, dived below aerodrome level. He then pulled the glider up and shot across the perimeter road right beside me just a few feet above the ground. I got a perfect shot, but at that moment the CO's staff car sped by and the glider's wing almost clipped it.

Later, Capt. Waldron told me that the CO really tore a strip off him.

Although the effects of war in Europe and the Far East called for the RAF's continuing support, there were more than enough aircrew to fly aircraft. Many RAFVR aircrew, depending on their age and length of service, were being demobilized. My number came up with a posting to No 100 PDC Uxbridge for "demobbing". On 18 June 1946 I left 1333 TSCU Syerston.

CHAPTER
SIXTEEN

Demobbed!

After departing Syerston I had a lot of leave due and the staff at PDC Uxbridge said, "Go home. We'll call you when we want you."

I moved to South Kensington and lived with my mother and new stepfather, Col Veysie Curran. I took in the sights of London and visited museums and theatres. What a life! No responsibility and full pay! But I missed climbing into a cockpit and heading off somewhere.

I went to Ireland and stayed with friends at Greystones for a few weeks. The Irish really know how to relax and take things in their stride. I also met a very pretty girl there.

Returning from Ireland on an Aer Lingus Dakota I was invited to the cockpit. It was very hazy. As we approached the London area the pilots, looking for Northolt, had difficulty picking out landmarks. I'd flown in and out of that aerodrome many times so I was able to guide them into the traffic circuit.

The war I had been trained for as a pilot had ended on VJ Day — 6 August 1945.

What now?

My only professional knowledge was how to fly aeroplanes and drop bombs, and I'd become quite good at it, but so had thousands of other young men. What would we do now? Where and how would we live?

Could I fly for an airline? With all the aerodromes around England, and the improvements in instrument flying, I was quite sure new airlines would soon spring up. But I couldn't wait that long.

Should I go back to school, to university as I'd planned back in 1940?

Since joining the RAF I'd travelled to Canada, the USA, India, the Middle East and most of Europe. I'd seen death, hunger and the ravages of war. I wondered if I'd be able to settle into an academic life?

Later, maybe. But certainly not now.

My mother no longer worked as a volunteer for the Canadian Legion Library Service and she planned to live with her husband in Canada. I'd trained at Carberry, Manitoba, with the Commonwealth Air Training Plan, and Canada appeared to be a land of opportunity and adventure; besides, England had the post-war doldrums.

At twenty-three I was alive, unscathed and needed to get on with my life, to look for greener fields and probably get married one day.

Plans were made and strings were pulled to get me a berth on a ship to Canada. One day a 'phone call came. If I could leave in ten days I had a berth on a ship docking at Halifax. I had to move fast. I called the 100 Personnel Demobilization Centre at Uxbridge and asked if I could be processed for "demobbing" right away. "Come on over," the voice on the 'phone said, "We're open until seventeen hundred hours."

I caught the tube and a bus and arrived at the centre at about 4 o'clock in the afternoon. I think I set a record for getting out of the service. I was the last person in the door and all the staff were still at their stations, so I was whipped down the line. Medical inspection here, pay settlement over there. I picked up my natty grey pin-striped "demob suit" and a tailor made a few quick minor changes; didn't make much difference though because it still didn't fit me!

Going out of the door, with a package of clothes in hand, I experienced a strange feeling. It wasn't elation as I expected, but sadness at the sudden realization. The war was really over and I was no longer a pilot. No longer a Flight Lieutenant in His Majesty's Royal Air Force.

Epilogue

For ten days I bounced over the Atlantic in a small freighter. The vessel had a short flight deck which enabled a Hawker Hurricane, carried on board to protect convoys, to take off. After the flight the pilot either ditched, or made it to an onshore aerodrome. During the voyage we were struck by a severe storm, and made very slow headway and a large wave knocked off one of the wartime gun emplacements. I arrived in Canada in December 1946.

I flew to Winnipeg and stayed with friends from my flying training days at Carberry. Several weeks later I moved to Toronto and got a job with E. S. & A. Robinsons (Canada) Ltd, a paper processing company.

After I'd learned something about manufacturing paper bags I was given the challenging task of setting up a production control system for the factory. I managed to create a procedure that worked, although I am sure it was later improved. During this period I gained my Private Pilot's Licence and at weekends rented small single-engined 'planes from Levens

Brothers at Toronto's Barker Field. Later I upgraded my license to a Limited Commercial Licence.

It cost me about $10 an hour to fly, but I occasionally took passengers for Levens Brothers on sightseeing trips around Toronto and the lake shore. I didn't get paid for this, but I got free flying time. Flying on skis in the winter was a new experience.

In 1947 I applied to join Toronto's RCAF 400 Auxiliary Squadron. The squadron mainly flew Harvards, but they also had a few de Havilland Vampires. I wasn't really thrilled about flying single-engined aircraft, but it would be free flying with fringe benefits.

I prepared a paper outlining the reasons why E. S. & A. Robinsons should buy an aircraft to fly their sales representatives around the countryside, and I should fly it. The company said it was a good idea, complimented me on my well-researched and well-written proposal, but they weren't going to do it!

Progress up the industrial ladder seemed very slow so when the RCAF recruiting officer told me that the RCAF was starting to train NATO aircrew, needed instructors and offered me a short service commission, I accepted the offer.

I had left the RAF in 1946 as a Flight Lieutenant and felt I should join the RCAF at that rank. I couldn't swing the Flight Lieutenant, but before I signed anything I managed to persuade headquarters that, as a Flying Officer, I should start with three years progressive pay.

I joined the RCAF on 1 November 1948 and on 29 November was posted to No 111 "K" Flight, Winnipeg. After a few weeks I complained to the Flight Commander, pointing out that I had more hours on Dakotas than any of the Captains with whom I flew.

Flt Lt Howie said, "You need a Green Ticket (Instrument Rating) to be a captain." He arranged for me to go to the No 1 Instrument Flying School at Centralia, Ontario.

After I'd completed the instrument flying course Wg Cdr Roberts, the CO, asked me to stay at the Instrument Flying School as an instructor. I instructed there until 1953. While at Centralia I married Barbara Mossop and my son Michael was born.

In ground school students reviewed Air Force and Department of Transport air regulations and instrument flying procedures. Because the wording of these two sets of regulations were contradictory, the ground school instructor had to explain where, and why there were differences.

To clarify and standardize our procedures I suggested to the CO, Wg Cdr Mike Michalski, that the Instrument Flying School should prepare its own training manual. "Good idea," he said. "How about you doing it?"

I spent about two months compiling the Instrument Flying Instructor's Manual. This standardization of procedures got me posted to Air Force Headquarters in Ottawa at the Directory of Air Staff Services, as DASS/S-2-2-2, to rewrite CAP 100, Flying Orders for the Royal Canadian Air Force.

One afternoon at Centralia a twin-engined Beechcraft from the Elementary Flying School, with an instructor and two flight cadets on board, crashed off the end of a runway while doing touch and go landings. I was assigned as investigating officer for the accident.

The investigation revealed that the instructor, Flt Lt Harris, cut an engine after a touch-and-go landing, the student pilot mishandled the engine controls and pulled the power back on the second engine. The aircraft hit the ground a short distance from the end of the runway, slid across an alfalfa field, hit a drainage ditch, broke up and caught fire. A nearby farm worker, recently arrived from the Netherlands, raced his tractor to the crash site and pulled flight cadets Vaughan and Blair out of the burning 'plane. Cutting a seatbelt with his knife, Harris was able to get out on his own.

In my findings and recommendations to the Board of Inquiry I suggested that Mr. Wilhem Koehle be rewarded for his heroism. I was gratified when, later, he was awarded the George Medal.

Before I left No 1 Instrument Flying School I was pleased to hear that my design for a squadron badge had been accepted and approved by the *Chester Herald* in England.

At Ottawa, in Wg Cdr Millar's Directorate of Air Staff Services, I shared a desk with my former Instrument Flying School instructor, Harry Pickard, now a Squadron Leader and known as Mr. Green Ticket, in charge of the air force's instrument flying programmes.

As secretary to the CAP 100 Committee I coordinated rules and regulations between Ottawa's Department of Transport and Air Force Headquarters: Air Transport Command, Fighter Command, Maritime Command and Training Command directories. Each of these air operations had its own role and staff officers often had conflicting views about how their pilots should be regulated. It was an interesting job that required a great deal of tact because, as a Flying Officer, I dealt with senior officers who were sometimes reluctant to accept changes.

Working with the Department of Transport I helped to produce a publication, *"A Guide To Instrument Approach and Landing Procedures"*, which established terrain clearances to ICAO standards for the preparation of let-down procedures. Because of my experience in this field I claim responsibility for the RCAF abandoning the newly-introduced élitist Blue Card instrument rating, which allowed a pilot to fly instrument procedures (unwisely) to "half" the published circling altitude and "half" the published distance ahead visibility.

During this period I also participated in NATO and American, British, Canadian standardization groups of inflight documents and attended meetings in London, Rome, Amsterdam and Washington. I frequently visited the Aeronautical Chart and Air Information Center at St Louis, Missouri, where the RCAF in-flight documents were published.

I declined a posting to 426 Transport Squadron, Montreal, to fly North Stars and in 1957 was posted to

412 Transport Squadron — the VIP squadron at Uplands in Ottawa.

Before joining the squadron I attended No 4 Transport Operational Training Unit at Trenton, Ontario, to learn how to fly a Dakota (DC-3) — again!

My arrival at the VIP squadron, from a desk job in Air Force Headquarters, was viewed by some senior squadron members with a certain amount of scepticism. Squadron aircrew usually had many years of experience in Air Transport Command before joining this squadron.

I was tolerated and, I think, over-tested, to see if they could find an excuse to get rid of me. But I'd learned to fly DC-3s in operational conditions with RAF 62 Squadron in India in 1944. I got my VIP pilot's rating and all was well from then on.

While at 412 Squadron I flew Beechcraft Expeditors and DC-3s and met many interesting VIP passengers; the flying was exacting and one had to be on one's best behaviour.

As the new arrival to the squadron, in July 1958 I was chosen to go on temporary duty to the United Nations detachment at El Arish, Egypt, to implement VIP procedures for aircrew at No 115 Air Transport Unit.

Once again I was not well received because aircrews resented the idea of someone from Ottawa telling them how they should fly their aircraft under desert conditions.

One of the first changes I proposed for the passenger and freight-carrying Dakotas was a reduction in fuel so that extra emergency drinking water could be carried on all flights. Pilots tried to convince me that they might need the extra fuel, but their argument was pretty thin and it fell apart when I asked, "When did you last fly IFR in cloud or rain?"

Aircrews also complained about a new procedure I was sent to El Arish to enforce; aircrews had to fly in their best uniforms when carrying VIPs.

One day we had an official function and I wore my tunic for the first time in the Mess. When the pilots noticed that I had both the Africa and Burma Stars their attitude changed. They were now eager to listen to me.

In September 1960 I received a posting to Air Transport Command Headquarters, Trenton, Ontario, to the Air Transport Operations Center (ATOC). Manned twenty-four hours a day by an aircrew Duty Officer, ATOC prepared operational orders for the squadrons and monitored the movement of command aircraft, organizing assistance when needed. I was responsible for the daily briefings given by the Duty Officers, and the presentation of visual displays.

In 1964, I moved from ATCHQ across the road to Base Operations at Station Trenton, where I remained until I retired from the Royal Canadian Air Force on my 45th birthday — 26 February 1968.

In 1946, at the age of twenty-three, I walked out of the demobilization centre in England with a bundle of wartime memories and a few medals. The 2nd World War had ended as had my wartime service as an RAF pilot. I looked ahead, with optimism, to a new life, a new career.

But it wasn't until four decades later that I finally left the Royal Canadian Air Force, with many thanks for a job well done and best wishes from my fellow officers. With the same optimism I'd had forty-two years ago, I again looked ahead to new ventures and horizons and wondered what they would be and where they would take me.